To John,
Best wishes
Cliff Jones

To John
Best Wishes
Terry Dyson

To John.
Maurice Norman

To John
Peter Baker

61

Published by Vision Sports Publishing Ltd 2010

ISBN 13: 978-1905326-88-4

© Tottenham Hotspur FC
Text © Martin Cloake, John Fennelly, Adam Powley and Julie Welch
Design: Doug Cheeseman

This book is an officially licensed publication

Tottenham Hotspur FC
Bill Nicholson Way
High Road
N17 OAP
www.tottenhamhotspur.com

Vision Sports Publishing
19-23 High Street
Kingston upon Thames
Surrey
KT1 1LL
www.visionsp.co.uk

Publisher: Jim Drewett
Club liaison: John Fennelly
Historical consultants: Andy Porter and Bob Goodwin

Printed in China

A CIP Catalogue record for this book is available from the British Library

61 THE SPURS DOUBLE

SATURDAY, AUG. 13th, 1960

COPYRIGHT

VOL. LIII. NO. I

ALL RIGHTS RESERVED

Secretary:
R. S. JARVIS

Manager:
W. E. NICHOLSON

Medical Officer:
Dr. A. E. TUGHAN

Chairman:
FRED. J. BEARMAN

Vice-Chairman:
FREDK. WALE

Directors:
F. JOHN BEARMAN, D. H. DEACOCK
S. A. WALE

TOTTENHAM HOTSPUR

FOOTBALL AND ATHLETIC COMPANY LIMITED

Official Programme

AND RECORD OF THE CLUB

THE OPENING OF ANOTHER SEASON

We are again on the threshold of another new season, and we welcome back our supporters with their appetites again doubtlessly renewed for the excitements of the months ahead. Although in 1959-60 the major honours eluded us in one of the closest-run finishes in the League on record we have memories of a most enjoyable season with the interest sustained right up to the closing day when the issues were finally settled. The public interest may be gauged by the attendance figures which gave us an average for our home League games of just under 48,000, the highest of any club in the country, and a sure testimony to the entertainment provided. In view of our encouraging record last season we think we can again face the new campaign in a spirit of quiet confidence believing that we are well equipped to meet the hazards that lie ahead. So far there have been no new professional signings to record since the close-down last May, and our playing staff consists of the 35 players who were re-

The Touring Party at London Airport before taking off on their flight to Milan.   Photo: Swissair Ltd.

In the Interests of Ground Conditions, Players on either side will not sign Autographs on the Field

PRICE TWOPENCE

Printed by Thomas Knight & Co. Ltd.,
The Clock House Press, Hoddesdon, Herts.

Contents

Foreword by Cliff Jones

It's 8 March 1961 and I'm waiting in the tunnel behind my pal John White. Alongside us are the Sunderland side we've got to beat in this sixth round cup replay to keep our dreams of the Double alive. The noise is unbelievable. The old East Stand is looming in front of us, its tiers crammed with 30,000 people. There are thousands more outside the gates. The whole of Tottenham High Road is at a standstill, ready to listen out for the oohs and aahs coming from inside White Hart Lane. And I'm thinking what I always think: "I'll have some of that. Let's go."

The rest is history, of course. Tottenham Hotspur 5, Sunderland 0. The match throbbed from start to finish and the whole world sensed they were witnessing something special that night. We'd played down what was happening most of the season, taking our attitude from Bill: "Ssh! Don't mention the Double. Just focus on each game as it comes." Now with Sunderland beaten, we really started to feel the pressure. We're in the semis! We can do the Double now!

Tottenham's glory years kicked off the sixties. We were a special team who were part of a special era in history. White Hart Lane is still a fantastic place, with fantastic supporters, but in the Double year 60,000 turned up every week. Wherever we went, the gates were shut. We were something unique and we knew it. We were a squad of players with different skills who complemented each other and who got on well with each other. It would be unfair to single out individuals but of course I have to mention Bill Nicholson and Danny Blanchflower. Bill was the main man. He worked harder than any of us, knew more about the game and gave us values and leadership. When we went on to the field of play, Danny Blanchflower took over. If it didn't work out, he and Bill would have words. But there'd be a handshake at the end. He was not just a great player but a great captain.

Memory's a funny thing. I don't remember scoring twice against Chelsea at the Lane at the end of March, only Ron Harris trying to kick me. But they were the goals that got us back on track in the League after going through the month without a win, and turned us into a team of champions in waiting again. And I'll never forget our last home game before the cup final – Spurs 1, West Bromwich Albion 2. Or rather, I'll never forget the rollocking Bill gave us afterwards: "You'd think West Brom were the champions, not Tottenham Hotspur. Hope you're going to do better than this in the cup final."

And we did. Fifty years later I count it as an honour still to be part of this great club and I enjoy every home match. Like everyone else I'd love to see the glory days back again. But that Double year was a moment in time that can never be repeated. Such a great side. Such a blend. It was unique.

Cliff Jones

Age of achievement

A shield presented to Ron Henry by a fan.

This is the story of the first league and cup Double of the 20th century, of why it was the greatest achievement in British football history and of how it changed the game forever. It's the story of the men who achieved it and of the people whose lives it changed forever. It is the story of how Tottenham Hotspur won the Double and why, half a century on in a very a different world, the Double of 1961 is still *the* Double.

Other clubs have won the league and FA Cup in the same season; other sides have notched that achievement more than once; one has gone even further and lifted the European Cup in the same season as winning the domestic double. Arguments will rage as to which is the best team from this elite group, its numbers swelled in recent years as England's regular Champions League qualifiers exert a near monopoly on trophy success. But 50 years on from Tottenham's triumph, that side is still regarded by many as the best of them all.

"I can hardly believe what Spurs did that year. Forget Liverpool, forget Manchester United, forget the Brazilians. Compared to Spurs in 60/61, the others were just donkeys." Those lines, from the final scene of Julie Welch's classic film *Those Glory Glory Days*, give an idea of the impact Bill Nicholson's Tottenham Hotspur made by winning English football's first modern Double.

It had been 64 years since a side had won the league championship and FA Cup in the same season. In 1897 Aston Villa secured the Double by beating Everton 3-2 in a thrilling game at Crystal Palace. As they lifted the FA Cup, news came through that Derby County had lost 1-0 at Bury – so ensuring that Villa were League Champions too. Eight years before, the first ever Double had been won by Preston North End. Supremely fit and

artistic, Preston won the league undefeated in 1888 and took the cup without conceding a goal. It was a sensational achievement, but one achieved over 22 games in the league and five in the cup. When the first modern Double was won, it would be achieved over 49 games – and fittingly enough by a side whose lilywhite shirts and blue shorts had been adopted in 1898 in honour of Preston's achievement.

Preston and Villa's Doubles came when English football was struggling to take shape, riven by disputes between the mainly amateur sporting gentlemen of the south and the professionals of the industrial north. Indeed, Preston's historic achievement may not have come about had Corinthians not clung so fiercely to the principles of amateurism that they refused to enter competitions. Although, it is worth noting, the Oxbridge gentlemen of Corinthians were paid more in 'expenses' than many professionals. But Preston represented the coming force, professionalism. They were the first club to make efforts to acquire the best players available and to use scientific training methods. Their Double set new standards, just as Tottenham Hotspur's would in a new century when football was very different – the dominant, professional, highly-organised new order forced into life by the achievements of Preston North End in that groundbreaking season.

In the 20th century, ten teams came within touching distance of the league and cup Double. In 1904, Manchester City won the cup but finished second in the league; the following year Newcastle United went one better in the league, but lost the cup final. In 1913, two teams missed out in the same season. Sunderland won the league, finishing a place ahead of Aston Villa, but lost the cup to the same opponents – each team

A pre-cup final feature in
Today – The New John Bull
magazine 6 May 1961.

11 MEN JUMP FOR JOY!

a trainer weighs up his team

Cecil Poynton takes a candid look at the pride of Tottenham as they prepare for the F.A. Cup Final

GOALKEEPER

BILL BROWN (29)

Born at Arbroath; a Scottish international who cost Tottenham about £17,000 from Dundee in 1959. A daring goalkeeper who rarely gets injured and a quiet, family man who shows few nerves before a match. 6 ft. 1 in., 12 st. 7 lb.

RIGHT BACK

PETER BAKER (29)

Born at Hampstead, he played for England youth teams while with the Enfield club in the Athenian League. Likes to loosen up before fixtures by kicking the legs of the dressing-room table. Has a very serious outlook and approaches a game coolly. 5 ft. 9 in., 10 st. 11 lb.

LEFT BACK

RON HENRY (26)

Born in London, he was evacuated to Redbourn during the war and played for the village team until Tottenham signed him six years ago. Needs a thorough massage of a troublesome back before every match. 5 ft. 10 in., 11 st. 13 lb.

RIGHT HALF

DANNY BLANCHFLOWER (35)

Born at Belfast and played for Glentoran, Barnsley and Aston Villa. Captained Northern Ireland to her first win in thirty years over England at Wembley in 1959. A non-stop, intelligent talker who has won friends and influenced fans on TV and radio. For all his donnish manner he is surprisingly tough in play. 5 ft. 9 in., 11 st.

CENTRE HALF

MAURICE NORMAN (26)

Born in Norfolk and played for Norwich City before joining Spurs in 1955. A natural worrier, he gets the full treatment from trainer Poynton both off and on the field. Subject to psychosomatic aches and strains. Just married. 6 ft. 1 in., 12 st. 1 lb.

LEFT HALF

DAVE MACKAY (26)

Fiery Edinburgh-born star. Cost Spurs £30,000 from Hearts in 1959. Toughest man in the side who, because he often gives out knocks as well as receiving them, is sometimes labelled "too rough" by rival fans. Has frequently appeared in the Scottish international side. 5 ft. 7½ in., 11 st. 2 lb.

OUTSIDE RIGHT

CLIFF JONES (26)

Cost Tottenham £25,000 from his home-town club of Swansea three years ago. Very quiet before matches. Likes to leave himself as little time to change as possible, then strips at high speed. Conscious of knee injuries before the match, but forgets them when racing down the wing. A regular Welsh international. 5 ft. 7 in., 10 st. 1 lb.

INSIDE RIGHT

JOHN WHITE (24)

Born Musselburgh, Edinburgh, he was with Falkirk before joining Spurs in 1959. A fine ball-player who has never needed attention from Poynton on the field. Extremely quiet, studious footballer, who likes a sniff of ammonia on leaving the dressing-room. A Scottish international. 5 ft. 8 in., 10 st. 7 lb.

CENTRE FORWARD

BOBBY SMITH (28)

Yorkshire born, he formerly played for Chelsea, but has found his ideal position as the spearhead of Spurs' ball-playing forward line. Highly strung in the dressing-room. Changes in a hurry and keeps up the pace for another ninety minutes. England's current centre-forward. 5 ft. 10 in., 12 st. 11 lb.

INSIDE LEFT

LES ALLEN (23)

Born at Dagenham; another player who came to Spurs from Chelsea. Scored five of Tottenham's thirteen goals against Crewe in a cup replay last season. Like many of the team, likes breakfast in bed on tour. Quiet and determined goal-getter. 5 ft. 9½ in., 10 st.

OUTSIDE LEFT

TERRY DYSON (26)

Born in Yorkshire, the son of a jockey, he was spotted by Spurs during his National Service. Live-wire of the dressing-room, he likes to bombard his colleagues with football kit. 5 ft. 4 in., 9 st. 8 lb.

PICTURE BY LAWRENCE HANLEY

18

19

AND OVERLEAF – THEIR OPPONENTS

The introduction

denied at the last by the other in a titanic tussle for immortality. In 1928 Huddersfield Town finished second in the league and lost the cup final. Four years later the same manager, Herbert Chapman, achieved the same feat with Arsenal. And in 1939, Wolverhampton Wanderers completed the unwanted Double of league and FA Cup runners-up.

In the 1950s the chase became more frantic. It was an age when great feats were being pursued – the four-minute mile, scaling the peak of Everest, a moon landing. Achieving more and better was the spirit of the age and the finest teams and players in football were becoming obsessed with the modern Double. In 1954, West Bromwich Albion won the cup but finished second in the league. In 1957 Manchester United's 'Busby Babes' won the league and were widely expected to secure the Double by winning the cup final against… Aston Villa. As it turned out, the Villa were able to hold onto their record of being the last Double winners, beating United 2-1. It was an agonising defeat for United because goalkeeper Ray Wood broke his cheekbone in a collision in the sixth minute. There were no substitutes then, so Wood was replaced in goal by Jackie Blanchflower – brother of Spurs captain and former Villa player Danny.

In 1960, Stan Cullis's great Wolverhampton Wanderers side looked set for the Double. Pursuing a third consecutive league title and having become the first team to score over 100 goals for three seasons in a row, they entered the final straight. On 23 April at Molineux, they faced a Spurs side which had lost two consecutive home games. A crowd of 56,283 saw Spurs tear Wolves apart. The Londoners' 3-1 victory not only denied Wolves the Double – Cullis's team did go on to win the FA Cup – it

signalled a power shift in the English game. The direct style of the old masters had been swept aside by the passing and movement of the emerging force. The significance was not lost on Danny Blanchflower, who wrote: "We made Wolves look old-fashioned that day and taught them that we were the new masters."

The contrast between the styles of Wolves and Spurs also provides a telling illustration of the state of the game in Britain at the time. Taking the then daring step to stage floodlit friendlies against European opponents at Molineux may have suggested an ambitious vision, but Wolves were exponents of traditional English virtues that prided physical teamwork over skill and individual expression. Their strategy and tactics mirrored the English game at large. Despite the 6-3 mauling handed out by Hungary to the England national side in 1953, giving football's founding nation a lesson in how to marry technique with tactical innovation, the insular English game was still stuck in a time warp. "When I returned to the hotel in London," said the Hungarian legend Ferenc Puskas, recalling the day the hubris of English football was so embarrassingly exposed, "a small boy came up to me in the foyer and said, 'Please sir, take me to your country and teach me to play football'." Such willingness to learn and improve was not shared by the sport's governing bodies, who refused to sanction participation by English clubs in European competition until Manchester United ignored what was effectively a ban in 1957.

Spurs were an English exception. The club had earned a reputation for innovation since its formation in 1882 and just two years prior to the Hungary game had thrilled crowds with the dash and verve of Arthur Rowe's title-winning side. Rowe lectured in Hungary in 1939, where he exchanged ideas with men

A signed autograph card of the Double winners.

The introduction

With Spurs on the brink of The Double the *Daily Mail* assembled as many of the 383 staff (including part-timers) it could muster for a squad photo. The 94 in the picture facing were captioned as follows: *First team*: D Mackay, J White, R Smith, W Brown, P Baker, W Nicholson, D Blanchflower, C Poynton (trainer), M Norman, L Allen, R Henry, T Dyson, C Jones. *Trainers*: J Wallis, A Thompson, J Coxford. Doctor: AE Tughan. *Groundsmen*: H Naylor (White Hart Lane), D Coulston (Cheshunt). *Maintenance Foreman*: E Watson. *Chief Scout*: N Liddle (one of 16). *Assistant Secretary*: A Leather. *Secretary*: R Jarvis. *Assistant manager*: H Evans. *Office staff*: H Mansfield, Mrs B Wallace, W Beeby, W Greaves, AH Joyce. *Office maintenance*: Mrs Naylor, Mrs Turner. *Catering*: E Phillips, Mrs Z Dobson, D Dixon (three of 54). *Reserves*: J Hollowbread, J Hills, J Ryden, F Saul, E Clayton, B Aitchison, M Hopkins, K Barton, T Medwin, T Marchi. *Directors*: S Wale, F Wale, Fred J Bearman (chairman), F John Bearman, D Deacock. *First aid*: Div Supt L Davis. *Chief Steward*: J Rist. Steward: G Anderson (two of 52). *Commissionaire*: A W Ferguson (one of 15). *Turnstile operator*: J Dearman (one of 53). *Programme seller*: J Aylward (one of 35). *Programme distributor*: S Hughes. *Band*: Secretary L Hatch (one of 35). *Reserves*: R Piper, J Fleming, R Moss, A Reed, B Fittock, F Smith, R Wilkie, J Collins, J Smith (capt), F Sharpe, W Dodge, N Lee, A Smith, C Brown, D Tharme. *Juniors with coach*: B Roffman, T Lloyd, P Beal, R Smith, S Tickridge (coach), B Embery, D Sunshine, R Low, B Lumley, A Davis. *Maintenance staff*: B Barnes, F Chapman, F Gold, M Stockwell, W Fox, F Murray, T Heathfield, G Dorling, M Moeser, V Knott. *Gateman*: W Elmore (one of two). *Ground pass official*: F Parrett.

whose tactical approach had been forged in the coffee houses of Central Europe. One of them was Gusztáv Sebes, who went on to coach the 'Magical Magyars' who humbled England at Wembley in 1953. Sebes drew on some of Rowe's ideas, which had their roots in the flowing football favoured by Peter McWilliam, who managed Spurs in the 1920s when Rowe was a youngster on the books. McWilliam's second stint as Tottenham boss entailed that he managed Vic Buckingham, who went on to help lay the foundations of Total Football at Ajax. The fires that forged the modern game glowed blue and white.

Rowe's innovation was to advocate the daring tactic of 'push and run' in which players traded passes in a whirl of fluid movement, in direct contrast to the more static manner of other teams. A key player in Rowe's side was Nicholson. His support for Rowe's tactics was to be given full and eloquent rein in his own team when he became manager in 1958. The belief, forged through the club, was that Tottenham's style would bring success.

So by the start of the 1960/61 season, the Double was football's and Tottenham's Holy Grail. For some, the frequency of the near-misses proved the Double was achievable. For others, the same circumstances proved the mental barriers became so great in the final stretch that no one could overcome them. But that's what they'd told Roger Bannister before he broke the four-minute mile in 1954, what Edmund Hillary and Sherpa Tensing had been told before they scaled Everest in 1953. This was the age of achievement and before 1961 was out, two more would be added to the list of human endeavour. On 12 April Soviet cosmonaut Yuri Gagarin became the first man to orbit the earth. Less than a month later Tottenham Hotspur won The Double.

Today, it may seem strange to mention the football Double in the same context as these other great firsts. Since 1961, the Double has been won by a further four teams on eight occasions. The achievement was bettered for good in 1999 when Manchester United won not only the league and the FA Cup, but the European Cup too. In fact, United have won the Double three times, as have Arsenal, with Liverpool and Chelsea forming the final members of this exclusive club. But many great sides have not won the Double; Don Revie's Leeds, Brian Clough's Nottingham Forest, the great Liverpool teams of the 1970s and early 80s.

That first modern Double still stands out in sporting history, and not just to supporters of Tottenham Hotspur. Indeed, the Double could be said to have become something of a millstone for the club, because Spurs have never equalled that achievement – or even won the league title – since. That team is still revered by football people, not only for what it achieved but for the way it achieved it. Describing them the sportswriter John Cottrell, in his book *A Century Of Great Soccer Drama* (Mayflower, 1970), said: "They were an outstanding side, offering the most exciting football of the day... Their greatness lay in their ability to produce the unexpected – the cheeky back-flick, the acutely-angled shot, the sudden switch of positions, the daring sally of a full-back into the attack."

Bill Nicholson's super Spurs were a sensation, the first superstars of the modern age. Their achievement helped take football to a wider audience and laid the foundations for the modern game. The Double side played a large part in helping to define how the game evolved – but the football they played belongs to a standard all of its own.

TOTTENHAM HOTSPUR FOOTBALL CLUB

MAINTENANCE STAFF

GATEMAN

GROUND-PASS ATTENDANT

JUNIORS WITH COACH

RESERVES

TURNSTILE OPERATOR

PROGRAMME SELLER

STEWARD

PROGRAMME DISTRIBUTOR

BAND

RESERVES

DIRECTORS

FIRST AID

CHIEF STEWARD

COMMISSIONAIRE

TRAINERS

DOCTOR

GROUNDSMEN

MAINTENANCE FOREMAN

CHIEF SCOUT

ASST. SEC.

SECRETARY

ASST. MANAGER

OFFICE STAFF

OFFICE MAINTENANCE

CATERERS

FIRST TEAM WITH MANAGER AND TRAINER

A
Daily Mail
PICTURE

The perfectionist

BILL NICHOLSON
(Spurs Manager)

"I want perfection," Bill Nicholson once said. Flawless football is a target most managers dream of – it's in the nature of their job. Most supporters can be just as unrealistically demanding. But it is a fair assumption to make that a good number of older fans of assorted allegiances would acknowledge that Nicholson came closer than perhaps any other British club manager to achieving the impossible and creating the perfect team. The Double was a venture that was years in the making, blending individual effort over time to forge a wonderful collective whole that reached its peak in 1961. The side's success may have owed credit to a lengthy list of contributors and, like the final step onto a mountain summit, proved relatively fleeting. But if one man deserves to be singled out for acclaim, it is William Edward Nicholson.

Steeped in Tottenham traditions and philosophy for the way the game should be played, Nicholson intuitively knew what made the club tick and spent a lifetime devoting himself to ensuring trophies and acclaim garlanded White Hart Lane. As a player, coach, assistant, manager, chief scout, president and elder statesman, he made a defining mark on the club like no one else has before or since. In time honoured and rather predictable fashion he has been dubbed 'Mr Tottenham' but the affectionate label rings true: Bill Nick was – still is – Spurs, and the Double is his shining legacy.

The detail of Nicholson's Tottenham career has become a club folk tale. He was scouted by Ben Ives and brought down from his Scarborough home as a 17-year-old to be trialled and groomed for future service in the Spurs defence. War intervened and by the time Nicholson was a first team regular he was 27. Unlike many of his contemporaries he had mercifully survived conflict, productively spending his time as a physical training instructor with the Durham Light Infantry, but had been robbed of a good chunk of his chosen career. Making up for lost time, he became a rock-solid part of the great push-and-run team that won the League in 1951. A solitary England cap does a disservice to his talents, but it was his involvement in Arthur Rowe's side that was to generate a more lasting influence.

Nicholson and Rowe were footballing soulmates. Rowe had carried a torch for the club's faith in stylish football and devised a revolutionary new template that was way ahead of its time in its use of swift movement and intelligent passing. Nicholson bought into this philosophy with relish and shared his mentor's liking for catchphrases that articulated his ideas simply and effectively. Nicholson often quoted Rowe's guiding principle: "Make it simple, make it accurate, make it quick; but above all make it quick," and added a few choice words of his own. Shrewd enough to know that it was preferable to instruct his players with easy-to-understand phrases rather than confuse them with long-winded analyses, he was a master of the pithy and profound comment. "When not in possession, get into position," was a Nicholson maxim; "When the game dies, make sure you come alive"

Bill Nicholson in conversation
with Cliff Jones, White Hart
Lane, 1959. Cecil Poynton
pours the half-time teas.

another and the witty observation that, "there's no spectating on the football pitch – people pay to do that" was a sharp rejoinder to the players that Nicholson would carry no passengers.

These were not empty statements. Nicholson strived to make sure his football wisdom was put to practical use from the moment he joined Jimmy Anderson's coaching staff once his one-club playing career drew to a close in 1955. When Anderson resigned three years later, Nicholson was the obvious choice to replace him. Anderson had bequeathed a decent inheritance. Though the team struggled in the 1958/59 season, there was a core of fine players at Nicholson's disposal including Blanchflower, Smith, Norman and Jones. His adeptness in the transfer market, one of his best qualities, soon added Mackay to the ranks with Brown, White and Allen to follow. He had assembled a brilliant team on paper in just a year. Now he set about translating that theoretical promise to substantive achievement.

The records and the memories express just how magnificent that accomplishment was. The team came close in the 1959/60 season, fading at just the wrong moment with two damaging defeats in April. But Nicholson used the experience to bolster the team's determination to make amends for the next campaign. Ably assisted by men such as assistant manager Harry Evans and trainer Cecil Poynton, with Blanchflower his idiosyncratic lieutenant on the pitch, Nicholson went to work on making the impossible possible. "I felt in 1960 I had a side well prepared to do something," he told Phil Soar. "You can't put it into words, it's a feeling you get." The rest is glorious Tottenham history.

Much is rightly made of the skills of the players in making the Double happen, though that tends to overlook Nicholson's tactical acumen. A push-and-run disciple of the short passing game, Nicholson introduced a delicious variation on Rowe's original. His teams could play the long ball as well – not aimless hoofs down the channels, or predictable wide deliveries to orthodox wingers, but precise, incisive passes that split defences asunder. The team had a fluid formation: players could swap positions at ease, forwards would track back and win possession deep in their own half, attacks would be built from the back. There was pace and power in abundance, too. It comprised an embryonic form of Total Football well before the Dutch made it their own.

Nicholson and Spurs were not to hit such a high as the Double again, for all the efforts of a very tight band of brothers. During his 16 years as manager, Nicholson fostered an *esprit de corps* via firm but even-handed man management. "Bill did things right – fair and proper," said Steve Perryman, who would later join Spurs because of the impression Nicholson made on him. The common portrait of Nicholson is of a serious, taciturn man, hard to please and difficult to warm to. The recollections of his players reveal a single-minded personality that brooked no compromise or distraction. Nicholson wanted to build and manage a successful football team, not indulge sensitivities and pamper egos. Alan Mullery recalled a story of how he and Terry Venables were one day called into Nicholson's office to be brusquely told that Mullery was going to be the new Spurs captain, to the obvious disappointment of the hopeful Venables. "Right, that's all," Nicholson said, forgoing any consideration that he might have hurt the younger player's feelings.

Yet he was no aloof martinet. "Morning boss," said Mullery on his first day of work at Spurs. "Don't call me boss, call me

Bill," said Bill. Nicholson could share a laugh and a drink with the people he commanded. He was clearly the man in charge but his set-up was no petty and restrictive hierarchy. Nicholson's Spurs was a side of talents adhering to an ethos of working together. Old-fashioned values of respect for colleagues, integrity, commitment and hard work underpinned the thoroughly modern skills each man brought to the collective. It was called teamwork and Nicholson made sure every man recognised how vital it was to the Spurs cause.

Never a truer word was said of Nicholson than from his own lips: "It's been my life, Tottenham Hotspur." Striving to do his best for the club became all-consuming, and entailed some personal cost. He and his wife Darkie remained devoted together right up to his death, but the sight of seeing his daughter Linda marry brought him to tears, not just out of happiness for his child but as recognition that he had missed out on seeing her grow up. The endless hours in his small office, on the training ground and in journeys up and down the country in a ceaseless search for talent took their personal toll.

But to those who really knew him Nicholson was a man of generosity with a friendly nature and a cheerful disposition. It's telling that his players called him 'Bill Nick' – not the more common 'gaffer' or 'boss' – and an indication that there was a real affection for a man who could be infuriatingly tough but commanded total respect. In later life especially, his warmer characteristics shone through. Freed of the weighty responsibilities of management he seemed to smile that bit more. For his neighbours on Creighton Road, just round the corner from White Hart Lane, Bill Nick was the kindly old bloke who lived in a modest but

Bill Nicholson just before the first away game of the Double season at Blackpool.

pristine house with his equally adored wife, tending his garden and providing a fund of marvellous Spurs stories for the many visitors who wanted a moment of his time.

In essence, Nicholson understood the fans. He would always emphasise how important they were and make his players aware they had a duty and responsibility to the people who paid at the gate and made the whole club a viable concern. At his memorial service in 2004, a moving occasion no one who was there will ever forget, Jimmy Greaves recalled one of Nicholson's pre-match team talks. "Whatever you're feeling now, remember: you're going to run out now in front of the people that pay your wages. Their expectancy is high, their value of you is high, their opinion of you is high. Do not let them down."

Nicholson never let Spurs down. He did not win as many titles as Ferguson, Paisley, Shankly, Clough or Busby, but more than holds his own in such esteemed company.

He broke records, paved the way for British teams to prosper in Europe and propelled the domestic game into the modern age. For Spurs he established the principles and standards that the club has strived to emulate ever since, but that has been an unenviable task. Perfection is a hard act to follow.

The Spurs files

Bill Nicholson kept meticulous records of players (*right*), detailing everything from their home address to their insurance value. He oversaw everything at the club, going round every Thursday with clerk of works Len Warren and jotting down every lightbulb that needed changing. The harsh reality of life as a professional footballer is illustrated by the red line through the entry for Tommy Harmer. Also featured are tactical plans and players on the retained list for 1960/61. The 'retain and transfer' system was scrapped in 1963, two years after the abolition of the maximum wage. Each player's wage (up to £20) and bonus are listed. Ron Henry's pay packet (*far right*) contained £17.64 after deductions.

80-61

PROFESSIONAL STAFF

NAME.	ADDRESS	HX	PLACE & DATE OF BIRTH	Signed Amateur	Signed Pro'	Height.	Weight.	Insce	Service with Previous Clubs
ALLEN.Leslie William.	Surrey Drive Hornchurch Essex.		Dagenham 4/9/37		11/12/59.		✓	20 000	Chelsea 4/9/54
AITCHISON.Barrie George.	Oxford Rd., Ponders End. Middlx.		Colchester 15/11/37.	2/6/54	11/1/55.		✓	3 000	Colchester Casuals.
BAKER.Peter Russell Barker.	Colney Hatch Lane. N.10.		Hampstead 10/12/31.	2/6/49	29/9/52.		+3	12 000	Enfield Town.
BARTON.Kenneth Rees.	Stannards Rd., Ponders End.		Caenarvon.20/9/37	28/5/53	4/10/54.		+2½	5 000	Caenarvon Boys Club
BLANCHFLOWER.Robert Dennis.	Morton Way Southgate.N.14.		Belfast. 10/2/26		8/12/54.		✓	15 000	Glentoran 46/48.Barnsley 48/51. Villa 51/5
BROWN.William. (ALIAS FYFE)	Melbourne Way Bush Hill Pk.		Arbroath. 8/10/31.		22/6/59.		✓	20 000	Dundee 9/9/49.
BROWN. Colin David.	Kings Ave., Watford.	HOME	Watford. 20/10/36	3/6/56	7/5/57.		✓	3 000	Juniors.
CLAYTON. Edward.	Brickley Rd., Hutton Essex.		Bethnal Green. 7/5/37	31/3/55	29/11/57.		✓	12 000	Eton Manor.
COLLINS.JAMES.	Penshurst Rd., Tottenham N.17.		Sorn(Ayrshire) 21/12/37		25/6/56.		+3	5 000	Lugar Boswell Thistle.
DODGE.William Charles.	Middleham Rd., Edmonton N.18.		Hackney 10/3/37	31/3/55.	7/10/57.		-3	8 000	Eton Manor.
DYSON. TERENCE KENT.	Colmore Rd., Ponders End.		Malton 29/11/34	18/12/54	1/4/55.		+4	8 000	Scarborough
FLEMING.Joseph.	St. Pauls Rd., Tottenham N.17.		Aberdeen 2/1/40.		24/10/58.		✓	1500	Banks o' Dee Aberdeen.
HARMER.Thomas Charles.	Mannock Rd., Wood Green.N.22.		Hackney 2/2/28	17/8/45	12/8/48.	Transferred to WATFORD.21.10.60		10 000	Juniors.
HENRY. Ronald Patrick.	Durrants Rd., Ponders End.		Redbourn 17/8/34	29/11/54	12/1/55.		+7	8 000	Redbourne.
HILLS. John Raymond.	Meophan Green Kent.		Gravesend 24/2/34	2/3/50.	17/8/53.		✓	6 000	Garvesend Northfleet "B"
HOLLOWBREAD.John Frederick.	Roedean Ave., Enfield.		Ponders End 2/1/34	3/6/50.	21/1/52.		✓	10 000	Enfield Town "B"
HOPKINS. Melvyn.	Connaught Gardens. N.13.		Ystrad. 7/11/34	10/5/51.	12/5/52		-5	20 000	Ystrad Boys Club. (Juniors)
JONES.Clifford William.	Connaught Gnds Palmers Green.		Swansea 7/2/35		14/2/58.		✓	35 000	Swansea Town. 1952/58.
LEE.Norman Thomas.	Grange Rd., Tottenham N.17.		Trelaw. 29/5/39	17/11/54	6/11/57.		✓	5 000	Ystrad Boys Club (Juniors)
MACKAY.David Craig.	Whitehouse Way. Southgate.N.14.		Edinburgh.14/11/34		16/3/59.		✓	32 000	Hearts 14/11/51/59.
MEDWIN.Terence Cameron.	Crawford Gdns.Palmers Green.		Swansea 25/9/32		1/5/56.		✓	15 000	Swansea 1949/56.
MOSS.Roy Graham.	Jersey Rd., Maldon Essex.		Maldon 5/9/41.		21/1/60.		✓	3 000	Juniors.
NORMAN.Maurice.	Collingwood Ave, Enfield.		Mulbarton 8/5/34		3/11/55.		✓	20 000	Norwich City 1952/55
REED.Alan James.	Lexden Drive,Chadwell Hth.Essex.		Ilford.31/3/41.	9/5/57.	10/6/59.		✓	3 000	Juniors.
RYDEN.Johnston John.	Tudor Rd., Edmonton. N.9.		Alexandra 18/2/31 Dumbarton.		2/11/55.		✓	12 000	Alloa 1949/53 Accrington 53/55
SHARPE.Frederick Charles.	Malpas Rd., Brockley. S.E.4.		London. 11/11/34	30/6/54	9/5/56		-3	8 000	Juniors.
SMITH.Anthony Brian.	Field Cres, Royston Herts.		Lavenham 5/10/41	4/8/57.	4/5/59.		+2	3 000	Juniors.
SMITH.Frank Anthony.	Eversley Ave.Barnshurst Kent.		Colchester.30/4/36	9/6/53.	24/2/54.		✓	3 000	Colchester Casuals(Juniors).
SMITH.Robert Alfred.	Connaught Gdns.Palmers Green.		Lingdale. 22/2/33		22/12/55.		✓	20 000	Chelsea 1950/55
SMITH.John.	Parminter St.Bethnal Green.E2.		Shoreditch. 4/1/39		15/3/60.		-1	21 000	West Ham 1956/60.
THARME.Derek.	Whitehawk Rd., Brighton Sussex.		Brighton 19/8/38	1/8/56	13/10/56.		✓	3 000	Whitehawk(Brighton).
THOMSON.Graham Nichol.Alex.			Kings Lynn.29/7/39	1/5/54	6/11/57.		✓	3 000	Kings Lynn (Juniors).

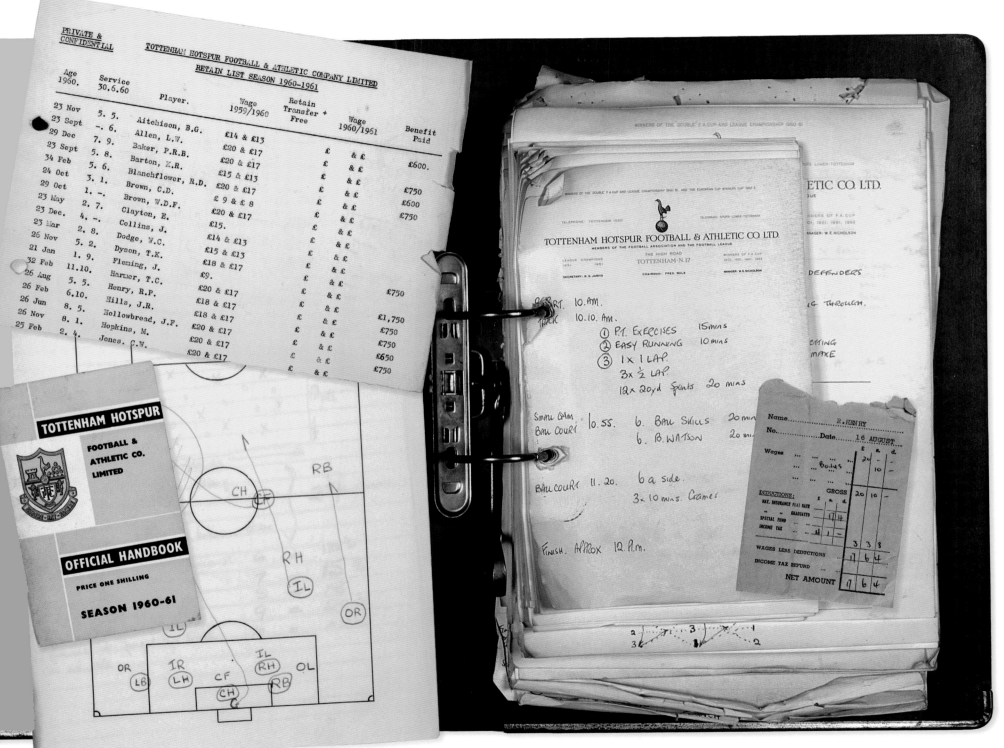

TOTTENHAM HOTSPUR FOOTBALL & ATHLETIC COMPANY LIMITED
RETAIN LIST SEASON 1960-1961

Age 1960.	Service 30.6.60	Player.	Wage 1959/1960	Retain Transfer + Free	Wage 1960/1961	Benefit Paid
23 Nov	5. 5.	Aitchison, B.G.	£14 & £13			
23 Sept	-. 6.	Allen, L.W.	£20 & £17	£	& £	
29 Dec	7. 9.	Baker, P.R.B.	£20 & £17	£	& £	£600.
23 Sept	5. 8.	Barton, K.R.	£15 & £13	£	& £	
34 Feb	5. 6.	Blanchflower, R.D.	£20 & £17	£	& £	£750
24 Oct	3. 1.	Brown, C.D.	£ 9 & £ 8	£	& £	£600
29 Oct	1. -.	Brown, W.D.F.	£20 & £17	£	& £	£750
23 May	2. 7.	Clayton, E.	£15.	£	& £	
23 Dec.	4. -.	Collins, J.	£14 & £13	£	& £	
23 Mar	2. 8.	Dodge, W.C.	£15 & £13	£	& £	
26 Nov	5. 2.	Dyson, T.K.	£18 & £17	£	& £	
21 Jan	1. 9.	Fleming, J.	£9.	£	& £	
32 Feb	11.10.	Harmer, T.C.	£20 & £17	£	& £	£750
26 Aug	5. 5.	Henry, R.P.	£18 & £17	£	& £	£750
26 Feb	6.10.	Hills, J.R.	£18 & £17	£	& £	£1,750
26 Jun	8. 5.	Hollowbread, J.F.	£20 & £17	£	& £	£750
26 Nov	8. 1.	Hopkins, M.	£20 & £17	£	& £	£650
25 Feb	2. 4.	Jones, C.W.	£20 & £17	£	& £	£750

TOTTENHAM HOTSPUR
FOOTBALL & ATHLETIC CO. LIMITED
OFFICIAL HANDBOOK
PRICE ONE SHILLING
SEASON 1960-61

TOTTENHAM HOTSPUR FOOTBALL & ATHLETIC CO. LTD.
MEMBERS OF THE FOOTBALL ASSOCIATION AND THE FOOTBALL LEAGUE

TELEPHONE: TOTTENHAM 1020

748 HIGH ROAD
TOTTENHAM · N.17

LEAGUE CHAMPIONS 1951

WINNERS OF F.A. CUP 1901, 1921, 1961, 1962

SECRETARY: R. S. JARVIS   CHAIRMAN: FRED. WALE   MANAGER: W. E. NICHOLSON

REPORT. 10. AM.

TRACK 10.10. AM.
1. P.T. EXERCISES   15 mins
2. EASY RUNNING   10 mins
3. 1 x 1 LAP.
   3 x ½ LAP.
   12 x 20 yd. Sprints   20 mins

SMALL GYM
BALL COURT   10. 55.   6. BALL SKILLS   20 min
                          6. B. WATSON   20 min

BALL COURT   11. 20.   6 a side.
                          3 x 10 mins. Games

FINISH. APPROX   12. P.M.

Name	R. HENRY			
No.	Date	16 AUGUST		
		£	s.	d.
Wages		20		
Bonus		10		
	GROSS	20	10	
DEDUCTIONS:		£	s.	d.
NAT. INSURANCE FLAT RATE				
" " GRADUATED			17	4
SPECIAL FUND				
INCOME TAX		2	1	
			3	3	8
WAGES LESS DEDUCTIONS		17	6	4
INCOME TAX REFUND				
NET AMOUNT		17	6	4

The Bill Nicholson I knew by John Fennelly

I'd heard that Bill Nicholson could literally stop the traffic. And he proved it one afternoon when I picked him up from his home just off White Hart Lane. Bill was well into retirement but had lost none of his authority as he showed when I prepared to drive forwards to find a place to turn before we headed to the stadium.

"Where are you going?" demanded Bill. "Just do a u-turn." I pointed to the heavy line of vehicles going in both directions but Bill was having none of it. As a double decker bus thundered along the road, Bill jumped out of the car and walked out in front of it with his hand in the air. The bus screeched to a halt and the driver's door was thrown back. I awaited a tirade of abuse but instead the bus driver shouted, "Hello Bill, how's it going?" The same thing happened on the other side of the road as a car driver wound down his window for a chat. Well you just did, didn't you? That was Bill, already 80 and still commanding authority. Just ask any of his players in that great Double side. Bill was the boss. And even when you thought you were doing him a favour by acting as his chauffeur, you still followed orders.

I first met him in the mid-1970s when I started on the *Tottenham Weekly Herald* with the sole role of following Spurs. By then he had returned from his brief sojourn at Upton Park and was very much in tandem with fellow Yorkshireman Keith Burkinshaw. His brief then was on the scouting side where he was exceptional, not just because of his vast football knowledge but because everyone knew him. In addition to respect, you sensed how he inspired real affection. Bill always had time for a chat. He never tired of talking football and I recall once getting into a lift with him to find a man already inside wearing an Arsenal shirt. Now beating the old enemy was crucial to Bill the eternal Spurs man, yet football in general was the key and I remember going up and down in that lift while the banter continued.

It was the same whenever I drove him to a local hospital to visit some unfortunate Spurs employee. Bill was so instantly recognisable that he would be chatting in reception for ages and then would light up the whole ward on entering as even people going through their own personal pain would be left smiling. And Bill gave them all the time in the world. In those days he smiled so much and that's how I'll remember him; with a smile. But it wasn't always that way. Woe betide me if I was ever late.

Back at his beloved Lane he had an office with the coaches in a wing of the West Stand with a view... of a brick wall! Yet you'd walk in there to see one of our scouts, who had also played at the highest level, crawling about on the floor as Bill pelted him with rolled-up pieces of paper to demonstrate the flight of the ball! Or his desk would be cleared while he explained a specific tactic or manoeuvre with the help of anything that came to hand. When I would drop in to see him and his lovely wife Darkie at their home, she would always produce a large tin of biscuits – and Bill would soon have the custard creams attacking the rich teas while he demonstrated a particular piece of play on the coffee table.

It was the same at the local café just outside the main gates where all the staff ate in those days. You had to borrow the 'centre-forward' to put salt on your chips because Bill had pinched all the condiments as part of a tactical talk. No specially designed boards in those days with magnetic discs; showing how the pepper marked the vinegar at a corner did the job just as well.

Even in later years his mind was as sharp as ever; his vast knowledge all there. He would always go that extra mile for

John Fennelly has worked for Spurs since 1984, for 15 years just down the corridor from Bill Nicholson's office. He was press officer for over 20 years and is now head of publications.

Spurs – as the signing of the likes of Tony Galvin and Graham Roberts from non-league football demonstrated. Other Spurs scouts tried the same on a more local scale but it just didn't work. They could spot a lot of things vital in the makeup of a top-flight footballer. But Bill saw into their soul.

Roberts was uncovered because Bill was recognised by a passenger at a railway station who recommended Graham, Galvin was snapped up because Bill braved a wild and snowy night across the Derbyshire hills to watch him play. And the legendary Gary Mabbutt. He wrote to many clubs as he looked to progress from Bristol Rovers. Few replied. But Bill did.

He also had an interest in the Spurs pitch. Not just because he believed the game should be played on the turf but because he had rolled up his sleeves, picked up a spade and helped create the thing in the first place. He was always on about "indentations" – try saying that in a typical Scarborough accent and you'll see why Colin 'Chalky' White, the groundsman at the time, went to sleep with that word running through his subconscious mind.

In fact, Bill maintained that need for a green and flat sward throughout his life. Ron Henry, our left-back in the Double side, told me how he would pick up Bill for games and Bill immediately took advantage of Ron's new career as a nurseryman to get him to mow his back garden. It was a small piece of green overlooking the cemetery, but the surface was like Wembley in spring.

Although Bill was always up for a chat, he was a quiet man in so many ways. He always ignored my attempts to wind him up by suggesting that 1960/61 was a particularly poor season anyway and that his players wouldn't cope in today's game! He knew what he had achieved but never banged his own drum.

John Fennelly and Bill Nicholson at the Double side's induction into the Spurs' 'Hall of Fame' in 2004.

He left that to others because the evidence of the magnitude of what he had built was there for all to see.

I once asked him how he felt as he walked home following our 10-4 triumph in his first game as manager, Bill said: "I knew I had to work on that defence!" He had many philosophies and loved a mantra, like "the man without the ball dictates the play," for example, as he stuck to the principles of our great push-and-run side that he was part of. Yet, although his massive concentration was always on the pitch, he drummed into his players how important our supporters were.

He had served a proper apprenticeship, not just as a player with our nursery side Northfleet, but also as a coach with England and Cambridge University. So when his time came it could never be transitory. Yet he was intelligent enough to appreciate the natural scheme of things, how times changed and life moved on, so never directly interfered with what subsequent managers looked to achieve. Bill was always ready with advice if asked, and thankfully most were sensible enough to do so, but all he cared about was his beloved Spurs.

How apt that they should name the old approach road to the stadium 'Bill Nicholson Way.' Because those three words represent a philosophy that any club would do well to follow.

Before the Double

Above: Danny Blanchflower's arrival at Tottenham is heralded by *Lilywhite* magazine in 1955.
Right: The architects of the Double side – managers on and off the pitch.

Bill Nicholson's long reign as manager at White Hart Lane began with a famous result that seemed to sum up the club's capricious nature. Within 90 minutes of drama that veered from unvarnished brilliance to occasional farce, Spurs thrashed Everton 10-4. Breathtaking in attack one minute, almost ineptly haphazard in defence the next, the display summed up the Spurs way of the time.

Wry comments from the players to Nicholson said it all. "We don't score ten every week, you know," said Tommy Harmer, scorer of a fabulous volleyed goal during the rout. "It's all downhill from now," Danny Blanchflower was reputed to have told his boss, the skipper's wit typically revealing a kernel of truth. The team struggled for the rest of the season and finished fifth from bottom, as injuries and inconsistency hampered stability. Cliff Jones laboured under the £35,000 price tag as Britain's most expensive winger, while Blanchflower spent a good part of the season in the reserves, played out of position and struggling to find form. A transfer was even mooted. Player, manager and all Spurs fans were left to thank their lucky stars that nothing came of any potential parting of the ways.

It was the next season, 1959/60, that was to provide the testing ground for the assault on the Double, and when the Glory Glory game really began to click. Save for a few additions, the team was in place and improving. The players had developed an understanding of how the manager wanted to play. They knew each others' strengths and how to get the best from each other within the team framework. With confidence returning, a momentum began to build that was to ultimately prove unstoppable.

Those additions to the squad and other changes, however, were pretty significant. Dave Mackay had crashed through the White Hart Lane front door in March 1959, bringing not just a fine set of skills but a fiery will to win that removed any of the vestiges of complacency that may have lingered around the club. Tony Marchi was brought back from Italian exile, ready to provide able back-up. Bill Brown donned the green jersey in August 1959, instilling a level of goalkeeping excellence any great side must have. Les Allen made his debut in December and Ron Henry took full advantage of the unlucky Mel Hopkins's injury to claim left-back duties. Meanwhile John White had arrived from Falkirk. Opposition defences would soon be aware of his talent, even if they were to catch all-too-rare sightings of the inside-right as he left them trailing in his ethereal wake.

Before the 1959/60 season got underway though, there was a tour to the Soviet Union. The three games between 27 May and 4 June provided a mixed bag of results – wins against Torpedo Moscow and Dynamo Kiev (1-0 and 2-1 respectively) before Tottenham went down 3-1 to a select Soviet XI in front of 100,000 in Leningrad. The value of the trip was not in the results, however. Nicholson saw it as a means to encourage team bonding and, with few other distractions, to concentrate on training and

Above: Arguably Bill Nicholson's greatest signing, Dave Mackay, on his debut. *Right*: 15 February 1958 and Cliff Jones signs on the dotted line, with Ron Burgess, his manager at Swansea Town, and Spurs boss Jimmy Anderson. Coveted by a whole host of clubs, Jones was told by Burgess, a former Tottenham playing legend himself, not to join Arsenal. "I couldn't understand why at first but now as a Spurs man, I now know why," Jones recalls.

playing. "I cannot overstate the value of that trip in terms of getting things together," he recalled to Phil Soar.

Results during the 1959/60 season soon proved Nicholson right. The side embarked on a 12-game unbeaten sequence, punctuated by four seminal 5-1 thrashings of vaunted opposition. First Newcastle were brushed aside in front of a disbelieving St James' Park crowd. Manchester United may have still been reeling from the Munich disaster, but were to finish runners-up that season and were trounced on their own Old Trafford turf. Preston suffered the same fate at Spurs a week later, before the best victory of them all, a humbling of reigning champions Wolves.

This game and the subsequent two meetings with the Midlanders together formed a pivot on which British football turned and took a different direction, as Wolves's energetic version of the long ball game was completely undone by Nicholson's modern faith in fluent control, passing and movement. Tottenham's unbeaten run came to an end at the hands of Sheffield Wednesday (so often the side that feature in milestone moments of Tottenham league history), but Spurs were top of the table for a three month period up to March.

Familiar inconsistencies meant the title and the cup slipped away, but finishing third, just two points behind champions Burnley represented impressive progress. The team scored goals with familiar abandon but, perhaps more importantly, the defence had tightened up and recorded the lowest goals-against tally in the division, conceding 50 compared to 95 the season before.

That Spurs team made a lasting impression. The venerable *Guardian* football writer David Lacey, recalling the great team displays of history in the wake of the modern Barcelona's exhibition at Arsenal in 2010, included a glowing tribute to the 1959/60 Tottenham side. "The pre-Double Spurs side stick in the mind," Lacey wrote, "because of the impact they had on an era dominated by the breathless, long-passing style of Stan Cullis's Wolves. The subtler, more-thoughtful football of Bill Nicholson's team gave the English game a new learning."

In the summer of 1960, the question was whether that learning could be put into action. Privately and off the record, Nicholson believed it could, but he kept his counsel during the tough summer months of pre-season training when he and Harry Evans put the squad through exhaustive preparations. Come August the team was fit, organised and ready.

It was left to Blanchflower to publically articulate Tottenham's attention-grabbing ambition. "I think we can do it," he would tell his audience. On the eve of the 1960/61 season, the campaign that was to become so important in the history of the game – let alone that of one north London club – the Ulsterman went one stage further and made it a promise. Asked by Chairman Fred Bearman what the team had in store, Blanchflower predicted "We'll get the Double for you this time – the league and the cup." Destiny awaited.

REYNOLDS NEWS
and SUNDAY CITIZEN
COLOUR PHOTO UNIT
presents

Tottenham Hotspur F.C.

Favourites for the League title

● Here are the players of Soccer's new "Bank of England" club, Tottenham Hotspur. The men who, under manager Billy Nicholson, are bidding to win the League championship for the second time in the 77 years of Spurs history.

● First title triumph was with the great Ronnie Burgess-led side of 1950-51. Since then Spurs have twice been runners-up and once finished third—but have just failed to take top place.

● The players in this Reynolds News colour photo (left to right in each row) are as follows:—

BACK ROW: Johnny Hollowbread, Bill Brown, Frank Smith, Ronnie Reynolds.

THIRD ROW: Jimmy Collins, Harold White,

Johnny Brooks, Bobby Smith, Maurice Norman, Tony Marchi, Dave Mackay, Tony Smith.

SECOND ROW: Johnny Hills, Dave Dunmore, Johnny Ryden, Peter Baker, Frank Teece, Norman Lee, Bert Wilkie, Ken Barton, Mel Hopkins, Ron Henry.

FRONT ROW: Billy Dodge, Terry Dyson, Joe Fleming, Tommy Harmer, Danny Blanchflower, Cliff Jones, Graham Thomson, Colin Brown, Alan Reed.

FOR YOUR RECORDS:
1959
Aug. 22—Newc'tle (A) 5—1
„ 26—W.Brom. (H) 2—2
„ 29—Bir'ham (H) 0—0
Sept. 2—W.Brom. (A) 2—1
„ 5—Arsenal (A) 1—1
„ 9—W.Ham (H) 2—2

Sept.	12—Man U. (A)	5—1
„	14—W. Ham (A)	2—1
„	19—Preston (H)	
„	26—Leicester (A)	
Oct.	3—Burnley (H)	
„	10—Wolves (A)	
„	17—Sheff. W. (A)	
„	24—Not'm F. (H)	
„	31—Man. C. (H)	
Nov.	7—Bolton (H)	
„	14—Luton T. (A)	
„	21—Everton (A)	
„	28—Blackp'l (H)	
Dec.	5—Blackb'n (H)	
„	12—Fulham (A)	
„	19—Newc'tle (A)	
„	26—Leeds U. (H)	
„	28—Leeds U. (H)	
1960		
Jan.	2—Bir'ham (A)	

Jan.	9—FA Cup	
„	16—Arsenal (H)	
„	23—Man. U. (H)	
„	30—FA Cup	
Feb.	6—Preston (A)	
„	13—Leicester (H)	
„	20—Burnley (A)	
„	27—Blackb'n (H)	
Mar.	5—Sheff. W. (H)	
„	12—Not'm F (A)	
„	19—Fulham (H)	
„	26—Bolton (A)	
April	2—Luton T. (H)	
„	9—Everton (A)	
„	15—Chelsea (H)	
„	16—Man. C (A)	
„	18—Chelsea (A)	
„	23—Wolvés (H)	
„	30—Blackp'l (H)	
May	7—Cup Final	

NEXT SUNDAY ● A WONDERFUL COL
PHOTOGRAPH OF ARSE

Above: The season prior to the Double. Spurs disappointed the headline writers, finishing third.
Right: John White arrives in London from Falkirk.

● JOHN WHITE signs for Spurs, watched by managers Billy Nicholson (left) and Tommy Younger.

Soviet Union 1959

Facing page: "We're going on a tour," said Bill Nicholson in the spring of 1959. "Great, we all thought," remembers Cliff Jones, "a nice trip to somewhere warm. Cyprus maybe. But Russia? 1959? During the Cold War? It was hard. But it did bond us." The players may have had their doubts but the trip was crucial to the evolution of the Double team.

Right: Vice-Chairman Fred Wale and his son Sidney (with cigar) relax on the plane while Danny Blanchflower and Ron Reynolds have a nap.

Below: The players take a stroll around the streets of Moscow.

Bottom right: Walking out for the Dynamo Kiev game. The tour party also went to the Bolshoi ballet at Bill Nick's insistence. He was impressed with the dancers' muscle conditioning and brought in a weight trainer with the aim of improving the players' physique and fitness.

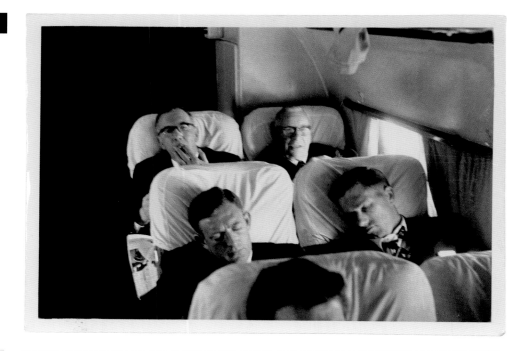

1

Bill Brown

Bill Brown
(Spurs)

1960/61	App/Gls	
League	41	0
FA Cup	7	0
1959-66	App/Gls	
All comps	262	0

It was not an easy task playing in goal for the greatest attacking team in English football history. So Bill Brown's powers of concentration were just as vital as his athleticism. While his team-mates tied their opponents in knots, Brown would pace his area, watching the play and organising his defence, or stand half-crouched between his posts, ready to spring into action. Dave Mackay observed that Brown would reach the dressing room after a supposedly easy game, "looking as tired as if our opponents had been peppering him all afternoon," such was his focus.

Brown's approach to the game was thorough and unfussy, something which means his role in this team of super Spurs has not always been appreciated. But he was the safest of goalkeepers, his performances for Scotland and Dundee – a club he played for as many times as he did for Spurs – attracting the attention of Bill Nicholson, who signed him for £16,500 in 1959.

Unlike many goalkeepers of his day, Brown cut a lean figure, meaning he was susceptible to heavy challenges. Lucky, then, that he had big Maurice Norman in front of him to deal with aerial threats. Brown's game was built on choosing the right position, and on a tremendous agility and sharp reflexes which made him a consummate shot-stopper.

Brown's reliability and unflappable personality meant that he asserted a calming presence on the team even in the tensest games. Having such a level head in the dressing room was every bit as important as having fiery, inspirational leaders.

The tendency is to look for the stars, the outstanding individuals, in any great team. But an assessment of Bill Brown's contribution to the Spurs Double side reveals just what a complete team this was. Brown's preference for finding a team-mate with a quick throw or even a longer kick often helped turn defence rapidly into attack and contributed enormously to the refined push-and-run style with which Nicholson wanted his team to play.

Brown reinvented the role of the goalkeeper. Previously, keepers had to impose themselves physically. Brown played as part of the defence, stopping shots still the main task, but also looking to change the play, retain possession and build from the back, often picking out Danny Blanchflower or John White with a precise delivery. During the Double season he missed just one game, away to West Ham on Boxing Day after picking up a slight injury against the Hammers in the preceeding match. He turned in an immaculate performance in the FA Cup final.

The home fans doubted Brown at first precisely because he was different. But they soon took to the man who would become one of the club's greatest goalkeepers, the chant of "Hovis, Hovis" (inspired by the famous brown bread) their expression of devotion. Brown stayed with Spurs until 1966, nurturing Pat Jennings before leaving for Northampton Town. He moved to Canada to play for Toronto Falcons in 1967 and worked in property development and for state government until he retired in 1995. He died in Simcoe, Ontario, on 30 November 2004, aged 73.

HOLD IT!

Previous page: Brown displays his agility in training in July 1960.
Above: Brown on the cover of the magazine *Lilywhite* (centre) with reserve keepers Frank Smith (left) and John Hollowbread.
Right: Sporting the latest in 'healthy' underwear in an advertising endorsement for Twilley's string vests.

Bill Brown

66 Bill was very agile, a great shot stopper and could handle the physical stuff. He was also the only Scotsman I ever understood! 99 Cliff Jones

1960

August

Left: Bobby Smith in typically combative action in the season's opening fixture, up against Jimmy Gabriel (No 4), Alex Parker and goalkeeper Albert Dunlop.

"The whistle blows, the cockerel crows, and now we're in the game" in the words of the Spurs anthem *MacNamara's Band*. Finally, after all the anticipation, the nerve-tingling hope, and the dreamy contemplation of doing the Double, the season for real at last got underway.

The pressure was considerable. Tottenham had disappointed many neutrals by just missing out on the league title the previous season and the tenor of some of the newspaper reports verged on the critical, as if it was demanded that Spurs live up to the billing the media had championed. Such was the beauty of Tottenham's football that they were not just tipped to win the title but to do so as a matter of duty. All England expected.

The initial task was not an easy one. Everton were tough opponents for an opening fixture and would go on to win the league two seasons later. Johnny Carey's team were resolute at keeping Spurs at bay, with keeper Albert Dunlop and his defenders in good form to snuff out the home side's attacking threat. Tottenham's patience was rewarded late on when goals from Les Allen and Bobby Smith secured victory. Though Cliff Jones limped off with an ankle injury that kept him out of the side for a month, Bill Nicholson expressed himself happy; his team had remained patient, played their football and got their reward. The players had bagged a morale-boosting win early on and the White Hart Lane crowd had got the early signs they were looking for. Spurs were setting the pace.

The inevitable question was whether the momentum could be maintained. The answer came as the Spurs roadshow hit the North. First stop was Blackpool, where Tottenham served up some thrilling end-of-the-summer-season entertainment that would have easily outshone the fabled illuminations. "London's Soccer showmen" the *News Chronicle* dubbed them, as they ran out comfortable 3-1 winners. Next up were another Lancastrian side and this time Spurs went one better, thrashing in-form Blackburn 4-1. Tom Finney described it as "breathtaking"; even the Ewood Park crowd were impressed, a measure of how Tottenham's style was winning admiration outside of north London.

Poor Blackpool had little time to recover from their defeat, swiftly making the return trip for another 3-1 humbling as August drew to a close. For man of the match Bobby Smith it was a milestone game. Not only did he score a hat trick, but with his first goal he broke George Hunt's record of 138 goals for the club that had stood for 23 years.

This blistering start left Spurs sitting proud at the top of the table, a point clear of Sheffield Wednesday and already with 12 goals to their name and just three conceded. It confounded the doubters and instilled renewed confidence within the club. Burnley and Everton, among the elite of the day, were no pushovers and though Blackpool were eventually to fall away and just avoid relegation, they provided a stern and robust test of Tottenham's mettle. The Lilywhites passed – and with flying colours.

MATCH 1. SATURDAY 20TH AUGUST. 1960

MATCH 2. MONDAY 22nd AUGUST. 1960

NEWS OF THE WORLD, Aug. 21, 1960

ODDS AGAINST SPURS? —TAKE THEM!

By HARRY DITTON
SPURS 2, EVERTON 0

IF anyone should be rash enough to lay you a shade of odds against Spurs winning the First Division championship, jump in quickly! True, they beat Everton only by dramatic goals scored in the 85th and 87th minutes when almost everyone was resigned to a draw, but Spurs had such a strong edge over their opponents in point of skill and pressure that any other verdict would have been a travesty.

And Everton are no mean side themselves, as you might expect with a forward line costing more than £100,000.

The power of Spurs unquestionably stemmed from their magnificent half-back line of Blanchflower, Norman and Mackay. All three were in tremendous form, with Blanchflower excelling in attack, Mackay unfailingly good both as an attacker and defender, and Norman utterly dominating at centre-half.

I have never seen Norman play better and he must have made a deep impression on the England Selectors present.

Maybe Spurs supporters will feel—and possibly Manager Billy Nicholson too—that with such strong support coming from the half-backs, the forwards should have settled the issue long before they did.

But I am not prepared to be unduly critical of Bobby Smith and his colleagues. True, as a line they did not move so smoothly as they so often can—and do, when little Tommy Harmer is in the line-up. (At the moment he has to be content with a place in the reserves.)

But the real reason goals were so long delayed was the superb goalkeeping of Liverpool-born Albert Dunlop. He gave a magnificent display.

A goalkeeper usually thrives on plenty of action, and Dunlop was never out of the picture. Even Blanchflower and Norman occasionally moved up to test him, but Dunlop's positioning was quite uncanny and he thoroughly deserved the great and spontaneous ovation a sporting crowd gave him at the close.

With Everton so heavily overplayed and little Bobby Collins and Vernon often forced to fall back and help out, little was seen of Johnny Carey's much-vaunted forward-line.

Such counter-attacks as were attempted usually came through the spirited raiding of outside-right Lill and from the long ball down the middle to centre-forward Harris. Neither looked like succeeding against a Spurs defence that was in tip-top form.

When Spurs went into the lead after 85 minutes, Bobby Smith fell heavily in the penalty area and there were frantic appeals for a penalty. The referee waved play on and Allen, cutting in quickly, scored with a low drive.

While the crowd were still cheering in relief and gratification, Spurs made another forceful raid on the right wing and from White's cross Smith scored with a beautifully-judged header.

SCORERS — ALLEN / SMITH

HALF-TIME — 0-0

ATTENDANCE — 53,395

OLD (WEST) STAND

1960 - 61

TOTTENHAM HOTSPUR

FOOTBALL & ATHLETIC CO. LTD.

Season Ticket - £8/8/0

DYSON no longer relies on spirit and nuisance value alone He has added considerable skill to his other attributes, in spite of his lack of size.

H.T.	LEAGUE DIVISION I	Gate
0-2 Blackpool 1	Tottenham 3	27,656
Mudie	Dyson 2, Medwin	

NEWS CHRONICLE, TUESDAY, AUGUS

Two-goal Dyson streaks in for slick Spurs

Blackpool 1   Spurs 3   By DENIS LOWE

SKILL : Blackpool 6, Spurs 8. Crowd 8. Control 9. GOALS: 0—3, 1—3.

TERRY DYSON doesn't really mind being overshadowed by his high-priced colleagues at Tottenham. But now and again, little Terry likes to make his presence felt. Last night, for instance. . . .

It was two-goal Terry who made sure of victory for London's Soccer showmen at Bloomfield Road. And it was a victory richly deserved.

Spurs served up some superb Soccer for the 27,656 holiday crowd.

Only nine minutes had gone when Spurs first struck. Les Allen pushed a short corner to Scottish international John White, and when the cross came over, Dyson soared high to beat Blackpool's giant keeper, Tony Waiters, with a fine header.

Squandered

Bill Brown brought off splendid saves from David Durie and Arthur Kaye before Blackpool squandered a penalty. Peter Baker fouled Ray Charnley in the 31st minute, and Kaye shot tamely past the upright.

Six minutes later Blackpool were two down. Terry Medwin and star-schemer White linked up delightfully for Medwin to fire in a right-foot drive.

Goal No. 3 for Spurs came in the 55th minute, with Blackpool's defence again caught on the hop. Baker came up in attack and squared across the edge of the box. Bobby Smith let it travel on to the incoming Dyson—and Waiters had no chance at all.

Blackpool sparked into life to score right from the kick-off, Jackie Mudie stabbing a Kaye pass into the corner of the net.

BLACKPOOL: Waiters 7; Armfield 7, Martin 7; Kelly J 6, Grarrix 7, Durie 6; Matthews 6, Mudie 6, Charnley 6, Kaye 6, Campbell 5.

TOTTENHAM: Brown 8; Baker 7, Henry 7; Blanchflower 8, Norman 8, Mackay 8; Medwin 7, White 8, Smith 7, Allen 7, Dyson 8.

REFEREE: N N Hough (Macclesfield). LINESMEN: L Barlow (Bury). H Burns (Leyland).

SCORERS — BLACKPOOL — MUDIE / SPURS — MEDWIN / DYSON (2)

HALF-TIME — 0-2

ATTENDANCE — 27,656

NEWS OF THE WORLD, Aug. 28, 1960

Breath-taking! That's Spurs

By TOM FINNEY as told to DON EVANS

BLACKBURN 1, SPURS 4

THIS was English soccer at its most superb—a solid slap in the face for the carping critics of our game, plus a 90-minute tip on who is likely to take the League title this season. Blackburn Rovers and Spurs, each with two great wins from two games, should have made the closest-fought match of the day. It proved to be a massacre.

An "I'll pick my spot" seventh-minute goal and another eight minutes later by centre-forward Bobbie Smith; a 17th-minute drive by inside-left Les Allen; a 48th-minute effort from outside-left Terry Dyson; and a 90th-minute header from Derek Dougan made it 4—1 at the final whistle. But the glory was in Spurs' game, not in their goals.

Spurs jingle-jangled their way to the back of the Rovers net with a classic display of controlled soccer, the sort which would have sent even the fabulous Real Madrid home rubbing their eyes.

The big difference between the teams was that every Spurs player was looking for the ball, while many Rovers men did not seem to realise it was about.

Even with wee Terry Dyson—and how well he played—in for Welsh international Cliff Jones, there was not the weak link in the Spurs team.

Like a machine

With Skipper Danny Blanchflower and Dave Mackay the kingpins, they moved like a machine, interchanged at will and with breath-taking efficiency, strode through the game like an English soccer colossus of old.

And if there is little of Blackburn in this report, that's how it should be, for that's how it was on the field. They came into the game occasionally, had bad luck at times, but lacked a schemer up front in the mould of Spurs inside-forward, John White.

Rovers' nearest efforts came with a handful of great drives by Chris Crowe, their best player afield, and two shots from Peter Dobing which Spurs goalkeeper Bill Brown only just managed to deflect.

But often Rovers seemed to be there solely to make up the required number.

However, Blackburn need not feel blue. To lose to such a side as Spurs is no disgrace. In fact to lose by only 4—1 to the Spurs of this fantastic football showing could almost be assessed as achievement.

LES ALLEN . . . goal-scoring inside forward obtained from Chelsea in exchange for Johnny Brooks.

SCORERS

BLACKBURN   DOUGAN
SPURS   ALLEN
             SMITH (2)
             DYSON

HALF-TIME   0-3
ATTENDANCE   26,700

DAILY MIRROR, Thursday, September 1, 1960 PAGE 19

Smith hat-tricks way to Spurs record

THE BOBBY DAZZLER...

By KEN JONES: Spurs 3, Blackpool 1

THE goals, the glamour and the glory went to Spurs centre forward Bobby Smith at White Hart-lane last night.

Battling Bobby, the never-give-up ruthless finisher of Spurs' football finery, hit Blackpool with what must have been his greatest "hat-trick"—and smashed a twenty-three-year Tottenham record.

Bobby kicked off on his night of nights, meaning to score just once to top George Hunt's 138 record goal total.

After only four minutes he'd done it—with a trip-hammer header that raked in under the bar.

It whipped him into gear as Spurs' one top-form forward, for their galaxy of stars never really clicked.

But what Spurs failed to achieve with artistry they made up for with fight—the stuff that wins championships.

In a rip-roaring last twenty minutes they hit Blackpool with everything and paved the way for Smith's triumph.

A deadly Blanchflower-Dyson move in the 75th-minute put Smith through for No. 2.

His Third

And he clinched his hat-trick eight minutes from time after right-winger Terry Medwin had carved out the chance.

Until Spurs finally ground them to the grass, Blackpool had always been in with a chance.

Leslie Lea, seventeen-year-old starlet inside right, raked in a 37th-minute equaliser, and Spurs' keeper Bill Brown had to pull out three top-class saves to keep out Jackie Mudie.

SCORERS

SPURS   SMITH (3)
BLACKPOOL   LEA

HALF-TIME   1-1
ATTENDANCE   46,684

BOBBY SMITH
Goal record for Spurs

	HOME						AWAY						
					Goals						Goals			
	P	W	D	L	F	A	W	D	L	F	A	Pts
Tottenham H. ..	3	1	0	0	2	0	2	0	0	7	2	6
Sheffield Wed. .	3	1	0	0	1	0	1	1	0	2	1	5
Wolverhampton.	3	1	0	0	4	2	1	1	0	5	3	5
Everton	3	2	0	0	7	1	0	0	1	0	2	4
Arsenal	3	2	0	0	4	0	0	0	1	2	3	4
Newcastle Utd .	3	1	0	1	7	3	1	0	0	3	2	4
Blackburn Rov.	3	0	1	1	5	5	1	0	0	3	1	4
West Ham	3	2	0	0	7	3	0	0	1	2	4	4
Birmingham	3	0	1	0	1	1	1	1	0	4	3	4
Burnley	3	1	0	0	3	2	0	1	1	2	2	4
Cardiff City	3	1	0	1	2	4	0	1	0	2	2	3
Manchester C..	2	1	0	0	4	2	0	1	0	2	2	3
Blackpool	3	1	0	1	6	6	0	0	1	1	3	3
Leicester City .	3	0	1	0	1	1	1	0	1	4	4	3
Fulham	3	0	1	0	2	2	0	1	1	6	9	3
Aston Villa	3	1	0	0	3	2	0	0	2	5	10	2
Chelsea	3	0	1	0	1	4	0	1	0	2	3	1
Bolton Wand. ..	3	0	1	1	2	4	0	0	1	1	2	1
Nottingham F. .	3	0	1	0	2	2	0	0	2	1	7	1
West Bromwich	3	0	0	2	3	6	0	0	1	0	0	0
Preston N.E.	3	0	0	1	2	3	0	0	2	0	3	0
Manchester Utd	2	0	0	1	1	3	0	0	1	0	4	0

2

Peter Baker

PETER BAKER
(Spurs)

1960/61	App/Gls	
League	41	1
FA Cup	7	0
1952-65	App/Gls	
All comps	342	3

In tandem with Ron Henry on the opposite flank, Peter Baker was a vital component of the Tottenham side and integral to ensuring its smooth running. He performed with precision and reliability, underpinning the flair for which the team became rightly famous. The Double side needed Baker.

Operating on the right-hand side of a three-man defensive line, he frequently had to cover for Blanchflower whose inspired sojourns were a joy to behold but could leave Spurs open on the right-hand side. Baker's efficiency, positioning and assured use of the ball provided the calm resolution in defence that ensured none of the fireworks up front went to waste. His preference for playing a short pass to Blanchflower, Henry or Norman was ideal for the team's push-and-run style.

In a team liberally served with individual brilliance his talent was often overlooked. This was as much to do with his unassuming character as with his playing style. It was an era when the maximum wage was doomed, a time when sportsmen were on the cusp of attaining celebrity status with the wealth to match. Yet Baker was perfectly content to simply get on with the job.

A locally born, home-grown veteran by the time the season got underway, Baker had been at Spurs for 11 years and had to fight for a place, his position in the first team occupied by no less a talent than Alf Ramsey. This testing experience helped make him such an accomplished defender, necessitating a level of consistency that his manager valued.

He certainly fitted Bill Nick's template, boasting character, composure, tactical know-how and technical skill coupled with physical strength and stamina.

Photographs of the team portray him as a figure with a ready smile but not as one to hog the gaze of the lens. Yet he was no introvert. In the aftermath of Tottenham's bruising defeat to Sheffield Wednesday that ended the unbeaten run, Baker remonstrated with opponent Bill Griffin and was ticked off by referee Reg Leafe. "One of my linesmen told me he had heard Baker make a remark," Leafe scolded. "Some players seem to think that my job is over when the whistle goes, and I reminded him a bit sharpish that I was still very much in charge."

Such displays of ruffled annoyance were the exception, however. Baker was both Mr Cool and Mr Dependable – he even went in goal during a defeat to Birmingham in 1959 and missed just one game in the Double season. He scored only once in the campaign, at Burnley. It was a reminder that this studious, industrious and reliable defender was a fine player and a fundamental part of the effective whole.

Given a free transfer in 1965 as injury brought his career to a close, Baker moved to South Africa where he managed Durban United before building up a furniture business. The charms of north London have proved hard to resist, however, and he has since returned to his old stomping grounds, where he remains a popular and gentlemanly figure on the Spurs old-boys scene.

Previous page: Baker defends on the goal line in the January 1960 derby against Arsenal. Spurs ran out 3-0 winners.
This page: Baker's no 2 shirt, worn in the 1961 FA Cup final against Leicester City.
Facing page: Training at Cheshunt, 28 February 1961. His elegant athleticism was a major feature of his game.

PETER BAKER, Tottenham Hotspur

"Peter Baker was one of the best all-round sportsmen I've ever met. Schoolboy cricket, county squash, junior Wimbledon... he was up there at all of them" Cliff Jones

1960

September

League

3rd	**Spurs 4 Man Utd 1**
7th	**Bolton 1 Spurs 2**
10th	**Arsenal 2 Spurs 3**
14th	**Spurs 3 Bolton 1**
17th	**Leicester 1 Spurs 2**
24th	**Spurs 6 Aston Villa 2**

Left: Terry Dyson heads the second goal past Arsenal's goalkeeper Jack Kelsey in the crunch north London derby, leaving defender John Sneddon a spectator.

Spurs got even better in September. They were so good that by the end of the month, just ten games into the season, the talk was not just of winning the English league title. That seemed a foregone conclusion. Already, the prospect of an assault on the European Cup the following season was being discussed.

The football press of the day was not as given to hyperbole as today's. So when the sober commentators of the nationals said: "There is no other team in the country that can live with Spurs" and: "It was impossible to imagine any British team stopping them at all," it really meant something. The warmth Spurs generated with their thrilling football not only appealed to lovers of the game, but to the pride of a nation in an age of ambition. For years the English football establishment had taken the view that English football was the best in the world because it was, well, English. But it was clear to all but the most blinkered that the European stage was the one upon which true greatness had to be demonstrated. Tottenham's September form gave a nation hope it could prove itself where it mattered.

By the end of the month a new record for consecutive league wins from the start of a season had been set – 50 years on it still stands – and Spurs had demonstrated just how they would come to achieve the glory of the Double. The wing-halves Blanchflower and Mackay were running games, keeping possession and distributing sweet passes for the forward line. White's passing and movement was also key, and goalscorers Allen and Smith thrived on the service they got. And at the back stood Norman, imperious in these early weeks.

A respected Manchester United team was beaten 4-1. Only an inspired display from United's goalkeeper Harry Gregg kept the score down. At Highbury, the old enemy were beaten 3-2 in what Peter Lorenzo dubbed: "Britain's finest soccer exhibition for years" and at Filbert Street Leicester City were swept aside. But there was steel to go with the silk.

Away at Bolton in midweek, missing Smith and Jones and with Henry labouring with a heavy cold, Spurs had to dig deep, eventually coming back from a goal down to win 2-1. The return a week later saw Spurs show they could win ugly in a tough game marked by a controversial penalty in the Lilywhites' favour, clenched fists on the pitch and robust abuse of the visiting keeper by Spurs fans. Even the torrential rain that night could not have a negative effect on Tottenham's parade.

Spurs also showed they had ammunition in reserve. When injury to Bobby Smith kept him out, some wondered if Spurs could replace a man who had scored eight times in five games. A 17-year-old called Frank Saul stepped in, scoring a screaming opener against Arsenal and setting up a second for Dyson. In the final game of the month, Spurs demolished a decent Aston Villa side 6-2 to set a new record of ten straight wins from day one. The final goal summed Spurs up – a five-person, pitch long passing move finished on the volley by a galloping Mackay.

MATCH 5 SATURDAY 3RD SEPT. 1960

MATCH 6 WEDNESDAY 7TH SEPT. 1960

EMPIRE NEWS and SUNDAY CHRONICLE, September 4, 1960

HEROIC GREGG VERSUS SPURS

BOBBY CHARLTON

Spurs 4, Manchester Utd. 1

by WALTER GREEN

GLORIOUS, wonderful Spurs! England's golden club team of the 60's might have hit Busby's bewildered boys for double figures, but for an out-of-this-world goalkeeping epic by Irishman, Harry Gregg.

At times it seemed that Gregg had been left to face Spurs' might all on his own. He dived, leapt and punched out blinding drives until he resembled a candidate for the Olympic jumps and boxing events combined.

His knuckles took a real pounding as one Spurs forward after another surged through to hit drives at him. Four times the magnificent Harry was beaten—but it might have been 14 against the one-way tide.

Gregg's ordeal was mainly due to those non-stop driving wing halves—Danny Blanchflower and Dave Mackay, and that automatic brain John White.

Lightweight White had some jolting experiences, especially one when he seemed to rattle and roll under the impact of a Maurice Setters charge.

Precise moves

But White—delicate, precise, ingenius—made the open spaces lured United's defence into one crisis after another, and laid passes on the line that would have done credit to the Continentals themselves. He made Bobby Smith's first goal (five minutes) wwhen he sized on an abbysmal Setters pass to send his leader through. Yet his most telling move only came in the 62nd minute, when United were trying to save at least their faces. He darted forward, changed pace and mesmerising United's defence, to give Les Allen an easy header to make it 3-1.

Allen—a very different proposition from the old Chelsea player—had got No. 2 (18 minutes) when he made Matt Busby's search for a defender look urgent by dribbling between three meen, then around Gregg, to tap the ball into the open net.

Six minutes from time, the player who has been reported to want to get away from Spurs, Terry Medwin, pulled the ball back from the line to give Smith a sitter.

Dennis Viollet got United's

goal three minutes before half-time to cut Spurs' 2—0 lead. He made the opening himself.

It was that way for United—individual efforts and precious little teamwork. They looked pale, disjointed and at times demoralised.

Bobby Charlton never stopped trying and hit two thunderbolts, but they were from too far out to worry Brown.

On the opposite wing, Albert Quixall looked lost and hopeless out on the line.

I wondered why United persisted in playing two of the cleverest inside men in the game out on their wings, when they so obviously lacked craft and thrust inside.

But United's main trouble is in defence. I rate them lucky to have got away so respectably after being so outplayed by what is clearly the most exciting League team of the day.

SCORERS
SPURS   SMITH (2)
          ALLEN (2)

MAN.U.   VIOLLET

HALF-TIME   2-1
ATTENDANCE   55,445

CLASH . . . between bustling Bobby Smith of Spurs and tough-as-teak Harry Gregg, Manchester United goalkeeper. It looks as if Smith is coming off worst . . . but it's Bobby who offers consolation in the end.   *Pictures by ROBERT STIGGINS*

NEWS CHRONICLE, THURSDAY, SEPTEMBER 8, 1960

Spurs surge back after early shock

— Bolton 1, Spurs 2: By FRANK TAYLOR —

SKILL: Bolton 7, Spurs 9. Sportsmanship 8. Control 8. Crowd 8. GOALS: 1—0, 1—1, 1—2.

PROUD Spurs hung on to their unbeaten record by their bootlaces at Burnden Park. It was a night that began in glory for Bolton . . . and ended in disaster.

Bolton grabbed a shock early lead. Spurs, the £200,000 Glamour Boys, were tottering to their first defeat. They were a goal down, and dithering against Bolton's power-play when brilliant full-back Tommy Banks tore his right thigh. From that point Spurs were fighting 10 fit men.

Now we saw the real Spurs' Soccer machine swing into action. They gradually ground down brave Bolton until they were leg-weary.

Five minutes after Banks' injury John White floated the ball over, Eddie Hopkinson failed to cut it out—his only boob of the game—and Les Allen equalised with a magnificent header.

Ten minutes from time Danny Blanchflower chipped over another glorious centre which White hooked into the net on the half-turn. A truly great goal.

That's how the game ended. But what a blistering start Bolton made. In the third minute Billy McAdams scored after Albert Holden had cheekily turned the ball back to him following a brilliant save by Bill Brown.

This goal really spurred Bolton. Freddy Hill was in tremendous form. Dave Mackay couldn't hold him, and I lost count of the near-misses. Ray Parry hit the oar. Hill shot wide, and McAdams blasted the rebound over the bar after Brown had brilliantly saved his initial shot.

Yet Spurs never flagged in their push-and-run style. Their new centre-forward, 17-year-old Frank Saul, looked a fast thinker AND fast mover.

SCORERS: Bolton: McAdams (3 mins.). Spurs: Allen (62). White (80).

BOLTON: Hopkinson 8; Hartle 7, Banks 8; Stanley 8, Higgins 7, Edwards 7; Birch 7, Hill 8, McAdams 7, Parry 7, Holden 7.

TOTTENHAM: Brown 8, Baker 6, Henry 6; Blanchflower 8, Norman 7, Mackay 7; Medwin 7, White 8, Saul 7, Allen 8, Dyson 7.

REFEREE. R T E Langdale (Darlington). LINESMEN: A Gorton (Macclesfield), K C Hesketh (Heald Green).

SCORERS   BOLTON : McADAMS
SPURS   ALLEN
        WHITE

HALF-TIME   1-0
ATTENDANCE   41,181

JONES BOY IN AGAIN!

GOLDEN BOY FRANK SAUL JUMPS TO IT FOR A GREAT GOAL

Arsenal 2, Spurs 3

CLIFF JONES, bought for £35,000 as a left-winger, will be back in Spurs team on Wednesday, helping them in the bid to set up an all-time record sequence of victories.

But he will be at outside right, in place of Terry Medwin, his Welsh international colleague, writes Bill Holden.

Spurs intend to persevere with Jones, fully fit again after injury, on the right wing, and he is willing to go along with the plan.

His appearance at White Hart-lane against Bolton should lead to Spurs notch-

Spurs out for all-time best start

ing their eighth win in a row.

When they beat Arsenal they broke the best-ever start by any club in the First Division and equalled their own 1919 record start in the Second Division.

On their first half showing against Arsenal it was impossible to imagine any British team stopping them at all.

Centre forward Frank Saul, playing only his second game, had the same master touch of his high-priced team-mates.

Brilliant

He blasted a brilliant goal in the twelfth minute and outside-left Terry Dyson headed the second in the twenty-third minute.

Only Arsenal 'keeper Jack Kelsey, with four dramatic saves, stopped a massacre.

The Gunners came fighting back after half-time and drew level with two goals in four fantastic minutes.

Centre forward David Herd thundered in the first

after 61 minutes, and right half Gerry Ward hit home a spectacular goal in the 65th minute.

Then Spurs, showing the stuff that makes champions, regained their grip, and inside left Les Allen raced through to lob in the goal which won the match in the 71st minute.

TOMMY DOCHERTY.

● It's just what the "doc" ordered! Arsenal's left-half Tommy Docherty takes time out for a rest in the derby clash with Spurs. Propping him up is Frank Saul, Spurs' young centre-forward

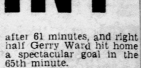

An anxious moment for Arsenal ends abruptly as Jack Kelsey gets his safe hands on the ball at Highbury this afternoon. Standing over him are John Sneddon and Gerry Ward. The Spurs player is 17-year-old centre-forward Frank Saul.

SCHEMED No. 1 — SCORED No. 3

LES ALLEN . . . the Spurs' inside-left, showed Arsenal the value of the long kick

SCORERS
ARSENAL: HERD
WARD

SPURS: SAUL
DYSON
ALLEN

HALFTIME: 0.2

ATTENDANCE: 60,088

MATCH 8 WEDNESDAY 14TH SEPT 1960

DAILY MIRROR, Thursday, September 15, 1960

Fury after penalty drama

PELTED BY FANS, SAYS EDDIE

By BILL HOLDEN

Spurs 3, Bolton 1

BOLTON broke their hearts in a vain bid to smash Spurs' 100 per cent. record last night.

And the startling penalty decision of referee F. Clarke in the sixty-fifth minute, which really swung the game, sparked five minutes of fury.

In that spell the referee took the name of Bolton right winger Brian Birch twice.

First he brought down Spurs left half, Dave Mackay, and then right winger Cliff Jones. Each time he was called up by the referee.

Policeman on Guard

And in the seventy-second minute, with the crowd booing continuously, Eddie Hopkinson, Bolton's goalkeeper, refused to take a goal kick until the referee had placed a policeman behind his goal.

He complained to the referee that fans were throwing litter at him.

It was a sad interval in an otherwise brilliant match, which drew 43,559 fans on the night of a downpour.

Spurs overcame the conditions and the impressive opposition to play fantastically good football.

Centre forward Billy McAdams, slammed Bolton into the lead in the seventh minute but centre forward Bobby Smith equalised in the twenty-fourth minute.

After the break Spurs were close to scoring four times before that fire-raising sixty-fifth minute exploded the game.

Smith crossed the ball from the left, Terry Dyson, outside left, went for the ball, was challenged, stumbled and fell.

Astonishing

Allen ran on to the ball and drove it wide. To the astonishment of most people, the referee pointed to the penalty spot.

Even Spurs players admitted afterwards that they were not sure at the time why he made the award.

It was officially announced afterwards that he had ruled that Dyson was fouled by being bundled off the ball.

Blanchflower, calmest man in a stormy ground, took the kick and scored. Then came the name-taking and the policeman posting.

Six minutes from the end, Allen put Smith through, and the centre forward ran on to lob the ball over Hopkinson and into the net.

" That's what comes of having one over the eight ! "

SCORERS

SPURS SMITH (2)
BLANCHFLOWER (PEN)

BOLTON MCADAMS

HALF-TIME 1-1

ATTENDANCE 43559

MATCH 9 SATURDAY 17TH SEPT 1960

EMPIRE NEWS and SUNDAY CHRONICLE, September 18. 1960

TOP TEAM CRUSH AS THEY DAZZLE

by ROLAND ORTON

LEICESTER CITY 1   TOTTENHAM HOTSPUR 2

MIGHTY Spurs march on with a 100 per cent. record. They contemptuously pushed aside a gallant Leicester City attempt to smash their proud sequence—now nine wins, which equals the Football League record for best-ever starts.

Two great goals by the hub of the relentless Spurs goal machine, burly centre-forward Bobbie Smith, took the heart out of Leicester, who up to half-time had been matching Tottenham's skill.

After being a goal down, Leicester played on undaunted to draw level with a never-to-be-forgotten goal by sturdy right-winger Riley, but it should not have been their first goal.

Centre-forward Len Leek had been guilty of two shocking misses, one from a perfect corner cross from Riley and the other when he shot over again after Jimmy Walsh had put him through.

With the home crowd near delirious at the way their team were holding their own, mood switched suddenly as Spurs went ahead after 19 minutes following a blunder by Colin Appleton.

The left-half had the ball dangerously near his own goal, and for some reason stood still, making no attempt to clear. Right-winger Cliff Jones whipped the ball from him and passed to Smith, who whipped it into the net.

Leek had another bad miss, but in the 30th minute put the ball to Riley to start Leicester's goal movement. The centre-forward passed cleverly, speedy Riley streaked goalwards, and then, with defenders jamming the goal-line, halted and hit a terrific shot into the net.

Spurs were now producing delightful football, particularly on the right wing. Just before half-time Tony Knapp stopped them from going ahead when he kicked a shot from inside-left Les Allen off the line.

But the inevitable second goal came in the 55th minute. It was an intricate piece of work, typical of wonderful Spurs.

Danny Blanchflower began it by switching the ball to Jones. There came neat inter-passing with inside-right John White before the ball was slipped inside for Smith's head to apply the finishing touch.

The goal shattered Leicester, whose only other threatening move was when Leek bulldozed goalkeeper Bill Brown into the net after a corner kick—but the quick-thinking Brown made sure the ball did not go in with him.

SCORERS
LEICESTER. RILEY
SPURS : SMITH (2)

HALF-TIME 1-1

ATTENDANCE 30129

There's no stopping Spurs: Nicholson's knockouts make it 9

IT seems nothing can stop Spurs — or Bobby Smith. Leicester City, the team who went to White Hart Lane last season and put the skids under Tottenham, went the way of the rest yesterday when Nicholson's knockouts chalked up their ninth successive win. Bobby Smith got both their goals to bring his total so far to a round dozen.

SMITH MAKES IT 12

What! No cheers you Leicester fans

SPURS SMASH RECORD

YES, SPURS ARE OUT ON THEIR OWN

By HARRY DITTON

Handwritten: MATCH 10 SATURDAY 24 SEPT '60

NEWS CHRONICLE, MONDAY, SEPTEMBER 26, 1960

TOTTENHAM 6, ASTON VILLA 2

WELL, the immaculate and irresistible Spurs did it. With another incredible show of brilliance they totted up their tenth victory since the season began, and in doing so set up a new Football League record. I am convinced that in their present mood there is not another team in the country that can live with the Spurs. Villa did not play badly. On the contrary, much of their midfield approach work was first-rate, and with any luck at all they would have had at least two more goals to show for it.

Gerry Hitchens had a particularly good first half against a rather uncertain Norman, and led his line with speed and intelligence.

Thompson at inside-right also repeatedly caught the eye and was dreadfully unlucky with a well-timed header which crashed against the crossbar.

There were a couple of other occasions when, with Spurs leading by only a goal, Villa were denied the reward which excellent approach work seemed to merit. So it was far from being a case of Spurs having nothing to beat.

Aston Villa were a good team but Spurs were a super side. That was the difference. There's nothing wrong with the British brand of soccer as Spurs interpret it.

From goalkeeper to outside-left, every man is playing with a wealth of confidence. There just isn't a semblance of a weak link anywhere.

Halves are the key

Nevertheless the key to the uncanny excellence of the team as a whole are those wonderful wing half-backs, Danny Blanchflower and Dave Mackay. If there is a better pair anywhere I have not seen them.

A forward line containing the punch and bustle of Bobby Smith, the sheer craft of John White and the speed and accurate finishing of Allen, Jones and Dyson can hardly fail to get a crop of goals. And of course they got six!

The first was delayed only seven minutes — a glorious Blanchflower and Jones movement which switched defence into attack in a twinkle, for White to score.

Two narrow shaves at the Spurs' end, and a great save by Brown from Deakin, was followed by the Spurs' second goal after 20 minutes.

Smith tactics

This time Dyson made the opening for White to finish the job, but much credit goes to Smith for his clever tactical move. As White shot, Smith ran across the flight of the ball and threw goalkeeper Sims completely off balance.

Nine minutes later Smith banged in number three, when Sims failed to hold a snorting drive by Mackay. Two minutes later Dyson gave Spurs a handsome first-half lead of 4—0.

But all credit to Villa. They refused to quit and, though Allen slammed in a fifth after 62 minutes, MacEwan (70 minutes) and Hitchens (81) got deserved goals for the visitors.

The intrepid Mackay rounded off quite a day by scoring Spurs' sixth goal five minutes from the end.

● Spurs' keeper Bill Brown and Villa's Bobby Thomson go for the ball. But Spur Ron Henry was racing across to Brown's rescue.

Hands go up in triumph as Spurs centre-forward Smith (No. 9) and inside-left Allen see Villa goalkeeper Sims beaten for the first goal at White Hart Lane today.

	HOME					AWAY						
	P	W	D	L	F	A	W	D	L	F	A	Pts
Tottnm	10	5	0	0	18	5	5	0	0	14	6	20
Shef W	10	6	0	0	12	2	1	3	0	5	4	17
Evertn	10	5	0	0	15	3	2	0	3	10	13	14
Blckbn	10	4	0	1	15	8	2	2	1	10	9	14
Wolves	10	4	1	0	11	5	2	1	2	9	9	14
Fulhm	10	5	0	1	14	8	1	0	3	8	15	13
Burnly	10	3	0	2	12	8	3	0	2	8	7	12
Man C	9	3	2	0	7	4	2	1	1	12	13	11
A Villa	10	5	0	0	13	7	0	1	4	9	21	11
Birgm	10	3	1	1	10	6	1	1	3	6	9	10
Arsenl	10	4	0	1	13	3	0	1	4	2	8	9
Chelsa	10	2	1	1	12	10	2	0	4	13	15	9
Leices	10	1	1	3	7	10	2	1	2	10	9	8
Cardff	10	2	1	2	5	5	1	1	3	7	11	8
Nwctle	10	2	0	3	12	11	2	0	3	8	17	8
W Ham	10	3	1	0	12	7	0	0	6	7	20	7
Prestn	10	2	1	2	10	9	1	0	4	3	11	7
W Brm	10	2	0	3	15	11	1	0	4	5	12	6
Nttm F	10	1	2	2	8	9	0	0	5	4	13	5
Man U	9	2	1	2	13	13	0	0	4	5	11	5
Bolton	10	1	1	3	10	11	0	2	3	9	9	5
Blckpl	10	1	0	4	8	15	1	0	2	3	9	4

Champagne flows for win No. 10

● ELATION . . . in Spurs' dressing-room (above): The champagne bubbles. And manager Bill Nicholson wears the chairman's bowler to add, according to Danny Blanchflower, a touch of distinction to the occasion. Standing: Bobby Smith, Terry Dyson, Cliff Jones, John White, Bill Brown, Maurice Norman, Ron Henry, vice-chairman Fred Wale. Sitting: Dave Mackay, manager Nicholson, Danny Blanchflower, Peter Baker, Les Allen.

● ELATION . . . on the field (left): Smith has just scored a goal made by Mackay.

—Pictures: ROBERT STIGGINS

Handwritten:
SCORERS
SPURS WHITE (2)
SMITH
DYSON
ALLEN
MACKAY

VILLA MCEWAN
HITCHENS

HALF TIME 4·0

ATTENDANCE 61356

45

3

Ron Henry

Ron Henry
(Spurs)

1960/61	App/Gls	
League	42	0
FA Cup	7	0
1955-65	App/Gls	
All comps	287	1

Left-back Ron Henry was a Spurs man. Signed in 1955 as an amateur, Shoreditch-born Henry was eventually to serve Spurs for over 50 years. He coached at the Centre of Excellence until 1997 and assisted the youth team on match days until 2006.

In his playing days, Henry was recognised as a cultured ball-player as well as a fine tackler and his abilities continued to draw people to Spurs long after he left the first team. A young Garry Brooke, turning up for a trial in the mid-1970s, remembers: "He had this drill where you had to knock a ball with your left foot, get it back and pass it again with your left foot. The bloke did it to perfection and said: 'If you think that was lucky,'... Bing, bong, he did it all again. Seeing him do that got me hooked."

With right-back, and room-mate, Peter Baker, Henry comprised an innovative partnership which embedded the Spurs crowd's love of quality, attacking full-backs. Like Bill Brown, Henry was a master of positioning. He rarely mistimed a challenge and would frequently shepherd an opponent away from the danger areas before pouncing to retrieve the ball. He thoroughly researched his opponents before every game to ensure he knew all their moves and tricks.

He could also pass the ball well, bolstering the backline platform Spurs liked to launch attacks from. The simple lay-off was key and Henry would follow up by immediately making himself available to receive the ball again. He was acutely aware of Bill Nicholson's doctrine that a player not in possession was still active and remembers that, "the one thing Bill insisted on was that we always had the ball in front of us".

Henry was a calming presence, injecting confidence into Baker and Maurice Norman. He linked up well with Danny Blanchflower and Dave Mackay, playing intricate passing triangles and covering for Mackay when the Scotsman marauded upfield. "Many times I thought 'Where's bloody Mackay?'," he jokes.

It was Henry's emergence in 1959 from the shadow of Mel Hopkins that began to hint that Spurs could do the Double. Hopkins was a fine defender, but when replaced by Henry due to injury, a new consistency and confidence spread through the rearguard. Once given the number three shirt, Henry didn't let it go.

His ability made him one of four players, alongside Blanchflower, White and Allen, to play in every game of the Double season. His finest hour came at Wembley in the cup final. With the squad drained after the efforts of the campaign, Spurs played a more cautious game in which their normal whirlwind attacking style was slowed in favour of an approach based on possession. Henry was pivotal in ensuring victory and a clean sheet.

By staying at the club until 1997, Henry holds the record for the longest-serving Spurs player, occasionally turning out for the reserves, who he managed for a while, even in his later years. He also ran a market garden from his home in Hertfordshire, an area his family was evacuated to, and maintained a connection with, after being bombed out of east London during the war.

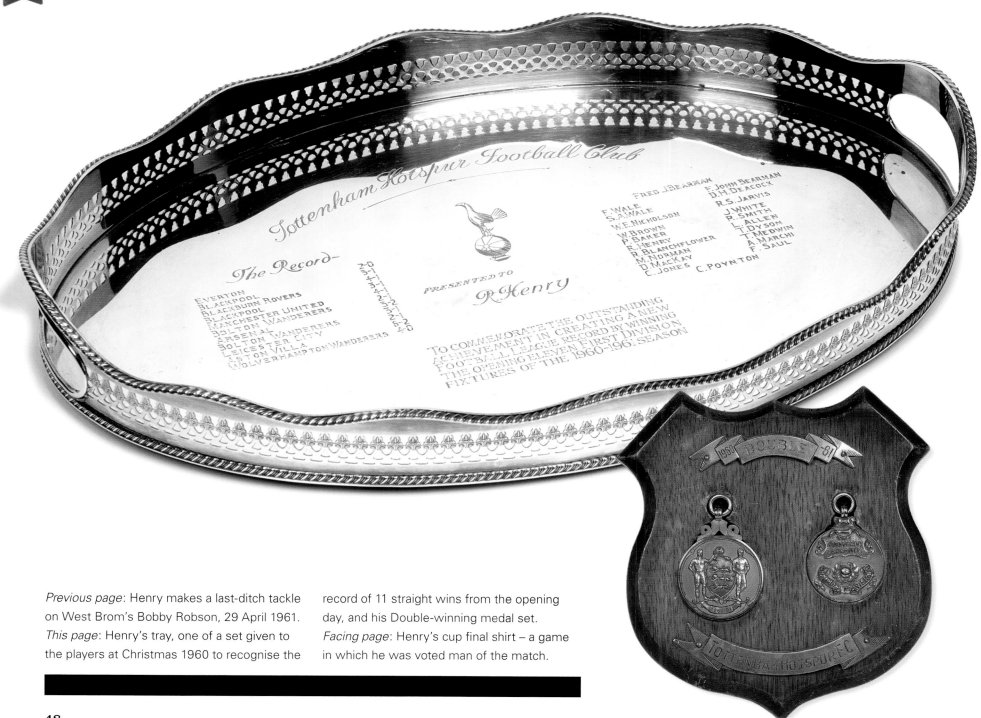

Previous page: Henry makes a last-ditch tackle on West Brom's Bobby Robson, 29 April 1961.
This page: Henry's tray, one of a set given to the players at Christmas 1960 to recognise the record of 11 straight wins from the opening day, and his Double-winning medal set.
Facing page: Henry's cup final shirt – a game in which he was voted man of the match.

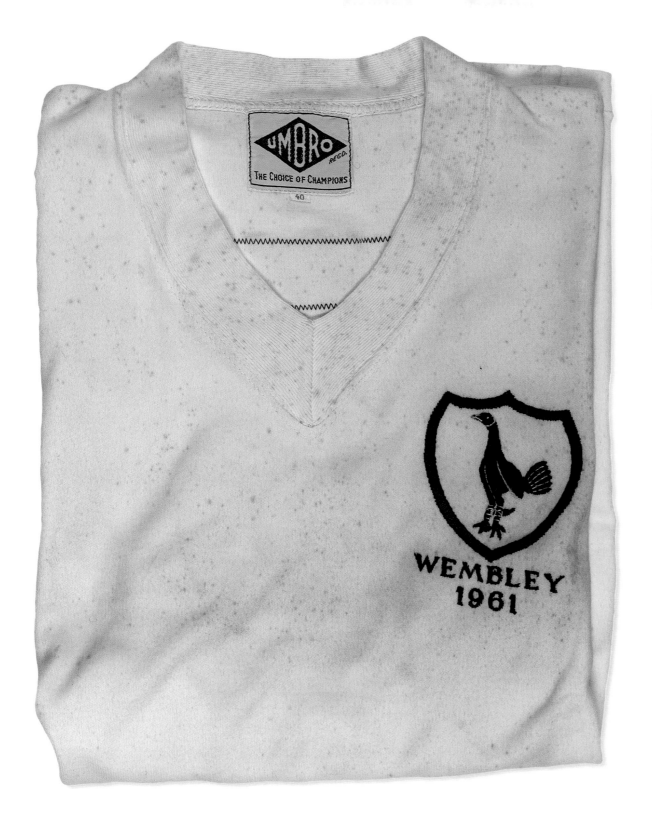

Ron Henry

66 Ron Henry was one of the quiet types, sound and shrewd. He used to go round to Bill's and mow his lawn for him **99** Cliff Jones

This page: Ron Henry's official club blazer and a commemorative memento of an epic season.

Facing page: The boots that won the cup – twice. Henry retained his footwear after the 1961 final, his sixth sense telling him they would be needed for the following season, as he explained in the accompanying letter.

Ron Henry   December 2000

I wore these boots in the 1960-61 Season, including at the F.A. Cup Final against Leicester City when we completed the 'Double'. After that game, in the dressing-room, Cecil Poynton (our physio) was packing the skip. He asked me to give him my boots to take back to White Hart Lane. I said "No, I'm taking them home, and I'll wear them again in next year's Final!" The following year we played Burnley in the FA Cup Final — and these boots probably became the only pair ever to be worn in 2 Cup Finals.

Best Wishes
R Henry

1960

October

Wolverhampton's goalkeeper Geoff Sidebottom gets that familiar sinking feeling at the hands of Spurs after the second Tottenham goal of a 4-0 rout hits the net.

Who can beat the super Spurs? That was the question rendered largely rhetorical by Tottenham Hotspur's extraordinary start to the league campaign. As autumn closed in Spurs played as if in an unseemly hurry to sew the title up before the clocks went back. It required a stretch of the imagination to wonder whether any side could possibly stop the relentless momentum of Tottenham's championship charge.

If anything, October's opening game presented even more emphatic evidence of Tottenham's invincibility with a 4-0 trouncing of Wolverhampton Wanderers in their own Molineux lair. The triumph of skill over physicality confirmed a handover of power as Spurs meted out unforgiving confirmation of the midlanders' declining status. At the inspirational behest of skipper Blanchflower and co, Wolves were reduced to mere also-rans.

Wolves were no conservative stick-in-the-muds; they had played an important part in ushering in a more enlightened approach with their pioneering floodlit matches against European opposition and their emphasis on fitness and organisation was forward thinking. Cullis was an innovative and intriguing manager fluent in French and Esperanto. But he and his team's brand of football was rooted in the long ball tactics promoted by the arch pragmatist Wing Commander Charles Reep, a football analyst whose views on the 'position of maximum opportunity' carried some considerable and debilitating weight within the British football establishment for a generation.

Spurs represented an irresistibly modern counter argument, and when the two philosophies clashed – Nicholson's expansive version of push and run versus Reep's cynical and colourless austerity, there was no contest. Cullis, magnanimous in defeat, pronounced Tottenham as "the greatest side I have ever seen" – no small praise from a man who had first-hand experience of Ferenc Puskas and his fellow 'Mighty Magyars'. Typically, Reep was more churlish. "I believe that a great deal of [Tottenham's] success stems from the fact they are meeting teams whose effectiveness is very much less than a few years ago," he opined.

Reep pronounced that Spurs needed to restrict their passing if they wanted to continue to succeed. He would have derived satisfaction from the next game, a 1-1 draw with Manchester City that finally brought the record 11-game winning run to an end. Spurs could have scored perhaps ten more from an almost ludicrous 39 attempts on goal and City's equaliser might have been disallowed for handball in the build-up. But, if anything, ending the winning streak was a monkey off Tottenham's back and the blip was only temporary. Forest were soon despatched 4-0, prompting *The People* scribe Ralph Finn to award every Spurs player an unprecedented 10-out-of-10 rating. A hard-fought win against Newcastle then wrapped up another glittering month. Still the Spurs marched on, remorselessly casting opponents aside with the kind of football excellence no one – Charles Reep aside – could even contemplate begrudging.

Soccer magic brings 11 wins in a row

WOLVES 0, TOTTENHAM HOTSPUR 4

SOCCER magic was on show at Molineux yesterday and Spurs provided it, of course. The scoreline shows that the polished maestros claimed four goals but they should have won by a hatful. So the sorcerers of White Hart Lane go striding on—eleven wins from as many League matches this season. And on this confident showing more are on the way.

Wolves? Well, what has happened to them? On this dismal showing that superb scoring machine is all messed up. At times they looked almost slap happy and only one or two looked like the great players of last season.

The goals came in the 32nd minute from outside-right Cliff Jones, the 44th minute from Danny Blanchflower, the 52nd from inside-left Les Allen and the 79th from outside-left Terry Dyson.

First Jones had only to turn a by-line-hugging cross from Allen home. Then, when Blanchflower accepted a loose ball 30 yards from goal he found no one to take a pass. With a grin he moved forward, veered to the right and did the only sensible thing, unleashing a terrific drive into the far corner of the net to leave Sidebottom hopelessly beaten.

The game was as good as over but after Allen had converted a White cross and Dyson had made it 4—0, the stands began to empty. Almost as much could be written about the Spurs efforts that nearly came off. Bobby Smith's upright rocker, his near-miss minutes later, and three great second-half drives from Dyson were but a few.

By Tom Finney

Write against this two great efforts by Mason, Flowers's header brilliantly beaten down by Brown and a swift cross which left Farmer and Mason immobile in front of an open goal, and there's little else left that Wolves did to enthuse over.

For just as Spurs were superb in confidence and controlled play, so were Wolves that much the opposite.

Seldom have I seen them look so ragged and lacking purpose in their play. I found young centre-forward Farmer a big disappointment.

Although Spurs centre-half Norman dominated the midfield, the Molineux lad was too often inclined to let his inexperience lead him astray.

Only one Wolves man stood out—wing-half Ron Flowers, and mainly for the work he got through. He never mastered John White, the architect of so many Spurs sorties.

Along with Blanchflower, Norman and Marchi, I name them my men of the match. And what a match!

One which sends Spurs striding on to even greater glory, and Wolves wondering just where along the way they've lost the incisiveness in attack and strength in defence which has kept them among the honours for so long.

Scorers
Jones
Blanchflower
Allen
Dyson
Half-Time 0-2
Attendance 53,036

SPURS, the greatest team I've seen, says STAN CULLIS

Wolves are well walloped by Britain's wonder team

SEND FOR REAL MADRID!

Wolverhampton W. 0, Tottenham H. 4   by CAPEL KIRBY

SEND for Real Madrid, Barcelona, Juventus, the lot. Let's get a team here capable of giving some idea of how good these super Spurs really are.

Wolves tried their best on a slithery, rainsoaked surface, but what Tottenham did to them was sheer audacity which, at the finish, was applauded to the echo by the crowd of 53,036 spectators.

This was a match to remember for the contemptuous ease in which Spurs tip-tapped their way to a comfortable four goals win to give them their 11th victory on the trot.

They carried out the most elementary moves at speed, walking pace and on occasions almost at a standstill. There were times when Wolves must have been given the impression that they were playing Tottenham's first team and the Reserves.

If ever there was a vacant space you could be sure it would be occupied by a white shirt. It was uncanny the way they found one another and moved into position if any of their colleagues slipped up.

THE NUMBERS ON THEIR BACKS MEANT NOTHING. IN FACT AT ONE STAGE No. 2, PETER BAKER, WAS IN WOLVES' PENALTY AREA LOOKING FOR A GOAL.

Cliff Jones was officially No. 7. Actually he spent most of his time in his natural position, at outside-left with Terry Dyson on the right. As for John White he was everywhere requiring a link.

In the early stages it looked as if the Spurs rhythm was going to be wrecked by the rock-like Wolves' half-back trio of Stuart, Clamp and Flowers. But it was not long before all, with the exception of England's international left half-back, were completely swamped and out-played by their ball seeking rivals.

SPORTING TYPES By JON

'Lovely side, the Spurs!'

● Don't give 'em a look in. That might have been Spurs' "battle plan" for beating Wolves. And that's how it was here as goalkeeper BROWN shares the picture with team-mates HENRY, BLANCHFLOWER and NORMAN when gathering a centre at Molyneux.

Skilfully led

No defence could have stood up to the persistent nagging and probing of Tottenham's attack as skilfully led by England's latest centre-forward Bobby Smith who proved that he can also play a bit of football apart from being a bulldozer.

Wolves held out for 30 minutes. Then Les Allen moved up the left wing and squared the ball hard and low for Jones to help himself to what must have been his easiest ever goal.

Give Wolves their due, they came back with a series of attacks from which Spurs survived by a combination of intelligent covering and not a little amount of luck.

Then came the knock-out blow. Two minutes from the interval Danny Blanchflower, throughout a perfect scheming old campaigner, did the coolest thing I've ever seen.

He killed a cross ball from Terry Dyson 25 yards out, spotted Wolves defenders setting their offside trap and promptly let fly with a shot which gave Sidebottom no possible chance.

The audacity . . .

This two-goals lead was all Tottenham required to switch on perfect combination. Never can any Wolves team have had such a lesson as well as they could have hoped against a side which was riding high and one which will be very difficult to beat as long as the reasonably dry grounds suit there type of football.

Five minutes after the interval White pulled down a difficult ball and almost in the same movement swung it across for Allen to flick the ball into goal, while ten minutes from the end Dyson took a pot shot which went in off a harassed Wolves defender.

From goal to attack Spurs were the complete and absolute audacity. Never can any Wolves team have had such a lesson and a battering before their own supporters.

Wolverhampton will have to go to market for an inside-forward to take the pressure off Peter Broadbent who was the only player to make any real impression.

Ted Fowler, the centre-forward who made his debut a week previously, was played right out of the game by Maurice Norman who must surely be given international honours before long.

THE BLANCHFLOWER WONDER-GOAL THAT WRECKED WOLVES

The razor-sharp Soccer brain of Spurs' skipper Danny Blanchflower notes Wolves rush forward to work the offside-trap. Danny springs the trap—with a great shot and a great goal.

Spurs record wrecked

FANS STILL GO WILD

Spurs 1 Manchester City 1: by JOHN CAMKIN

SKILL: Spurs 8, Manchester C. 7. Sportsmanship 8. Crowd 7. Control 7. GOALS: 1—0, 1—1.

THAT Tottenham record of invincibility was broken last night. But this was still a feast of fine football by the maestros of White Hart Lane.

Let me paint the picture that was spoiled by a goal from Clive Colbridge, former Crewe winger. For 45 minutes, magnificent Spurs scaled the very peaks of Soccer perfection.

At half-time, nearly 60,000 people gave Danny Blanchflower and his men one of the largest ovations I have heard. The 12th win in a row looked inevitable. Spurs had smashed in a fantastic total of 25 shots to City's five.

So it resumed. In the first three minutes of the second half, John White and Bobby Smith almost added to the goal which England's Smith had nodded past Bert Trautmann in the 27th minute.

Then Barry Betts, City right-back whose career was once "ended" by medical experts, prodded a long pass down the centre. George Hannah headed it back to Joe Hayes.

Protest !

A quick forward pass by Hayes saw Colbridge cut in from the left. Spurs protested that he had handled the ball before he shot into the far corner. *Referee Gilbert Pullin pointed firmly to the centre.*

For 40 more minutes Spurs strove like Trojans to cancel out the indignity. But the blond Trautman was in superb form.

Now some of the magic have departed from the League competition for this season. If there is a note of sorrow in North London, we can at least rejoice at the superb quality of this match—which could not be surpassed in Brazil, Spain or any other land.

City who might have been five goals down at half-time, still had the courage to match Spurs at their own game. The prompting of two elegant wing-half-backs made them the equal of the masters in the last half hour.

Irony

Colbridge, in fact, almost crowned a night of glory with a sparkling run in the 80th minute.

He made an open goal—which right - winger Colin Barlow wasted with a hasty high shot. The end of a glorious sequence was, of course, inevitable for Spurs at some stage. It is ironic that the ability to seize chances, which has been their strength this season, should be the instrument of eventual failure.

They finished with the incredible total of 39 shots against nine, 14 corners against two. We must hope, for the sake of English football, that these sparkling Spurs will not often squander such crushing supremacy.

SPURS: Brown 7; Baker 8, Henry 8; Blanchflower 8, Norman 8, Mackay 9; Jones 7, White 9, Smith 8, Allen 7, Dyson 7.
MANCHESTER CITY: Trautmann 8; Betts 7, Sears 7; Barnes 8, Plenderleith 7, Shawcross 8; Barlow 6, Law 7, Hannah 7, Hayes 7, Colbridge 7.
REFEREE: G Pullin (Bristol). LINESMEN: W T Castle (Colchester), J C Jays (Leamington Spa).

SCORERS
SPURS SMITH
MANC. C. COLBRIDGE

HALF-TIME 1—0
ATTENDANCE 58,916

Super Spurs should be in Super League

By DOUG WILSON
NOTTINGHAM FOREST 0, SPURS 4

ONE day we shall get that super League. But until we do I suppose we'll have to go on suffering these cruel, painful and pathetic spectacles between giants and minnows. The Spurs were so devastatingly superior that they became arrogant, bored and, let us admit it, at times just a little indulgent.

But you can't blame them. They probed and penetrated at will and even with the brake on scored three goals in the first 25 minutes.

The Forest's 37,000 supporters, the biggest crowd of the season, seemed to accept the situation.

I thought the red and white scarved Nottingham fan summed it up nicely as he left the ground with:

"We couldn't expect to get any points off Spurs but it was a privilege to play against them."

Spurs opened the scoring in the seventh minute. The talented John White completed a Terry Dyson move, steering the pass cleanly and effortlessly over the head of goalkeeper Charlie Thompson.

With the Spurs making it look "Oh, ever so easy," a Dave Mackay cross in the 20th minute, with plenty of side on it, was deflected off centre-half Bobby McKinlay into the net.

Cliff Jones made it 3—0 in the 25th minute. A Jones header put Spurs four-up after the interval and from then on it was just playful exhibition stuff by the Londoners.

It would be unfair to criticise the Forest. They were playing against a super team in which the football was of a different brand to theirs.

HENRY : Efficiency and concentration.

SCORERS WHITE MACKAY JONES (2)

HALF-TIME 0—3
ATTENDANCE 37,198

CLIFF JONES—two goals for Spurs

SCORERS
NEWCASTLE: WHITE (2) HUGHES
SPURS: NORMAN, WHITE, JONES, SMITH

HALF-TIME 2—1

ATTENDANCE 51,368

	HOME						AWAY					
	P	W	D	L	F	A	W	D	L	F	A	Pts
Tottenham H.	14	7	0	0	19	6	6	0	1	26	9	..27
Sheffield Wed.	14	8	0	0	18	2	2	3	1	8	9	..23
Everton	15	6	1	0	19	5	4	1	3	18	19	..22
Burnley	15	5	0	3	23	13	5	0	2	18	10	..20
Wolverhampton	15	5	2	1	17	12	3	2	2	15	14	..20
Manchester C.	14	5	2	0	16	6	2	2	3	15	18	..18
Fulham	15	5	2	1	17	12	3	0	4	16	22	..18
Arsenal	15	7	0	1	18	5	1	1	5	7	12	..17
Aston Villa	15	7	0	1	22	12	1	1	5	12	23	..17
West Ham	15	6	1	0	24	14	0	1	7	8	22	..14
Blackburn Rov	15	4	0	3	18	16	2	2	4	12	18	..14
Leicester City	15	2	2	3	11	13	3	1	4	15	15	..13
Chelsea	14	2	2	2	17	19	3	1	1	5	21	..12
Birmingham	15	4	1	2	12	8	1	1	6	12	21	..12
Preston N.E.	15	3	1	3	11	11	1	1	5	3	16	..12
West Bromwich	15	3	1	4	16	13	2	1	5	9	13	..11
Newcastle Utd	15	3	1	4	29	14	2	0	5	10	22	..11
Cardiff City	14	3	1	3	7	7	1	2	4	9	18	..11
Manchester Utd	14	4	1	2	18	11	0	1	6	8	21	..10
Blackpool	15	2	0	5	14	20	1	2	5	7	15	..8
Bolton Wand	15	2	1	4	5	11	16	2	0	5	6	13..8
Nottingham F.	15	1	2	5	10	17	1	0	6	6	18	..6

Spurs a bit lucky, admits Danny

By GEORGE TAYLOR
Newcastle ..3 Tottenham ..4

BACKSTAGE, when this drama had been played out and the Tottenham side had departed for the first available train, Newcastle's team and officials were still up in arms.

They claimed they had been robbed by referee F. V. Stringer's refusal to veto Spurs' third goal, scored by Cliff Jones, as offside.

Jones looked offside when he received the ball. The linesman's flag was raised. But Mr. Stringer of Liverpool refused to investigate.

Cold comfort

"There was no need to," he told me afterwards. "I was sufficiently up with the play to see that a defender had played the ball on to Jones. It was a goal all right."

So Tottenham keep their unbeaten record. Danny Blanchflower's frank confession: "I thought we were a bit lucky," was cold comfort.

The first half was quiet until a three-minute scoring spree brought a trio of goals—two for Newcastle, from the thrust of centre-forward Len White, and one from an adventurous advance for a corner by Spurs' centre half, Maurice Norman.

Seven minutes after the interval John White levelled the score. Then came the dubious Jones goal.

Faint hopes

When a long, dipping centre from right-winger Gordon Hughes dropped into the net, with Spurs' keeper Bill Brown concentrating more on the advancing Len White, Newcastle seemed to have a few faint hopes of toppling Tottenham.

But they were denied even one point when Bobby Smith cracked home the winner four minutes from time.

So victory went to a side whose wing halves, Dave Mackay and Danny Blanchflower, have found the magical touch of the crack continentals.

Newcastle Utd.—Harvey; Keith, McMichael; Scoular, Stokoe, Bell; Hughes, Woods, White, Allchurch, Mitchell.
Tottenham Hotspur.—Brown; Baker, Henry; Blanchflower, Norman, Mackay; Jones, White, Smith, Allen, Dyson.

55

4

Danny Blanchflower

1960/61	App/Gls	
League	42	6
FA Cup	7	0

1954-64	App/Gls	
All comps	382	21

Danny Blanchflower believed. He was a fine player in a fine team, but he knew ability alone would not secure the glory he strove for. It was his belief that the Double could be done that sprinkled a vital element of stardust, infusing the entire team with a spirit that became an unbreakable determination to scale new heights. "It can be done," said Danny, "but you've got to believe."

Blanchflower was the finest attacking wing-half of his day, his ball control and passing on the pitch as immaculate as his appearance off it. He wanted the ball all the time and he used it to devastating effect; short passes to the inside-forward, switching the ball long and right into the stride of a winger, splitting a defence to send his forwards away. He conducted affairs on the pitch, putting Bill Nicholson's ideas and values into practice. He made it simple, he made it quick. He made it effective.

If there was a weakness to his play it was in the tackle. He took on his defensive duties, but was better at intercepting the pass or harrying opponents away from danger areas. The presence of Dave Mackay alongside him gave him the freedom to concentrate on doing what he did best, going forward and creating the play. But a proper assessment of Blanchflower's influence requires more than simply understanding how he played the ball and used space.

Many footballers achieved greatness because of those qualities but, as Spurs historian Bob Goodwin says: "Few have left their mark because of the man they were." Danny did.

The man was a romantic, a thinker, a free spirit who understood how the sum of the parts made a greater whole. The element of magic that runs through the story of the Double always leads back to Blanchflower. His sense of romance attracted him to the glory of the achievement, his free-thinking shimmied around the obstacles to it, his belief kept Spurs marching on.

He was fond of lofty oratory, but even when it went over the heads of his team-mates they trusted in his sincerity and integrity. He was a truly inspirational captain, but off the field he kept his distance. "You can't lead from the middle of the pack," he said. He was the team's beating heart.

In typically contrary fashion he was downbeat on the lap of honour at Wembley, the Double now secured. "The whole point to me wasn't in winning the Double. It was in believing we could win the Double," he said. There was the glory 1961's Footballer of the Year so famously believed in, something he described as "a season of victory and crowds, a season for Tottenham Hotspur and football to remember." He was the embodiment of that triumph, something recognised when he was selected from that great team by the football writers as their player of the year.

Blanchflower stayed at Spurs until injury ended his career in 1964. He went on to become a fine journalist and to manage his country, Northern Ireland. He died on 9 December 1993 in Cobham, Surrey, at the age of 67. His name was Danny Blanchflower. He was the leader of the band.

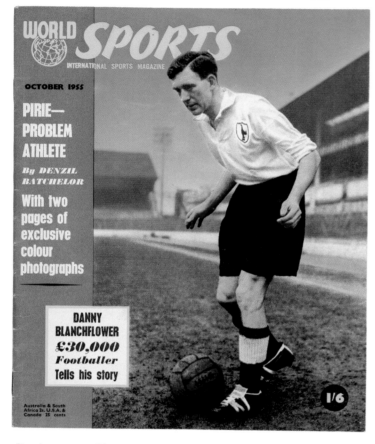

Previous page: Two young star-struck admirers with the most famous footballer of the era and his team's trophy haul.

This page: From the moment he signed in 1955, Blanchflower was perfect front-cover material. His superstar status resulted in club rosettes being fashioned in his honour.

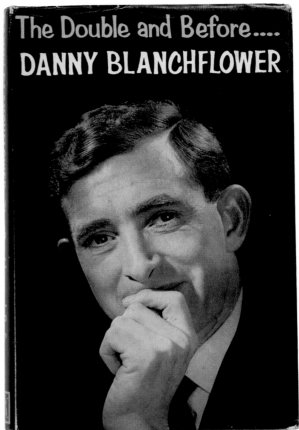

Left: Welcomed back by his adoring fans at White Hart Lane on 27 April 1963. It was his first appearance after a near four-month injury layoff.
Above: On the cover of his 1961 autobiography, in which he observed: "On the field I am the club's authority, the manager's agent on the spot."
Following pages: Blanchflower's famous No 4 shirt and engraved Double watch. One was presented by the club to each player.

66 **Danny Blanchflower was just the man. When we went on the field of play he became the manager** 99 Cliff Jones

1960

November

League

2nd   **Spurs 3 Cardiff 2**

5th   **Spurs 5 Fulham 1**

9th   **Sheff Wed 2 Spurs 1**

12th **Spurs 6 Birmingham 0**

26th **WBA 1 Spurs 3**

Friendly

14th **Spurs 5**

       Dinamo Tbilisi 2

Left: Maurice Norman (falling) takes a tumble as he scores Tottenham's only goal in the clash with Sheffield Wednesday. Dyson and Allen (right) celebrate but it was Wednesday who prevailed.

There is an imperceptible line between the momentum of achievement and the burden of expectation it creates. As November chased away the vestiges of autumn, that line was crossed and a winter chill began to gnaw at the hot Spurs.

A nervous display against Cardiff saw Spurs, without the injured Jones, a goal down and floundering until they woke up to score two in a stunning ten-minute burst just before half-time. A contentious penalty capped a win labelled "barely deserved" by the *Daily Mail*. Nicholson gambled on Jones's fitness for the game against Fulham and the Welshman inspired a 5-1 drubbing. But again, Spurs did not live up to the standards they had set until the last 15 minutes, with only the profligacy of the Fulham forwards taking the shine off the Cottagers' display.

The Fulham win was vital, steadying nerves and showing Spurs could dig in when necessary. The timing was just right, because Tottenham's next game was away to Sheffield Wednesday. The Owls were a bit of a bogey team having ended Tottenham's 12-game unbeaten run the season before at Hillsborough, a ground at which Spurs had won only once in half a century. With Wednesday seven points behind Spurs in second place, the stage was set for a battle between two styles of play, one based on defence and closing down, the other open and attacking.

Wednesday hadn't dropped a point at home, Spurs hadn't lost a game, so something had to give. Looking back with the benefit of hindsight, the encounter marked a turning point in the season, resulting in a defeat which released the pressure that had been suffocating Spurs' style.

The game was every bit the titanic struggle predicted. It was physical and exciting, the initiative swayed back and forth, Wednesday led and then Spurs equalised, then eventually Wednesday inside-left John Fantham ghosted in to slam home a ball in the midst of a goalmouth melee. Blanchflower urged his men on, Mackay whirled ferociously across the pitch, Norman ran repeatedly from his own half at the resolute Wednesday defence… but at the whistle the bubble had been burst.

The players now admit the reverse was something of a relief. And how that relief showed. After warming up with a 5-2 defeat of Dynamo Tbilisi in a home friendly, Spurs smashed six past Birmingham. It was a display to match the sensational performance against Nottingham Forest, with fluent passing and wonderful goals, including three in the first 18 minutes. As the season unfolded, each one of the Spurs team would put their own special stamp on particular games and this match was Les Allen's. He didn't score, but he made three and was faultless throughout. A player who had initially lacked confidence and been regarded with suspicion by the Spurs crowd was now firmly established as a vital part of the country's finest football machine.

Allen was on the scoresheet as Tottenham saw out November at The Hawthorns, Bobby Smith grabbing the other two in a 3-2 defeat of West Brom.

MATCH 15 WEDNESDAY 2ND NOVEMBER 1960

MATCH 16 SATURDAY 5TH NOVEMBER 1960

Spurs win but lose that top class lustre

Tottenham Hotspur ....3 **Cardiff City** 2

By JOHN CAMKIN

SPURS, now holding an astonishing 29 points from 15 First Division matches, did not wear the mantle of great champions at White Hart-lane last night. They barely deserved to beat Cardiff.

For the first time Danny Blanchflower and his men used a pitch kept in fine trim by the new £1,000 plastic covers, which could change the whole conception of winter football.

Even on the dry, green surface, Spurs showed signs of dangerous tactics. Both David Mackay and Blanchflower took chances in defence which were unnecessary and unprofitable.

Cardiff, who used an intelligent 4-2-4 system, were beaten only by ten minutes of vintage Spurs football before half-time and a penalty kick for hands in the 60th minute.

Dragged

At the end of the first half, Spurs showed all the old thrust and power. From 0—1 down they went into a 2—1 lead, had five corners and nearly scored with three further efforts.

Little Terry Dyson, popping up at inside right, headed the first from Mackay's centre in the 35th minute.

Les Allen brilliantly designed the second for Terry Medwin two minutes before half time.

In the 60th minute Cardiff right half Steve Gammon, the auxiliary centre-half, dragged the ball forward with his hand with no imminent danger to

justify it. Blanchflower rammed home the penalty.

Cardiff scored twice through Donnelly—in the 20th and 86th minutes.

It will be a tragedy if Spurs throw away the advantage they have built up in these last ten weeks. They would be well advised to remember that straightforward Soccer has given them their success.

Tottenham: Brown. Baker. Henry; Blanchflower, Norman, Mackay; Medwin. White. Smith. Allen. Dyson.
Cardiff: Vearncombe; Harrington. Edwards; Gammon. Malloy. Baker; Walsh. Sullivan. Tapscott. Donnelly. Hogg.

SCORERS SPURS DYSON
MEDWIN
BLANCHFLOWER (PEN)

CARDIFF DONNELLY (2)

HALF-TIME 2-1
ATTENDANCE 47,605

THOSE SLICK SPURS AGAIN

Allen and Jones smash poor Fulham hopes

TOTTENHAM 5, FULHAM 1   By HARRY DITTON

IN a grandstand finish, Spurs scored three times in the last 15 minutes against Fulham at White Hart Lane to record their 15th victory in 16 games. But to be fair to Fulham, a 5—1 trouncing was rather more than they deserved.

Until that last fatal quarter of an hour Spurs did not produce that soccer *par excellence* we have become accustomed to expect from them. A simple explanation is that there was too much tension and even some needle which indifferent refereeing did not improve.

The turning point was a brilliantly-taken opportunist goal by Cliff Jones after 75 minutes. Before that, Fulham, inspired by the superb ball distribution of Johnny Haynes, were only a goal behind, and every time Haynes had the ball an equaliser looked a probability.

But the Jones goal took all the stuffing out of Fulham in the literal sense, and a defence which had hitherto covered magnificently collapsed like a pack of cards.

As the leg weary teams trooped off at the end of the game the referee shook hands with Roy Bentley, the Fulham centre-half. The tribute was richly deserved.

No bigger compliment can be paid Bentley than to say that he played the baffling Bobby Smith so effectively and fairly that England's centre-forward—watched by Walter Winterbottom—was never a menace inside the penalty area.

But by the same token this serves to demonstrate what a well-built and powerful side Spurs have become. Allen and Cliff Jones wore the mantles of match-winners with devastating effect. Indeed, the first three goals scored by Spurs—two by Jones and one by Allen—were masterpieces of quick thinking and could so easily have been missed.

MISTAKE

The first, taken by Allen after 22 minutes, was the direct result of a badly-taken goal-kick by Macedo that went to Mackay. With a first-time volley he found Allen, who pivoted quickly and scored a clever goal.

After 35 minutes the ball was swung out to Dyson on the left wing. His centre fell short but Jones, moving to the near upright, headed through a wonder effort.

Fulham produced their best form after this and in the 51st minute Leggat met a partial clearance from Cook's shot to slam through from close range.

This really set the game alight with Fulham in with a chance. Only the soundness of Norman prevented first Leggat and then Cook improving on several great defence-splitting passes by Haynes.

But the pressure eased, and from Dyson's centre Jones stabbed in No. 3 after 75 minutes. With Fulham wilting badly. White (85 minutes) and Allen (88 minutes) completed the rout.

LES ALLEN

Les Allen, of Spurs, has not been taking a shot at Tony Macedo's head. He's putting in one of Spurs' five goals against Fulham.

● Gotcher! gasps Fulham's busy goalkeeper Tony Macedo as he dives once more into the White Hart Lane mud to keep out goal-hungry Spurs. Poised for any slip by Tony are Dave Mackay (right) and Les Allen.

SCORERS

SPURS. ALLEN (2)
JONES (2)
WHITE

FULHAM LEGGAT

HALF-TIME 2-0
ATTENDANCE 56,270

MATCH 17 SATURDAY 12TH NOV. 1960

SPURS RECORD GOES

FANTHAM HAUNTED SPURS

SHEFFIELD WEDNESDAY SHATTER TOTTENHAM RECORD, KEEP THEIR OWN

John Fantham

Hillsborough rocked in this gigantic struggle

Sheffield Wednesday .... 2 Tottenham Hotspur 1

AT last the mighty have fallen. After their great run of 16 games without defeat, Spurs crashed to the glittering steelmen of Sheffield in a rip-roaring tussle of temper, tantrums and tremendous excitement. But make no mistake, Wednesday deserved their win. They matched Spurs for craft and skill, outstayed them for stamina and kept their heads better in a gigantic struggle that turned Hillsborough into a searing furnace.

By GERRY LOFTUS

And at the end, torn programmes and crushed matchboxes littered the terraces from fans who had died a thousand deaths.

For the goals that rocked the terraces three times, bringing elation, despair and finally elation again, join me five minutes before half-time as the game is flowing from end to end.

Wednesday had held the whip hand, looking far more likely to clinch the points. Their super defence was masterly and never in real trouble but their forwards could not force home an advantage.

Near disaster

Then disaster almost hit Wednesday as Peter Swan, this giant centre half who blotted England leader Bobby Smith from the match, made his one mistake.

A bad back pass gave Les Allen an easy opening. A goal seemed certain. But reserve goalkeeper Roy McLaren made the save of his life.

The ball was cleared upfield. Little Bobby Craig whipped it in from the right and Billy Griffin, who had changed wings, carefully took aim and slammed it past despairing Bill Brown.

In a couple of minutes the triumph was cut short. Spurs hit back and Allen tore down the left wing. A linesman flagged for a goal kick and undoubtedly the ball was over the line but referee Leafe awarded a free kick.

Quickly Dave Mackay took the kick and from a ruck of players centre half Maurice Norman hurled forward to head the equaliser.

It was a psychological blow for Spurs coming at a vital point and I felt it would probably swing the match their way.

And so it looked in the first 10 minutes of the second half as Spurs rolled the ball round and seemed to be carving out a winning move.

But you can't do that long against these Wednesday defenders. Left half Tony Kay hurtled back into the game, his red head flaming everywhere under the lights. And Wednesday again took over.

Kay himself slashed in a 20 yarder that Brown luckily caught second time. Alan Finney was within inches of a goal. Then the winner came in the 67th minute.

Burly left-back Don Megson, must have recalled his days as a winger. He ran up and centred a beauty. Keith Ellis headed it over Norman then hit the ball against an opponent's legs.

In one lightning split second the game was won and lost as John Fantham crashed the ball home.

Gambled

Blanchflower smacked his hands trying to rally his team. Mackay did the same and tore round and round. Norman twice gambled on upfield runs. But Wednesday had the gleam of victory and would not let go.

There was only one more real attack by Spurs that nearly ended in a bitter brawl when McLaren was almost knocked out.

A pity the Spurs tarnished their reputation by giving so many fouls. And the excitement was not over when the whistle ended, for a linesman reported Peter Baker to the referee who lectured the left-back severely.

- **Eighteen League clubs have visited Sheffield this season—and not one has collected a point. Wednesday and Second Division leaders United have each won all their nine home games.**
- **Spurs have failed to equal the League record of 19 matches without defeat at a start of a season. Yesterday also broke their run of ten winning away games, two at the end of 1959-60**
- **Tottenham first visited Hillsborough in 1910. Their League statistics at the ground are played 24, won one, drawn four, lost 19, goal-average 21-54.**
- **Johnny Morrison, Jackie Gibbons and the late Fred Sargent scored the goals when Spurs gained their only Hillsborough win, 3-0 in a Second Division game on Thursday, September 16, 1937. They drew in 1909-10 (1-1), 1949-50 (0-0), 1950-51 (1-1) and 1954-55 (2-2).**

SCORERS
WEDNESDAY GRIFFIN
FANTHAM
SPURS NORMAN

HALFTIME 1-1
ATTENDANCE 56.363

MONDAY 14TH NOVEMBER 1960

DAILY MIRROR, Tuesday, November 15, 1960

Russians take five-goal hiding—with not a ghost of a fight-back

BILL BROWN

THE HOT SPURS AGAIN

By BILL HOLDEN: Spurs 5, Tbilisi Dynamo 2

WHATEVER confidence Spurs may have lost when their record-breaking League run ended on Saturday was restored last night.

But that is the best thing that can be said for their victory over the Russian Cup finalists, who shared ten goals in a thriller with Wolves last week, after crashing 5—0 to Sheffield Wednesday.

The Russians showed none of the fire or determination they had at Molineux.

At times, after Spurs had run into a commanding lead, they seemed careless and disinterested.

It was exactly the same team which battled it out with Wolves, yet performing altogether differently.

The result was another nightmare for goalkeeper Kotrikadze, who, for all his brilliance has had fifteen goals hammered past him in three games.

He saved from inside left Les Allen and right half Danny Blanchflower before right-winger Terry Medwin made it 1—0 in the 18th minute.

Allen was twice more foiled by Kotrikadze.

Then Russian left winger Meshki showed his true form with a run that ended in a cross for right winger Melashvili to equalise.

Three minutes before the interval Dave Mackay put Spurs ahead again from a Medwin cross.

Header

Two minutes after the interval, outside left Terry Dyson swung over a cross which England leader Bobby Smith nodded down for Mackay to drive in.

Five minutes later, Medwin made it 4—1.

And Dyson got a fifth, before Barkaya clipped Spurs' lead five minutes from time.

No. 570
TOTTENHAM HOTSPUR
Football & Athletic Company Ltd.
Block L WEST STAND
TOTTENHAM HOTSPUR
v.
DYNAMO CLUB (U.S.S.R.)
On MONDAY, NOV. 14th, 1960
Kick-off 7.30 p.m. Floodlit Friendly
Row Q 35
Seat No.
PRICE 10/-
The Tottenham Hotspur Company do not Guarantee that the proposed match will be played.
R. S. JARVIS
Secretary
Ticket Holders are requested to be in their seats 15 minutes at least before the Kick-off.
WEST STAND—Entrance HIGH ROAD
Printed by Thomas Knight & Co. Ltd., The Clock House Press, Hoddesdon, Herts.

DAVE MACKAY thumps in his second goal against the Russians last night.

SCORERS WHITE
DYSON (2)
JONES (2)
SMITH (PENALTY)

HALF-TIME 3-0
ATTENDANCE 46,010

MATCH 18 SATURDAY 19TH NOV 1960

MATCH 19 SATURDAY 26TH NOVEMBER 1960

NEWS OF THE WORLD, Nov. 20, 1960

WHITE-HOT SPURS

Six-goal blitz spoils Bloomfield debut

By Harry Ditton

SPURS 6, BIRMINGHAM CITY 0

THIS was another runaway win for the immaculate Spurs, and they took only 15 minutes to achieve it. In that short space of time they scored three of their six goals, and what wonderful goals they were !

Within three minutes of the kick-off Jones, Smith and White combined in a glorious passing move, and it was literally White-hot Spurs as the Scot crashed the ball high into the roof of the net from an almost impossible angle.

Six minutes later Mackay seized on a goalkick from the Birmingham end, and pushed the ball through to Allen who took it right to the by-line. There, little Terry Dyson picked it up, and again the shot literally rocketed into the roof of the net.

While Birmingham were still wondering what had hit them, Smith, Allen and Jones again carved through the City defence with their speed of thought and movement for Jones to finish with an unstoppable drive.

This was super Spurs at their irresistible best.

Not unnaturally, perhaps, they eased up for a time after this, and Birmingham came more into the game.

But when Spurs turned on the heat again, Birmingham were "blitzed" for another three goals by Dyson, Smith (penalty) and Jones in the last 20 minutes.

INVINCIBLE

No defence can live with Tottenham when they are in such a mood, and I felt sorry for Birmingham.

The goal rush gave Birmingham's young Colin Withers the sort of League debut he is never likely to forget.

But let it be said at once he was in no way responsible for the defeat. Indeed he can look back on his performance with pride.

COURAGEOUS

In the face of the most fiery ordeal he displayed great courage, and two great saves from Bobby Smith and Cliff Jones nearly lifted the roof off the Tottenham stands.

Jimmy Bloomfield, whose £25,000 transfer to Birmingham from Arsenal was sealed a couple of hours before the game, had a less notable debut.

In a Birmingham attack which seldom carried a serious threat, he used the ball neatly, but seemed reluctant to try his luck as a marksman. He lost more than one good chance of narrowing Spurs' victory margin.

To praise the Spurs individually is superfluous.

They are, apparently, a tremendously powerful and well knit team capable of giving most opposition a two or three goals' start—and a licking !

Another three-goal spell for the Spurs

By W. CAPEL KIRBY

WEST BROMWICH 1, TOTTENHAM 3

WEST BROMWICH fans who went to see the smooth soccer which has established Tottenham as the team of the season, went away not only satisfied, but pleasantly surprised. They had seen their team respond with a brand of football which was every bit as good as that of the opposition.

Tottenham excelled only in the fact that they had one of their devastating three - goal spells. Afterwards they indulged in some fancy interpassing, which might have got them into a great deal of trouble if the Albion forwards had had a little more luck in front of goal.

Referee J. S. McLoughlin came in for considerable criticism from the crowd after allowing Tottenham's first goal in the 20th minute, I agreed.

Smith offside

Smith appeared to be at least three yards offside as he collected John White's side-footed flick. It seemed that England's centre-forward also considered himself offside in the manner that he slammed the ball into the net—more to express annoyance than having scored a goal.

Whether he was offside or not, the fact is the referee was on the spot, and it should teach Albion's defence the foolishness of relying on the offside trap.

Seven minutes later Smith struck again with a magnificent header from Les Allen's centre, while Allen himself scored shortly afterwards with a shot that was only partially saved by Jock Wallace.

Instead of folding up, West Bromwich settled down to a series of well-combined attacks. This new-look forward line, with the introduction of full-backs Don Howe and Graham Williams, moved confidently.

Howe fitted in and scored Albion's only goal at inside-right, but Williams did little to suggest that he is the solution to the outside-left problem.

From start to finish the match was fought at breathtaking speed, and produced a standard of football which we have come to regard as exclusive to the star-studded Spanish and Italian teams.

Through it all Spurs' wing half-backs Danny Blanchflower and Dave Mackay were brilliant.

Tottenham must rid themselves of the irritating habit of having a goal spree, and then playing for keeps.

Watch Albion climb the table. On this form they will beat most clubs who visit the Hawthorns.

LOOK at those two Spurs in the picture on the left. They're full of themselves. That defeat by Sheffield Wednesday didn't shake their confidence. Look, again—at Terry Dyson's dance of joy after Cliff Jones has scored the third against Birmingham yesterday.

SCORERS WHITE
DYSON (2)
JONES (2)
SMITH (PENALTY)
HALF-TIME 3-0
ATTENDANCE 46,010

SCORERS WBA HOWE
SPURS ALLEN
SMITH (2)
HALF-TIME 1-3
ATTENDANCE 27,800

	HOME						AWAY						
					Goals						Goals		
	P	W	D	L	F	A	W	D	L	F	A	Pts
Tottenham H.	19	8	1	0	33	9	9	0	1	30	12	35
Sheffield Wed	18	9	0	1	21	5	2	4	2	9	11	26
Everton	19	7	2	0	25	6	4	2	4	21	23	26
Wolverhampton	19	7	2	1	25	15	4	2	3	21	20	24
Burnley	18	6	0	3	28	16	6	0	3	23	15	24
Aston Villa	19	9	0	1	26	13	2	2	5	15	25	24
Arsenal	19	8	0	2	22	11	1	2	6	8	19	20
Fulham	19	6	2	2	22	17	3	0	6	18	29	20
Leicester City	19	4	2	3	18	16	4	1	5	19	19	19
Blackburn Rov	19	5	1	3	22	18	3	2	5	15	22	19
Chelsea	18	4	2	2	27	24	4	0	6	20	19	18
Manchester C.	17	5	2	1	17	8	2	2	5	19	27	18
West Ham	18	7	1	1	32	18	1	1	7	10	23	18
Newcastle Utd	19	5	1	4	31	23	2	0	7	12	31	15
Cardiff City	19	5	2	3	11	8	1	3	6	14	29	15
Birmingham	19	5	1	3	15	11	1	1	8	12	29	14
Manchester Utd	18	5	2	2	21	11	0	1	8	9	27	13
Preston N.E.	18	4	2	3	14	12	1	1	7	7	24	13
West Bromwich	19	3	0	6	18	18	2	2	6	10	17	12
Blackpool	18	3	1	5	21	22	1	2	6	10	19	11
Bolton Wand	18	2	2	6	17	22	2	1	5	8	15	11
Nottingham F.	19	2	3	5	14	20	2	0	7	13	25	11

International caps of Spurs players from the British Isles. *Clockwise from top left*: Danny Blanchflower, Northern Ireland; Bobby Smith, England; Bill Brown, Scotland; Cliff Jones, Wales. For all the camaraderie that existed between the Spurs players, friendships would be suspended when they were pitted against each other at international level. Cliff Jones remembers that: "Dave Mackay would say: 'We might be mates but not today, laddie. Not today.'"

5

Maurice Norman

1960/61	App/Gls	
League	41	4
FA Cup	7	0

1955-66	App/Gls	
All comps	411	19

His team-mates nicknamed Maurice Norman 'swede' because he used to gather the root vegetables by hand on the farm in Mulbarton, Norfolk, where he worked as a youngster. But while big Maurice was strong, his approach was anything but agricultural. Like the rest of the Double team's back line, there was a sophistication to his play which forever changed the way his defensive position was viewed.

Norman was a centre-half, the rock around which Bill Nicholson built the side. "I remember Norman standing on the goal line on many occasions clearing with his head, his feet and his body after the rest of the defence had been beaten," says Spurs fan Richard Porter. Interviewed by *Charles Buchan's Football Monthly* on the eve of the Double season, the player explained the thinking behind an experiment that his manager had tried with him on the Russian tour of 1959. "It was decided by our manager Bill Nicholson that instead of playing the orthodox centre-half game, I should stay deep behind my full-backs and allow our wing-halves to control the midfield play entirely. My task would be to pick up the loose balls and generally cover the penalty area, making use of my height to head away the high centres and lobs from the opposing wingers."

This not only gave goalkeeper Bill Brown the physical protection he needed, it allowed half-backs Danny Blanchflower and Dave Mackay to push forward, safe in the knowledge that Norman would cut out counter-attacks. He was strong and quick but,

oddly enough, not the greatest tackler. He compensated with a sharp positional sense which he employed to intercept the ball with his long legs before opposing forwards could latch on to it.

In the first seven games of the Double season, Norman was outstanding. Standing six feet and one inch tall he was a powerful, athletic presence, a giant with jet black hair who filled the gaps left by his more creative team-mates and truly dominated the rearguard. He missed only one game, the 1-0 away win over Manchester City, all season.

But it wasn't just his defensive contribution that marked him out. "Tottenham are so much a ball-playing team," he said, "that the centre-half job at White Hart Lane is anything but static." And Norman loved to get forward, his ungainly running style – memorably described by Ivan Ponting as looking like "some fantastic cross between runaway giraffe and quick-stepping spider" – taking him deep into opposition territory for a careful lay-off.

He was the first central defender to push up for set plays, something Blanchflower encouraged by urging him forward while he dropped back to cover the space. Norman scored some vital goals this way, but more importantly his presence created mayhem which enabled Bobby Smith and Les Allen to score more.

Norman would return to Norfolk in the summer to work the fields, something which kept his fitness levels up and ensured, "I have none of the weight problems that plague some big fellows like myself." A broken leg in 1965 ended his playing career.

Previous page: Norman in resolute mood, defending against Crewe in the FA Cup fourth round 5-1 win in January 1961.

Below: Now retired, Norman mans the pumps (left) at his garage in Southgate in 1968.

Below right: He later owned a wool shop in Frinton-on-sea with his wife Jacqueline; Norman then returned to Norfolk where he worked as a gardener.

Facing page: The Normans were married on Easter Monday in the Double season and gave this signed wedding photo to Norman's team-mate John White.

66 Maurice Norman was a good lad and a gentle giant. He was the only one Bill wouldn't have a go at. Bill would put an arm round him instead and tell him what he wanted 99 Cliff Jones

Best Wishes
Jacqueline & Maurice

71

1960

December

League

3rd   **Spurs 4 Burnley 4**

10th   **Preston 0 Spurs 1**

17th   **Everton 1 Spurs 3**

24th   **Spurs 2 West Ham 0**

26th   **West Ham 0 Spurs 3**

31st   **Spurs 5 Blackburn 2**

December loomed with a testing six games to play on pitches turning into the quagmires common to the era. The defeat to Sheffield Wednesday had shown the super Spurs could be beaten and, with difficult away trips and a summit meeting with the reigning champions to contend with, December would reveal much about Tottenham's title challenge.

That the team emerged unbeaten and having dropped only one point effectively determined that the trophy was bound for north London. The sequence of one draw and five wins left Spurs ten points clear of second-placed Wolves and well positioned to focus attention on the other side of the Double coin.

The month opened with what was the best league game of the season – or the "match of the century" as the *Evening Standard* put it, venturing into excited if understandable theatrics. Holders Burnley arrived with a deserved reputation for fine football and the game did not disappoint. Inspired by White at his coruscating best, Spurs raced into a 4-0 first-half lead, a blistering assault that featured a three-goal salvo in just three minutes. The result appeared to be secured, but the Lancastrians were made of nerveless stuff and bounced back with a dashing display of their own to earn a remarkable but deserved point. "We scored eight goals and only drew," was a dumbfounded Nicholson's reported post-match comment after a lengthy dressing room inquest; Mackay was less sanguine and rightly fumed about a dropped point from a seemingly unassailable position.

The team needed to respond and get back to winning ways quickly. They did so with five wins in succession, 14 goals scored and just three conceded. First Preston were defeated with a rather underwhelming 1-0 win secured via scorer White and an impressive rearguard display from Norman, Baker and Henry. Fluency was restored with a 3-1 beating inflicted upon Everton at a foggy Goodison, with Mackay's outstanding long-range effort the highlight.

Next was a London derby double-header against West Ham either side of Christmas Day. In the White Hart Lane meeting, two goals without reply from White and Dyson were a modest return from a one-sided encounter. The Hammers struggled to contain Tottenham's bewildering movement and seemingly took no heed in the return at Upton Park, going down 3-0.

December was wrapped up with the best performance of the month. Despite missing the injured Mackay and Jones and with Tony Marchi playing through the pain barrier, Spurs hit peak form. Once again it was poor Blackburn who were on the receiving end, thrashed 5-2. Smith got back on the scoresheet after a curiously barren spell with two goals, Allen followed suit with a brace of his own and Blanchflower completed the spree.

Spurs were super once again. White in particular had been in sensational form and in a sure sign of the team's brilliance, the shrewdest judges of all served notice. The bookies were now refusing to take bets on Spurs winning the title.

Left: Bobby Smith bears down on goal during the epic 4-4 draw with Burnley at the start of the month.

THIS WAS MATCH OF THE CENTURY

TOTTENHAM 4, BURNLEY 4
From BERNARD JOY: Tottenham, Saturday

This was not the match of the season—it was the match of the century. Spurs, hitting three goals in a fantastic three-minute spell here at White Hart Lane, jumped into a 4—0 lead. Then came the magnificent fight back by the reigning champions, Burnley. And the result was a 4—4 draw.

Spurs' first-half onslaught came with a ferocity and suddenness which shattered Burnley. I doubt whether any team would have stood up to it.

The man who sparked off the spell was inside-right John White. He refused to panic when Burnley had his colleagues reeling with beautiful football in the opening 15 minutes.

Two for Jones

By continuing to play methodically he steadied the other forwards. It was from a corner by White that the first goal came after 18 minutes. The ball went wide to Mackay, who hit it straight back and NORMAN scored with a diving header.

Within another three minutes Spurs were 3—0 up. Jones scoring both goals. For the first a long throw by Mackay was helped on by Smith, who was playing despite a cold, and JONES crashed it in first time. A minute later Allen and White combined on the left and Smith jumped over the centre leaving JONES an open goal.

I give full credit to Burnley for fighting back despite the heartbreaking position of being three down after all the early running. It was thrill-a-minute football now, with Spurs just holding the edge. If Spurs are the prospective champions, then Burnley are worthy to hold the title at present. Spurs were a well-oiled machine while Burnley exploited the open game to perfection.

Connelly's miss

Two fine saves by Brown were followed by Connelly missing a fine chance from Pilkington. At the other end pile-drivers by Allen and Mackay were scrambled away.

Burnley had another heartbreaking experience in the 36th minute, when Blacklaw misjudged a 30-yard shot from MACKAY and the ball slipped out of his grasp into the goal.

Burnley still refused to give up and two minutes later CONNELLY obtained the goal they richly deserved.

Just on half-time a shot by McIlroy hit Brown on the foot as he dived, went straight up in the air and fell into Brown's arms. That was the sort of luck Burnley were having—and yet there was no doubt that Spurs well deserved their lead.

Half-time: Tottenham 4, Burnley 1

Despite the heavy pitch—the covers were removed early today—the speed, skill and thrills were maintained after the interval.

In the very first minute after the restart Jones made a fine run from the half-way line, took a return pass from Allen and crashed in a low shot which brought the save of the match from Blacklaw.

Burnley immediately retaliated with a combined move in which the forwards interchanged brilliantly. McIlroy shot and Brown got it away with a desparing dive.

Jones was now the mainspring of the Spurs' attack and was as likely to turn up at centre-forward as on one of the wings. He had fine service from Blanchflower.

Dangerous wingers

The raids of wingers Pilkington and Connelly were very dangerous and Spurs backs looked uneasy under the pressure. Within two minutes, Burnley took advantage of two defensive errors to reduce the lead to 4—3 after 60 minutes' play.

Henry tried to stop a fierce cross-shot from Pilkington which was going wide, and the ball slithered away from him to ROBSON, who scored easily.

Then Norman only partially cleared from a goalmouth scramble. POINTER snapped up the ball and ran on to beat Brown with a cross shot.

There were breathtaking escapes at both ends as each team flung in everything for another goal. The 58,000 spectators were enthralled at this vigorous and brilliant battle for mastery between two great teams.

Best of all

CONNELLY equalised after 74 minutes with the best goal of the match, after a lightning exchange of passes with Robson. Immediately afterwards Allen hit the Burnley post.

White saves the Spurs' pride at Preston

By TOM FINNEY

PRESTON 0, SPURS 1

SPURS inside-right John White scored with one of his left foot specials yesterday. Time: 3.14. Location: the Preston goalmouth. Result: a match winning goal for Spurs. White waved his arms in delight and with good reason. Spurs never looked like scoring again.

So Tottenham take home another two points. Against poorly-placed Preston, Spurs should have managed a much bigger win. Yet North End—the team that has not had a win in its last seven games—could easily have got away with a draw.

True Spurs were faster, and in midfield they were certainly superior to Preston.

But in the number of scoring chances, it was Preston who piled up the lead. Three times outside-left Peter Thompson brought full length saves from Spurs goalkeeper Bill Brown.

Twice centre-forward Alex Alston was within a coat of goalpost paint of scoring and once inside-left Seddon sent a header just over the bar.

Spurs seldom showed anything up front to match this — a great second-half try from outside-right Cliff Jones apart.

Even then Preston goalkeeper Fred Else was on hand to save. The one that got away, the one that moved past him, came after Else had fisted out two successive headers.

But as he chopped down the second John White was there waiting to flash the ball past him.

JOHN WHITE
scored vital goal

Brilliant

Had Preston had as much bite in attack as they had brilliance in defence, Spurs would certainly have been beaten.

But Preston too often played it square instead of forward. Time and again they allowed the Tottenham defence time to clear back and cover up before Preston put in a shot.

At times they livened up. And the fact that 17-year-old Frank Saul had to come in at the last minute for centre-forward Bobby Smith was not the reason that they failed to score again.

But the Spurs defence is good too—and they held out.

● As told to DON EVANS.

(handwritten notes:)

MATCH 20 3RD DEC 1960
SCORERS
SPURS NORMAN MACKAY JONES (2)

BURNLEY ROBSON CONNELLY (2) POINTER

HALF-TIME 4-1
ATTENDANCE 58737

SCORERS 0-1 WHITE
HALF-TIME
ATTENDANCE 21,657

THIRD ROUND DRAW

PLAYED on January 7, kick-off 2.15 or, if floodlit, no later than 3 p.m.

Preston	v. Accrington or Mansfield	Brighton	v. Derby Co.
Reading	v. Barnsley	Sunderland	v. Arsenal
Manchester U.	v. Middlesbrough	Tottenham	v. Charlton
Plymouth	v. King's Lynn or Bristol C.	Scunthorpe	v. Blackpool
		Lincoln	v. West Bromwich
Wolves	v. Huddersfield	Gillingham	v. Leyton Orient
Aldershot	v. Shrewsbury	Sheffield W.	v. Leeds
Tranmere or York	v. Norwich	Everton	v. Sheffield U.
		Liverpool	v. Coventry
Chesterfield or Oldham	v. Blackburn	Southampton	v. Ipswich
		Nottm. Forest	v. Birmingham
Luton	v. Northampton	Leicester	v. Oxford United
Cardiff	v. Manchester C.	Newcastle	v. Fulham
Rotherham	v. Crystal Palace or Watford	Portsmouth	v. Peterborough
		Darlington or Hull	v. Bolton
Bristol R.	v. Aston Villa	Burnley	v. Bournemouth
Swansea	v. Port Vale	West Ham	v. Stoke C.
Stockport	v. Bangor City or Southport	Chelsea	v. Halifax or Crewe

MACKAY BRINGS SPURS JOY

His 35-yard rocket dims Everton hopes

By BOB PENNINGTON   **EVERTON 1, SPURS 3**

A ROCKET drive from mighty Dave Mackay blazed 35 yards through the dank murk of Merseyside to evade the clawing fingers of goalkeeper Albert Dunlop and flash high into the corner of the Everton goal. And a deathly hush fell on this frenzied crowd of 61,000 as the Spurs players hugged the craggy Scot, Mackay, and went wild with joy and relief. For the second time in this momentous, magnificent seesaw of a match, Spurs were two ahead.

This time you felt that only the fog, swirling in from the river, could stop them celebrating an epic victory that deserved to clinch the championship.

Spurs manager Bill Nicholson and his directors sat in agonised frustration as the gloom deepened, and finally dimmed the skill of two Super-League stature sides, valued together at half a million pounds.

From the Press Box you could just see a Bobby Smith goal disallowed for handling, a Jimmy Gabriel header tipped against the Spurs bar, and a Cliff Jones header pounding against the Everton post.

My last clear memory before the grey blanket rolled over was of Britain's costliest centre-forward, Alex Young, missing a gift chance that would have crowned his English debut. Young, playing his first match for five weeks, looked what he is—a fine player only 75 per cent fit.

But it was not the need to gamble on Young through Roy Vernon's absence that cost Everton almost their last hope of catching Spurs. They should have been two up before Spurs even had their first shot at goal, yet never did they have the wit to try a long shot through the fog.

With Blanchflower making a strangley tentative start, outside-left Derek Temple and inside-right Frank Wignall had simple scoring breaks before Spurs surged into their true form after half an hour.

In the 36th minute Blanchflower and Jones joined in creating Spurs' first goal, scored by White with an elegant glide past Dunlop.

THAT DANNY BOY

And Blanchflower again, fighting back against his early failure, made a superb run from which Allen crashed the ball into the net for No. 2 four minutes later.

Three minutes after half-time Alec Parker, Billy Bingham and Young schemed a clear opening for Wignall, who drew out goalkeeper Bill Brown before side-stepping the ball into an open net. And Mackay's clincher came in the 59th minute from a Blanchflower throw-in to Jones.

The only tragedy was that the fog should have marred what would have been a match good enough for a Cup-final.

Everton : Dunlop ; Parker, Thompson ; Gabriel, Labone. Harris ; Bingham, Wignall. Young, Collins, Temple.
Tottenham : Brown ; Baker, Henry ; Blanchflower. Norman. Mackay ; Jones. White. Smith, Allen, Dyson.

SCORERS
EVERTON   WIGNALL
SPURS   WHITE
ALLEN
MACKAY

HALF-TIME   0-2

ATTENDANCE   61,052

TENSE TOTTENHAM TRIO, Norman (left), goalkeeper Brown, and Henry waited anxiously in the goalmouth for this Everton shot to determine its course—but the ball skidded wide of the post. Spurs continued their winning ways with a 3-1 win at Everton.

CLASSY TOTTENHAM PUT ON SPARKLING SHOW

White Hits the Hammers

RHODES KEEPS WEST HAM IN WITH A CHANCE

By VIC RAILTON

CLASSY Spurs played thrilling Christmas Soccer against West Ham in the local " derby " at Tottenham. Their forwards provided more pin-pricks for the West Ham defence than could be found on a holly bush, yet at half-time all they could show was a 25th minute headed goal from John White.

Wes Ham had to thank goalkeeper Brian Rhodes, that although technically outplayed, they were still in the game with a chance.

There was no goodwill among a small section of the 54,880 crowd. Police led away a spectator after a scuffle.

Apart from a couple of sorties by Musgrove on West Ham's left wing it was shooting in for Spurs for most of the first half. Jones and Dyson baffled Hammers in the early stages with bewildering switches and the only relief for the visitors came as Smith was twice caught offside.

Breakaway

It was 13 minutes before West Ham broke away, then they nearly scored through Dunmore, made skipper for the day on his first return to his old club. He eluded Norman, slid the ball between the wide-playing Spurs' backs, but Musgrove hammered the ball wide of an upright.

West Ham looked thrustful in mid-field, with Woosnam constantly probing for openings, but even two free kicks could not shake Spurs out of their calm.

Why West Ham are seeking a goalkeeper is a mystery for Rhodes saved his side several times, particularly when he dived to cut out a dangerous move following a Jones shot.

Spurs went through WHITE after 25 minutes. Smith, out on the right, crossed hard and shoulder high. White, though harassed, got his head to it and deftly flicked the ball into an empty corner of the West Ham net.

Rhodes continued to be the goalkeeper of action. He saved from Jones full stretch, while his opposite number, Brown, had scarcely a worthwhile shot to save.

Annoyance

The ball play of Jones and White, particularly, made the Hammers' defenders wonder where to go next. They tried to gain a respite with off-side tactics. So Spurs took a breather and held the ball almost at walking pace to the annoyance of the jam-packed crowd.

A foul by Mackay on Grice brought Spurs their first anxious moments just before the interval. Bond put the free kick in the goalmouth where Dick let fly with a left-foot drive which cannoned off Malcolm and over the bar.

This scare prompted Spurs to speed up again, but their finishing efforts were off target.

H.-T.: Spurs 1, West Ham 0.

The second half opened at the fastest pace of the match. Jones hurt a knee and Rhodes his right arm as the West Ham goalkeeper beat the winger for possession.

Rhodes had to use his damaged arm to tip over a point-blank shot from White. Then Jones went off for treatment and then returned ten minutes later with his right knee heavily bandaged.

Spurs: Brown; Baker, Henry; Blanchflower, Norman, Mackay; Jones. White. Smith, R. Allen, Dyson.
West Ham: Rhodes; Bond. Lyall; Malcolm. Brown. Moore; Grice, Woosnam. Dunmore. Dick. Musgrove.

John White

SPURS 2, WEST HAM 0

● Spurs master-mind John White flings himself at Bobby Smith's centre West Ham goalkeeper Brian Rhodes moves to his right, but White's header streaks the other way into goal.

SCORERS   WHITE, DYSON

HALF-TIME   1-0

ATTENDANCE   54,930

Match 24 Boxing Day. Monday 26th Dec. 1960
Match 25 Saturday 31st December 1960

DAILY MAIL, Wednesday, December 28, 1960

Spurs give West Ham double hiding to nothing

West Ham 0   Spurs 3

BLANCHFLOWER, I believe, has brought the Spurs team very close to his ideal of how Soccer should be played, closer than any other tactician has been able to mould a side to his personal ideas. His leadership, which is strictly by example, showed up clearly at Upton Park on Boxing Day when Spurs completed a holiday double over West Ham.

The first half of the double, at White Hart Lane on Christmas Eve, was disappointing, because West Ham's challenge when Spurs were only one goal up, and one man (Jones) short, looked lukewarm, to say the least.

On West Ham's smaller ground, where the gates were closed with the tightly packed crowd roaring a mere handsbreadth from the touchline, the contest was much more fierce, the quality of play higher. Excitement was a natural and plentiful by-product of this happy state of affairs.

And, since Spurs are so much an expression of Blanchflower's personality, there was humour too, of a puckish Celtic variety. For a Spur to lose possession is to lose face. Blanchflower has amusing methods of avoiding deprivation.

LYALL BAMBOOZLED
Cross-Legged Pass

Once, in the fiercest part of the battle, with his team leading through a goal scrambled through off Brown by Allen in the 24th minute, he trotted along in the inside-right position, seeking to make a break for Medwin on the wing.

Lyall was right on top of the winger, though. Blanchflower induced him to leave his post by switching the ball to his left foot, as if to cut infield; then, curling his right leg behind his left, he flipped the ball out to Medwin, who now had space to centre almost at leisure.

West Ham looked tired at the end. Their inability to depend on the exact timing of a team mate's pass, and the sad inaccuracy of Woosnam's distribution, meant that their danger men —Musgrove, Dick and Dunmore— had to depend upon strength and speed to make progress.

But a Spur (vintage 60-61) never runs when he can trot, and never trots when he can walk. Medwin, in the injured Jones's shirt, fell in with this idea at once and Hollowbread marked his return with the best save of the match from a first-timer by Moore off a centre by Malcolm.

MACKAY'S PASS
Convenient Bounce

Allen was a trifle lucky with his second goal, not long before the interval. Mackay's pass across goal was not exactly made to measure and hit Allen hard high up on the chest; but it bounced forward conveniently to give him an easy shot.

White got the third, nine minutes from the end, running unmarked on to Smith's flick from the left, and stroking the ball in-off the far post. Yet West Ham's much publicised search for a goalkeeper could well be abandoned on Rhodes' present form, for all Spurs' three goals.

West Ham.—Rhodes; Bond, Lyall; Malcolm, Brown, Moore; Grice, Woosnam, Dunmore, Dick, Musgrove.
Spurs.—Hollowbread; Baker, Henry; Blanchflower, Norman, Mackay; Medwin, White, Smith, R. Allen, Dyson.

Scorers: Browne (own goal) Allen & White
Half-time 0-2
Attendance 34,481

Peter Baker is a product of the Enfield nursery club, Peter joined Spurs as an amateur in 1949 and three years later signed professional forms. Since then he has never looked back and has now established himself as a firm favourite at White Hart Lane.

76

---

16 NEWS OF THE WORLD, Jan. 1, 1961

SPURS (A GOAL DOWN IN 13 MINS) KEEP A SECRET

Marchi crippled—but still they hit back

SPURS 5, BLACKBURN 2   By BOB PENNINGTON

TONY MARCHI, Spurs' £35,000 stand-in left-half, played on in pain for most of this amazing match with a crippled back—and a silent determination not to let Blackburn know his grim handicap.

Only after Spurs had stormed back to win one of their greatest triumphs, did manager Bill Nicholson reveal to me: "Everyone thought Marchi had a poor game. If they had only known what he was up against they would have realised it was one of his greatest. The injury came in the first few minutes when he leapt to head a ball.

"He kept quiet about it and the lads tried to keep the ball away from him. But it was an enormous handicap."

Even before the match Spurs were in trouble. No Dave Mackay, no Cliff Jones and Marchi only just recovered after treatment for an earlier back injury.

In 13 minutes they were a goal down—a brilliant solo and a rocket drive from England right-winger Bryan Douglas.

By half-time Bobby Smith had levelled the score from a centre by Terry Dyson, who had been wisely allowed to continue his left-wing surge after a clumsy foul had given variety to Blackburn's effective offside trap.

But still the odds were very much with the Cup finalists. "I thought that if we were going to lose at home, this was it," Nicholson confessed.

ARTISTRY

Blackburn, with strolling Derek Dougan, the artistry of Douglas, and a refreshingly consistent Peter Dobing were playing all the football in front, with old trusty Ron Clayton uncompromising in his treatment of Spurs key forward John White.

Danny Blanchflower was out of touch with his passes and with Marchi only conspicuous when he lobbed the ball on his own goal-net in a grotesque attempt to turn, the Tottenham attack was denied almost any constructive wing-half service.

HEART, FIGHT

But the heart and the fight were still there, from white-faced Marchi to men who were fit but out of form, like Blanchflower and Smith.

And in two minutes of glory, two great goals from Les Allen (56 minutes) and Blanchflower (58 minutes) crushed this once tight Blackburn defence into a demoralised rabble.

The rest of the game was just a question of how many the now-rampant Spurs would choose to score.

Allen (68 minutes) and Smith (73 minutes) after Allen had hit the post, made it five before Dobing scored a fine 75th-minute goal that brought little consolation.

As Nicholson said with a glow of pride: "What a team, what fighters. This bunch deserve nothing but the best."

After this I believe even the impossible is possible. And I mean the League and Cup double.

Scorers
Spurs: Smith (2) Allen (2) Blanchflower
Blackburn Douglas Dobing
Half-time 1-1
Attendance 48,742

	HOME				Goals		AWAY				Goals		
	P	W	D	L	F	A	W	D	L	F	A	Pts
Totnhm	25	12	0	0	44	15	12	0	1	37	13	46
Wolves	25	10	2	1	39	21	6	2	4	27	27	36
Burnley	24	8	0	4	37	26	8	1	3	35	21	33
Shef. W	24	11	1	1	29	10	2	6	3	14	18	33
Everton	25	8	1	2	30	14	5	1	5	29	30	32
Aston V	25	10	1	2	33	18	3	2	7	21	32	29
Arsenal	25	9	1	3	30	18	2	1	7	17	28	26
Man U.	24	8	2	2	33	12	2	2	8	16	33	24
Leicestr	25	6	3	3	25	18	4	1	8	22	29	24
W. Ham	24	9	1	2	29	17	1	2	9	16	33	23
Blackbn	25	7	1	4	30	21	1	5	6	21	34	22
Cardiff	25	7	2	3	18	10	1	5	7	16	33	23
Fulham	25	7	3	3	28	23	3	0	9	21	39	23
Chelsea	24	5	2	4	37	31	4	0	9	23	33	20
Man C.	24	6	2	3	23	16	2	2	8	21	38	20
NottmF	25	4	2	3	21	16	4	1	7	17	27	20
Birham	25	6	3	4	21	18	2	2	9	16	34	20
Nwcstle	25	5	4	4	38	30	2	0	10	17	40	18
W.B.A.	25	4	2	6	24	22	3	2	8	14	28	18
Bolton	24	5	2	6	24	24	2	2	7	11	24	18
Blackpl	24	5	1	6	29	25	1	3	8	13	26	16
P.N.E.	24	4	3	5	15	15	1	2	9	7	27	15

● One at a time, gents please! Over eagerness by Spurs' inside-right John White (second from left) cost skipper Danny Blanchflower an almost certain goal against Blackburn. Danny looked all set to give the League leaders a 2—1 lead after 40 minutes when White beat him to the ball and crashed it wide of the post. Not to worry. Danny scored No. 3 when Spurs cracked on the pressure to win 5—2

The hosts with the most

The tension of serious football business was put on hold at the club's Christmas Party. These lighthearted snapshots reveal the country's best team letting their hair down with management and directors.
Above: Terry Dyson and Bobby Smith receive their silver trays (see page 48).
Top right: Board members Fred Wale, Fred Bearman, Douglas Deacock and Sidney Wale get in the festive mood.
Bottom right: Cliff Jones, Bill Brown and reserve Norman Lee share a tipple.

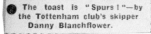
The toast is "Spurs!"—by the Tottenham club's skipper Danny Blanchflower.

And Mr B, at 88, gets his Lady C

By PETER MOSS

EVERYBODY agreed that Tottenham Hotspur's Christmas party yesterday was the best ever.

After all, they have the most to celebrate. The League table proves it.

First, the formal presentation of engraved silver trays to the players who had helped to set up the record of 11 wins to start the season.

Then the other gifts . . . TERRY DYSON, who is only 5ft. 3in. tall was given a copy of "Little Women."

Promise

MR. FRED J. BEARMAN, the 88-year-old chairman, was presented with a copy of "Lady Chatterley's Lover." "After I've read it I'll tell you boys all about it," he said.

BOBBY SMITH. England's centre forward, received a model of a petrol filling station. This is because he has a reputation for borrowing his team-mates' cars and forgetting to refill the tanks.

Then in came third-team goalkeeper FRANK SMITH, wearing a ragged suit and carrying a tray of matches. Smith is serving a two-week suspension. He collected more than £9 for his wares.

The happy reflections captured by Sportsmail cameraman RONALD FORTUNE belong to Terry Dyson and Bobby Smith.

6

Dave Mackay

1960/61	App/Gls	
League	37	4
FA Cup	7	2
1959-68	App/Gls	
All comps	318	51

"He was fantastic. The minute the ball was kicked off he was screaming, urging everyone on, swearing at every mistake... there aren't the characters like Dave Mackay today." Former player and physio Cecil Poynton lamented in Hunter Davies's classic *The Glory Game* that Mackay's successors were mere shadows in trying to emulate his greatness. But such comparisons are unfair. Whatever the era, whatever the team, there has never been a footballer quite like Dave Mackay.

A phenomenally combative midfielder, Mackay was the unquenchable heart of the Double team. Forming one of the game's finest half-back partnerships with Blanchflower, he was a dynamic force of nature who rampaged from box to box to utterly dominate opponents. But there was craft, wit and poise too. Mackay was a fine footballer who slotted into Tottenham's pass-and-move style with ease and he chipped in with some important and deftly executed goals. Half a century before the all-purpose midfielder became the vogue, Mackay created the template. Subsequent imitations have never bettered the original.

As effervescent a personality off the pitch as on it, Mackay was a Scotsman who embodied all the best qualities his nation's footballers were then famous for. He arrived from Hearts for £30,000 in 1959 – great value even then and a price he began to repay several times over as soon as he pulled on a Spurs shirt.

"The main job of a wing-half is to *get* the ball," Mackay informed *Charles Buchan's Football Monthly*. And through the

Double season, get it he did, often in uncompromising but rarely illegal fashion. He was a hard man but not dirty and never a bully. His unblemished disciplinary record in having never been sent off in his professional career tells any critic all they need to know. Mackay tackled with an almost scary intensity, but cleanly.

The remainder of his contribution to the Double cause was just as vital. He didn't score after December in the league, but his leadership was key. He was simply a born winner and evident to all eyes was his relentless, remorseless pursuit of victory. His team-mates loved him for it, the crowd worshipped him for it and Nicholson, perhaps, couldn't do without it. Of all the losses that cut to the core of the Double side after 1960/61, Mackay's two-year absence due to a twice-broken leg was arguably the most keenly felt, as it deprived the side of its most competitive element. The bond between manager and player was strong, and when Nicholson received the news of Mackay's second fracture, his was visibly upset. "They say tough men don't cry, but believe me, they do," recalled Alan Mullery in his autobiography.

Typically, such hard knocks did not curtail the Mackay career. He recovered, won the FA Cup again in 1967 before leaving for a successful post-Spurs career as manager and player, including a title-winning spell at Derby, for whom Brian Clough had signed him. Old Big 'Ead said Mackay was the best piece of business he ever did. Few would dispute that David Craig Mackay was the best player Tottenham ever bought into the north London fold.

Charles Buchan's
FOOTBALL
MONTHLY

DAVE McKAY
Hearts

" Dave Mackay was a winner. A complete winner and a good character. He added the commitment that might have been missing. He was like Bobby Smith; they were both tough but they were so skilful as well " Cliff Jones

Previous spread: Mackay with his jaw set square at the club photocall, 4 August 1961.
Left: A young Mackay, wrongly captioned 'McKay', at Hearts where he played and won honours from 1953 to 1959.

Top left: Dave Mackay, back row centre, part of the 1960s Scottish team that included Bill Brown, John White, Denis Law and Ian St John.
Above: Cartoonist and Spurs fan Paul Trevillion's strip from *Football Supporter* magazine, 1969.

DAVE MACKAY
Spurs

8 JUNE, 2967

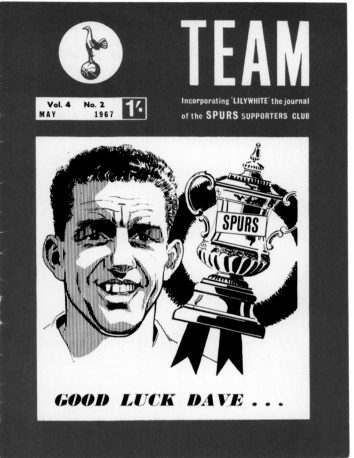

TEAM

Vol. 4   No. 2   1/-
MAY   1967

Incorporating 'LILYWHITE' the journal
of the SPURS SUPPORTERS CLUB

GOOD LUCK DAVE . . .

Facing page: Mackay ushers Danny Blanchflower's son Richard towards the bus before the trophy parade. Assistant secretary Alan Leather is also pictured.
Far left: Bill Nicholson checks an injury in June 1967.
Above: Captain in 1967.
Left: Photobooth fun with Cliff Jones and John White.

1960

An inside view

In December 1960 French magazine *Miroir Sprint* commissioned its chief correspondent Francois Thebaud and photographer Louis Lucchesi to cover Spurs' Christmas Eve match against West Ham. Thebaud adopted a rather critical stance. Under the heading *'Une équipe Britannique de série'* (A typical British team) he wondered if Spurs would shine in the European Cup, despite their brilliant individuals and ten-point lead in the championship. Lucchesi shot a series of unique documentary photos, providing a rare glimpse of White Hart Lane on a matchday and an evocative taste of the atmosphere at the club.

First, the pictures reveal the build-up to to the game as the fans mingle and players arrive, greeted by enthusiastic young autograph hunters. Then, inside the ground, the players and staff begin their preparations with Bill Nichoslon meticulous to the last. Then a flurry of action; Jones, Allen, Smith and White swirling through the matchday mud. Afterwards the wind-down. The players collect their weekly pay packets – dilligently issued by Nicholson himself – and head off to the players' lounge beneath the West Stand. Here, Cliff Jones admits, many a week's wages were won or lost on the snooker table. Finally the players retire to The White Hart pub where Dave Mackay holds court at the bar and the Christmas celebrations start in earnest.

This rarely seen photography is a journey in time back to the heart and soul of Tottenham Hotspur in the middle of its most famous season. Take a trip…

1. Fans queuing to enter the West Stand look over the car park as it begins to fill up.

2. Eight shillings got you a place on the terraces.

3. Two young supporters wear their customised colours to the ground.

4. Bobby Smith in demand for autographs from young fans.

5. A stare from Dave Mackay as he steps out of his Jag.

6. Bill Nicholson (far left) and Cecil Poynton at work in the heart of the dressing room…

7-8. Danny Blanchflower and Terry Dyson tie their laces.

9. Jones, the winger who became an extra attacker when the ball was on the opposite flank, heads for goal.

10-13. Les Allen evades West Ham keeper Brian Rhodes on the goal line, then darts past Bobby Moore and Ken Brown, a move Allen may have honed when he and Brown grew up on Bonham Road, Dagenham. Bobby Smith is also seen tussling with Brown.

14-17. John White glides across the muddy turf to unleash a drive, Allen shoots and Terry Dyson jinks in front of the East Stand.

18. Bobby Smith stops briefly to draw breath.

19. Dyson and White console Jones after the game. This injury put him out for the FA Cup third round.

20. Assistant manager Harry Evans, one of the best-loved but least-known figures of The Double era, takes care of the paperwork.

21. John White collects his weekly wages from Bill Nicholson.

22-25. Tony Marchi signs in to the players' lounge. Jones and Ron Henry unpack the Christmas drinks. Marchi sets out the snooker stakes. Jones gets to the table.

26. Getting a round in at The White Hart pub.

27. Rosettes for sale.

Cliff Jones

CLIFF JONES
(Spurs)

1960/61	App/Gls	
League	29	15
FA Cup	6	4

1958-68	App/Gls	
All comps	378	159

During the Double season, Cliff Jones played fewer games than any of the men now recognised as the first eleven who won it. But it is his pace and skill that is seared into the memory. Described by writer Ivan Ponting as "the most thrilling, eye-catching entertainer in Spurs' greatest team," and by Terry Venables, who as a boy watched Jones from the terraces, as "magnificent... possibly the best winger the club had," Jones was pivotal.

The Welshman combined sublime skill with fearlessness. He refused to wear shinpads because they slowed him down. So he collected knocks and his willingness to stick his head in to the thick of the action not only brought goals aplenty but facial lacerations. "There was no braver player in the game," said Bill Nicholson. But for all the times he was sent flying, Jones kept an even temper. He hated any form of violence on the pitch, once saying: "Football was never meant to be a game of biff and bang."

Jones could play on either wing, but was no orthodox winger. He could hug the line and beat his man to send in a cross, but he'd also cut inside or run straight at defenders after picking the ball up from deep. His dribbling and ability to change direction destroyed opponents, his passes to Smith and Allen created chances, his powerful shot and ability to leap high and thump home headers provided the finish. "The way we were playing," he wrote in 1962, "made for more fluid forward disposition and I knew that when I went into the centre, someone would automatically be in my position." Jones was the only player Nicholson would allow to hold the ball. His team-mates joked that if they tired they could just "give it to Jonesy." He didn't give it away.

As the team's great start began to falter, Nicholson gambled on playing a not entirely fit Jones. Against Fulham his two headed goals helped Spurs to a 5-1 victory. As Spurs pushed for the title, it was Jones's contribution against Chelsea and Preston in the Easter double header which drew plaudits. Two goals in the first, and a superb hat trick capped with an overhead kick in the second secured his reputation as the best winger in the world.

Jones's first goal against Preston finished a move that summed this team up. Blanchflower started from deep, Tony Marchi helped it on to Les Allen at the corner of the opposition box, who checked and rolled it onto the penalty spot for Jones, who nimbly changed feet twice before slamming home. Incisive, direct, controlled brilliance.

Off the pitch, Jones and his great friend John White were the resident pranksters, always up to some trick, egging each other on or playing practical jokes on their team-mates. When the mood needed easing, they would do it.

Jones was the last of the Double players to leave, joining Fulham in 1968. He went on to teach PE and continues to work as a match-day host for Spurs. He retains a tremendous affection for the club and for that Double season. "It was something special," he says. "A buzz all the time. Particularly on a match day. We were something special and we responded to it."

The players **Cliff Jones**

Previous page: Jones scores against Chelsea, Easter 1961.
Above: In the Spurs dressing room, pre-season 1959.
Top right: Part of the great Wales team which reached the quarter-finals of the 1958 World Cup, the summer that Jones (front row, far right) signed for Spurs. The side also included the club's Mel Hopkins (back row, third right) and Terry Medwin (front row, far left).
Right: In 1958, Gunner Jones lined up for the British Army side alongside Fusilier AH Parker, a Scottish international from Falkirk. Parker played against Jones in the 1960/61 opener for Everton at White Hart Lane. Jones recalls: "First game of the season, I got injured by Alex Parker. I was in the army with him and he done me like a kipper! Right across my ankle. It was a bad smack but I couldn't go off. They stuck me into the middle of the field so I was a nuisance factor – someone had to mark me. As a result I missed six of the first seven games, but I wasn't worried. I was Bill's number one winger. I could play outside-right or outside-left. I just understood it – that I wouldn't lose my place."

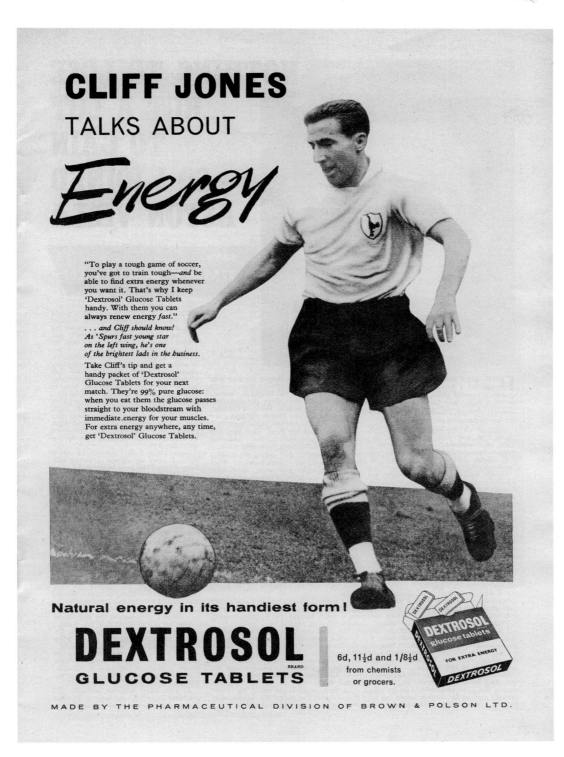

CLIFF JONES
TALKS ABOUT
Energy

"To play a tough game of soccer, you've got to train tough—*and* be able to find extra energy whenever you want it. That's why I keep 'Dextrosol' Glucose Tablets handy. With them you can always renew energy *fast*."

. . . and Cliff should know! As 'Spurs fast young star on the left wing, he's one of the brightest lads in the business.

Take Cliff's tip and get a handy packet of 'Dextrosol' Glucose Tablets for your next match. They're 99% pure glucose: when you eat them the glucose passes straight to your bloodstream with immediate energy for your muscles. For extra energy anywhere, any time, get 'Dextrosol' Glucose Tablets.

Natural energy in its handiest form!

DEXTROSOL
GLUCOSE TABLETS

6d, 11½d and 1/8½d from chemists or grocers.

MADE BY THE PHARMACEUTICAL DIVISION OF BROWN & POLSON LTD.

Jones recalls his off pitch ventures being less than successful. A deal with Dextrosol (left) pocketed him £35 and was considerably more lucrative than a venture in to the meat trade (right) with a friend ("now ex-friend" says Cliff) which ended up costing him money.

Top: Jones's hero was Stanley Matthews who he played alongside in a farewell match in 1965. Matthews gave him his pre-match meal secret – a raw egg beaten in a glass of milk with glucose powder. Cliff adds: "It worked! Well, if it was good enough for Stan..."

Cliff Jones and John White formed an instant friendship and roomed together on away trips. "He was my pal, one fantastic character. When he played well, the team played well."
Top: Shopping for shoes on tour in Mumbles, Wales, 1961.
Above: White plays mother for post-training tea-time in 1962.
Facing page: "Look at that for a six pack!" says Jones.

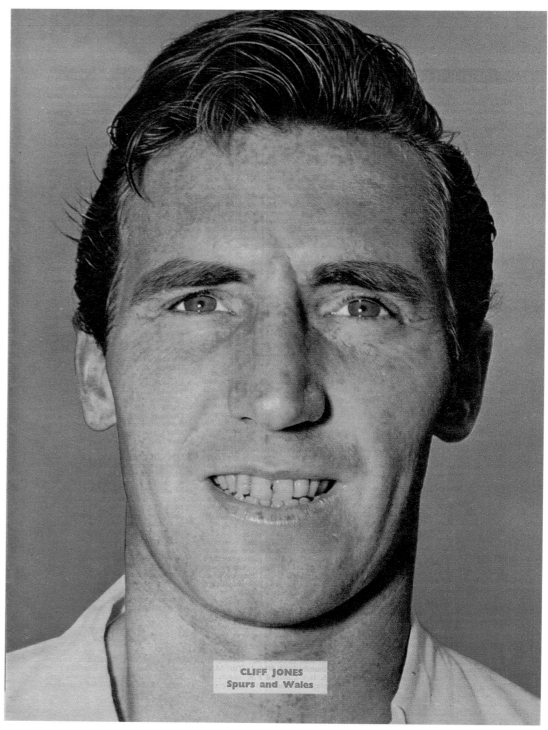

CLIFF JONES
Spurs and Wales

“ I was someone who enjoyed what I was doing and thought I was very fortunate. My style for Spurs was 'Have ball, will travel.' I didn't just stick to one side and when I got the ball there was an expectancy from the crowd. I could sense it **”**

1961

January

Left: With the season's focus turned towards the cup, Charlton Athletic goalkeeper Willy Duff springs to save a shot from John White (hidden between Charlton's John Sewell and no 2 Gordon Jago).

The New Year came in screaming. With the third round of the FA Cup came renewed excitement as the second front opened. Expectation was heightened as statisticians latched on to a sequence now legendary in Lilywhite lore, the fact that Spurs tended to win the cup when the year ended in '1'. Spurs were ten points clear at the top of the league, seemingly unstoppable. And in the background, a dispute over the transfer and wage system would be resolved, with far-reaching significance for football, only after last-ditch talks prevented a national footballers' strike.

Spurs drew Charlton in the cup and more of their fans turned up to watch the tie at White Hart Lane than had attended a game at The Valley all season. Spurs led, but let the Addicks back into the game before Blanchflower stepped in to calm the pace. It was the worst display of the season, not exactly ideal preparation for facing an improving Manchester United side at Old Trafford.

Saturday's game was called off because of fog, so Spurs had to return to Lancashire on the Monday. In the interim, Peter Baker pulled a muscle, which meant Spurs took to the pitch without him, Jones or Medwin, giving debuts to Ken Barton and John Smith on the wing. Spurs began confidently, but the axis of Mackay and Blanchflower were soon ground down by the close attentions of a hungry United side. In the end, the Reds' handsome display sent Spurs to only their second defeat of the season.

The following Saturday also threatened to be a free day, with the League poised to shift the programme to Friday in order to stymie the footballers' strike. It was a move that attracted huge public criticism and contributed to an eventual settlement which, in the short term, meant the weekend's matches could go ahead on the Saturday and in the long term would see footballers take home pay beyond the wildest dreams of the stars of the sixties.

The largest crowd to watch a match in London all season, 65,251 – an official figure that probably does not include the 300 who stormed the gate and got in for free – had cause to be grateful as Spurs gave an inexperienced Arsenal side a lesson in football. The sweetest moment in Tottenham's sixth double of the season came when Mackay and Smith combined in the flowing manner more reminiscent of Blanchflower and White to score the home side's third, the culmination of a move described as "the season's pièce de resistance" by journalist Julian Holland.

In the fourth round of the cup, Crewe were the opponents for the second year running. Determined to avoid a repeat of the 13-2 scoreline which is still a Tottenham club record, they tried to kick their opponents off the pitch.

Goalkeeper Brian Williamson restored some Fourth Division pride with a great display that restricted Spurs to five goals, but there was still plenty of opportunity for Tottenham's players to celebrate with the kind of "kissin' and cuddlin'" behaviour which had earned a midweek rebuke from the FA and criticism in the press. For all the admiration for modernist Spurs, some more traditional attitudes persisted.

F.A. Cup 3rd Round, Saturday 7th Jan. 1961

SPURS v CHARLTON

The Evening News & THE STAR

World's largest evening sale

LONDON, SATURDAY, JANUARY 7, 1961

Another Bid For That Cup And League Double

By JOHN OAKLEY

COCK-A-HOOP Spurs start their bid for the coveted Cup and League double with a third round tie against Charlton Athletic to-day . . . and they should make no mistake in passing this first Wembley milestone.

But don't think Spurs are taking this match lightly. They know they have the finest chance of the double since Aston Villa last achieved the feat 63 years ago, so they intend to go all out from the start.

With a lead of 10 points over Wolves in the First Division, Spurs can afford to concentrate on the Cup. But for those fans who consider Spurs, on their present form, unbeatable let me remind them of last season.

Then Spurs went into the Cup three points clear in the League and again all talk centred on their chances of the double.

West Ham Bid

They strode confidently through to the fifth round but then, in a disastrous 90 minutes on a mud-bound pitch at White Hart-lane, they went out 3-1 to Blackburn and two further home defeats by Manchester City and Chelsea over Easter killed their League hopes.

So Spurs, like many great teams before them, finished up with nothing.

To-day Charlton could be dangerous. They come to White Hart-lane with nothing to lose and a free-scoring attack that has netted 57 goals in 24 League games.

West Ham, who played in the first Wembley Cup Final in 1923, have rarely gained glory in the F.A. Cup. Yet they have always struck me as an ideal team for the cut and thrust of knockout competitions.

Though they can be deplorably bad at times, West Ham can also produce soccer unequalled by any other team in the country outside of Spurs and Burnley.

Manager Ted Fenton is hoping for a repeat of their outstanding form against Wolves three weeks ago for the Cup battle against Second Division Stoke City at Upton Park to-day.

Scorers
Spurs Allen (2)
       Dyson
Charlton Leary
          Lawrie
Half-Time 3-1
Attendance 54,969

A QUESTION BY DANNY

By RON BEAGLEY
Spurs 3, Charlton 2

AFTER this tie, Spurs' skipper Danny Blanchflower wanted to know why Charlton were not among the top clubs of the Second Division.

The answer was supplied by Charlton manager, Jimmy Trotter, who said: "We don't get the same support at home as we got today.

"If only the fans would cheer the boys every week, instead of just on special occasions, the team would produce the good football they played today."

Trotter may be right, for Charlton were terrific, and gave the Cup favourites and League leaders one of their toughest games this season.

Charlton fans roared as their heroes played Spurs at their own game, with fast, attacking Soccer. Their nippy attack repeatedly broke through, and Spurs defenders were often lucky to block shots as they rocketed towards goal.

Spurs were inspired by Blanchflower, his usual brilliant self at right half, and by some snappy shooting from inside left Les Allen.

Left winger Terry Dyson deserves a mention for grabbing Spurs' third goal despite an injured leg muscle.

Scorers.—Spurs: Allen (7, 28 minutes), Dyson (86). Charlton: Leary (33), Lawrie (46).

DANNY BLANCHFLOWER
Schemed Spurs win

Terry Medwin deputising for the injured Cliff Jones.

By J. L. MANNING
Tottenham 3   Charlton 2

DAILY MAIL, Monday, January 9, 1961

Nicholson escapes the doghouse—jus

MR. BILL NICHOLSON would have been in a very distinguished managerial doghouse this morning, with no more than a replay on Wednesday to cheer him, if Charlton's plan had not gone wrong.

It went wrong at the very time this Cup-tie hung in the balance and Spurs, with a bit of luck, escaped temporarily from the wearying effect of growing staleness and mounting injuries among their wingers.

January will be a hard month for them. League matches at Old Trafford and with Arsenal, followed by another Cup-tie, will stretch to the limit the club's resources and the players' spirit.

Three incidents

Charlton revealed how slender is the thread of success. They would have snapped it rudely if their match-winning winger, John Summers, had been given the ball when the Spurs were worn and wide open in the second half. Mr. Jimmy Trotter ruefully agrees with me on this tactical point.

The idea was to keep Summers as a threat to prevent the Spurs concentrating their defence on Leary. But Charlton went too far, and nothing could be done from the touchline to correct the error. The lesson is that a roaming winger is never a threat to anyone unless he gets the ball.

Despite all this, three incidents in the last few minutes decided the game in favour of Spurs:

Spurs' back Baker had quickly to beat three Charlton men in the tackle to stop the equaliser;

Spurs' goalkeeper Brown had to leap and clutch the ball desperately when Norman was bustled into a pass-back that nearly scored;

Edwards, from the left wing, put a centre over the bar with three Charlton forwards waiting unmarked for the pass, from which they must have scored.

That was how Spurs escaped. In the first half Blanchflower and Mackay drove the team not only to three goals but to what looked an unchallengeable triumph.

In front the forwards made what they could of this remarkable service, but when Dyson was injured and Smith clearly was floundering on the mud and sand pitch, Charlton had no great defensive problem.

Astonishing shot

They turned the corner in the second half as soon as Blanchflower fell from the thick of the fight. If, at this stage, Summers had been set free I do not think Tottenham would have won.

Allen (33 minutes) gave Spurs a two-goal start within 28 minutes. Leary made it 2—1 and the limping Dyson was lucky to be thought onside when he made it 3—1 nine minutes before half-time.

Immediately after the interval Lawrie scored an astonishing shot which brought Charlton back with a chance.

I can say only that Charlton were clearly the better team for the rest of the match and everyone in the crowd knew it

No. 570

TOTTENHAM HOTSPUR
Football & Athletic Company Ltd.

Block L   WEST STAND

F.A. CUP, 3rd ROUND

TOTTENHAM HOTSPUR
v
CHARLTON ATHLETIC

On SATURDAY, JAN. 7th 1961
Kick-off 3.00 p.m.

Row Q   35
Seat No.

The Tottenham Hotspur Company do not Guarantee that the proposed match will be played

R. S. JARVIS
Secretary

PRICE 10/-

Ticket Holders are requested to be in their seats 15 minutes at least before the Kick-off.

WEST STAND—Entrance HIGH ROAD

THEY COULDN'T BELIEVE IT!

'THIS TIME WE WON'T BE HUMILIATED'

By JACK WOOD

SMILES, cheers, amazement. As you can see from the picture, that was the spontaneous reaction of the giant-killers of Crewe Alexandra, on hearing they had been drawn against Tottenham in the fourth round of the Cup for the second successive year—a 960-to-one chance.

Five nervously chewed cigarettes, two drinks, and 40 hectic minutes after this incredible Cup pairing had come through were in the tiny boardroom on a hired portable radio, we began to get the whole thing into perspective.

'No jeers'

Manager Mr. Jimmy McGuigan, a quiet and efficient Scot who has spent his life among football's working classes, said: "The cheers of the lads when the draw came through were instinctive. But all of us realise that this dream match could again turn out to be a nightmare.

"I would rate Spurs among the top three club sides in Europe. We cannot hope to beat them. But this time there will be no humiliation. No jeers, that we heard last time from the Londoners."

Mr. McGuigan, 56, was Crewe's trainer then. "I have never felt worse than on that night last February when Spurs beat us 13—2. We never got settled into the game, and as the goals kept smashing in I wanted the ground to open and swallow me."

DRAW FOR ROUND 4

To be played on January 28.

Sheffield Utd.	v. Lincoln
Scunthorpe	v. York or Norwich
Sheffield Wed	v. Manchester Utd
Swansea	v. Preston
Southampton	v. Leyton Orient
West Ham or Stoke	v. Aldershot or Shrewsbury
Peterborough	v. Aston Villa
Brighton	v. Burnley
Birmingham	v. Rotherham
Wolves or Huddersfield	v. Reading or Barnsley
Liverpool	v. Sunderland
Newcastle	v. Stockport
Leicester	v. Bristol C.
Tottenham	v. Crewe
Bolton	v. Chesterfield or Blackburn
Luton	v. Cardiff or Manchester C.

AS THEY CAME OUT OF THE HAT . . SPURS v. CREWE

Pearson, Quixall, and Stiles bemuse Tottenham

Dawson excels himself in goal

BY ERIC TODD

Manchester U. 2, Tottenham H. 0

In the presence of 65,295 wildly enthusiastic spectators Manchester United gave Tottenham Hotspur a forthright example of their new-found strength at Old Trafford last night when they beat the League leaders and beat them handsomely 2-0. It was only Tottenham's second defeat in 26 games.

Victory against such redoubtable opposition would have been notable at the best of times; on this occasion its merit was enhanced by the fact that Gregg was injured and played at centre-forward for the whole of the second half, and Dawson took his place in goal. Such is United's spirit these days that the inconvenience was not noticeable. United played well to a man and one would not presume to give individual praise, although a possible exception might be made of Dawson who, stormed at with all sorts of shots and subjected to all sorts of bodily assaults, did not flinch. Never before this season has one seen a better example of team work.

Tottenham may plead that they had to make late changes. With Jones already out of action Medwin and Baker had to cry off at the last minute because of injury and were replaced by J. Smith and Barton, the latter making his first League appearance, not inappropriately at this stage since he is Tottenham's delegate to the Professional Footballers' Association. But it is doubtful whether at full strength Tottenham could have made much of this United side.

R. Smith generally was mastered by Foulkes and Allen and White found progress nearly impossible against first-time tackling. Even Blanchflower and Mackay were so overworked by Pearson and Stiles that only in the early stages were they given time to set the Tottenham forwards in anything like their regular motion. Long before the end Tottenham had to admit defeat and they were obviously exasperated by United's confidence that at the last amounted almost to impertinence.

Tremendous spirit

Defences were so much on top in the early stages that, apart from a near miss by R. Smith with a header and an excellent hook shot by Stiles neither goalkeeper was given cause for embarrassment. Tottenham played the more classic football with Blanchflower pushing some lovely passes down the middle, but United fought with tremendous spirit. On one occasion when Henry kicked the ball well into the United half, J. Smith ran on to it with an anticipation matched only by that of Charlton, who chased the outside right and dispossessed him. In the thirteenth minute United took the lead and an excellent goal it was. Pearson and Quixall combined well on the right, each shaking off two tackles, none of which was particularly gentle, and when Pearson eventually put the ball across, Stiles hit it first time past Brown. It was a triumph for sheer persistence.

Shortly afterwards there occurred one of those incidents that will be talked about for a long time. J. Smith found a way through a ruck of players and a splendid shot was saved brilliantly by Gregg, who appeared to hurt his shoulder as he fell. He recovered after attention and the crowd expected a bounce up since no player of either side was anywhere near Gregg at the time. The referee awarded United a free kick three yards out, but no sooner had the ball cleared the penalty area than the referee ordered the kick to be retaken. In fact, there were four free kicks, two to each side in rapid succession, but the reasons were not apparent. When the excitement died down Brennan made one of his infrequent miskicks and J. Smith, possibly through over eagerness, followed suit when it might have been easy for him to have scored.

Score disallowed

United's defence played magnificently against a clever side and five minutes before the interval Charlton, who previously had been beaten twice for possession in races with Brown, went close after receiving a fine pass from Stiles. Just on half time Gregg made a great save from Allen and there was a terrific scramble before R. Smith headed the ball into the net, but the goal was disallowed. Alas for United Gregg aggravated the injury to his shoulder and was led off the field and Dawson went in goal. Dawson was still wearing the goalkeeper's jersey at the restart and there was a great cheer when Gregg, his right shoulder heavily bandaged, returned to play at centre forward, a position one understands he has coveted for most of his life. It now remained to be seen whether he could make it a fairy tale ending by scoring a goal—preferably the winner.

Gregg, who appeared to have read about the deep lying centre forward plan, wandered about quite happily and put in one shot that was nowhere near the target, but at least it was an effort and no praise can be too high for him. Dawson also enjoyed himself thoroughly and he made some good looking saves, especially one from Allen that Gregg himself could not have improved upon. Try as they did, Tottenham could make little headway against a defence that really excelled itself and in the seventy-fourth minute United were rewarded with their second goal and another beauty it was. Stiles, Quixall, and Pearson made all the running and when Pearson slipped the ball out to Gregg, he let it run past the centre as though he had been doing this sort of thing regularly. Tottenham were bewildered by this astute move—but not Pearson. He brought the ball under control and Brown had no chance of saving.

MANCHESTER UNITED.—Gregg; Brennan, Cantwell; Setters, Foulkes, Nicholson; Quixall, Stiles, Dawson, Pearson, Charlton.

TOTTENHAM HOTSPUR.—Brown; Barton, Henry; Blanchflower, Norman, Mackay; Smith (J.), White, Smith (R.), Allen, Dyson.

Referee: W. T. Surtees (Durham).

111

Match 27 Saturday 21st Jan. 1961

TOTTENHAM BEAT ARSENAL 4-2

SPURS v CREWE

Players crowd in front of Arsenal goal for a corner at White Hart Lane this afternoon.
From left, are: McCullough, Arsenal, Norman and Smith Spurs, and Neill (on ground and Docherty of Arsenal.

DOCHERTY HAS NAME TAKEN

TOTTENHAM 4, ARSENAL 2

From HAROLD PALMER: Tottenham, Saturday

Spurs, after the shock of an Arsenal goal in the eighth minute, beat their North London rivals in a rousing match at White Hart Lane this afternoon. It was rugged stuff at times and international referee Arthur Ellis, who had taken a firm line over some of the tackling, eventually took Arsenal left-half Docherty's name.

About 65,000, biggest crowd of the season here, saw Spurs attack from the kick-off. Smith headed in from a corner and Irishman McClelland, deputising in goal for Kelsey, looked really spritely as he leaped to hold the ball.

There was early evidence it was going to be tough and Jones, back on Spurs wing, soon showed he could take it as McCullough swept his feet from under him.

Next Mackay served up the rough stuff to bring down Eastham and got a talking to from the referee.

After eight minutes a spectacular goal from HENDERSON put Arsenal in the lead. Docherty, deputy for Groves as both centre and left-half, made the chance—if chance you could call it. Henderson, from 25 yards, suddenly whipped in a terrific low shot that out of Brown's reach.

Two minutes later Spurs were level. White changed the point of attack as he screwed a pass to his left. ALLEN ran onto the ball and his shot went in off the far post.

Arsenal were rather unlucky to concede a penalty for a late Neill tackle on Dyson after 23 minutes, and McClelland could not reach BLANCHFLOWER'S well-placed kick.

Referee Ellis was clamping down on some of the over-eager tackling. He had a word with McCullough after a rugged tackle on Dyson.

Clapton was hurt and went off for a few minutes.

It was full-blooded football and even those, and there were many, who bought 8/- tickets off the touts for £2, must have felt they were getting their money's worth.

As far as artistry was concerned, none provided this more than Blanchflower and Eastham, who always seemed to be in an open space and used the ball so intelligently.

Docherty, at 32, was no sluggard and his use of the ball was thoughtful. I can understand his reluctance to give up playing, but he told me before the game that he is prepared to do so to get established as a coach or manager.

Mackay made a dazzling start to a third Tottenham goal two minutes before half-time. Jones carried on the good work and, after Magill had passed back to McClelland, SMITH rounded the goalkeeper and had only to chip the ball into an open goal.

Half-time: Tottenham 3, Arsenal 1

Clapton resumed with his left knee bandaged.

Arsenal did not deserve to be two goals down. They built up their attack with accurate passing and quick positioning.

But Spurs looked more dangerous when they broke away. There was a wonderful move in which Jones and White combined smartly, but in the end McClelland saved easily from Jones.

Rebound

Spurs were lucky after 56 minutes when a shot by Henderson rebounded into play off a post.

Eventually Docherty had his name taken. He brought down Smith and then appeared to argue with the referee.

White chipped a pass out to the right to give Jones a chance. The winger worked the ball up the goal-line before passing back to ALLEN, who scored from short range. That was after 15 minutes of this half.

Less than a minute later Arsenal replied through HAVERTY, whose effort from the left wing sent the ball curling in just under the bar.

The ball may have touched Baker en route, but I would hate to rob Haverty of the credit for his first League goal this season.

Brave effort

There was another brave effort by Arsenal, and Clapton in particular. Henderson and Eastham made a chance for the crippled winger, who drove over the bar.

Mackay had revelled in this game. No one was more often in possession. He seemed tireless as he laboured like a sixth forward. Spurs were in charge now.

SPURS — Brown; Baker, Henry; Blanchflower, Norman, Mackay; Jones, White, Smith, Allen, Dyson.
ARSENAL — McClelland; Magill, McCullough, Neill, Young, Docherty; Clapton, Eastham, Herd, Henderson, Haverty.

Scorers
SPURS:
ALLEN (2)
BLANCHFLOWER (pen)
SMITH

ARSENAL:
HENDERSON
HAVERTY

HALF TIME 3-1
ATTENDANCE 65251

THE VISITING FIREMAN SAYS: SPURS 5-0

FIRST man to wish Crewe's Cup heroes good luck when they arrived in London yesterday was a Spurs supporter—Stan Fitton, fireman on the express train that brought them to Euston Station ten minutes ahead of schedule, writes GERALD WILLIAMS.

"They'll need it," he cracked. "It's obvious Spurs will win, isn't it? I'd say 5—0."

Fireman Fitton's one regret is that he will not be at White Hart-lane to see whether his prediction comes true. "I'll be miles away in Blackpool," he said.

Little Welsh outside-left Merlyn Jones, one of the three survivors of the Crewe side which lost 13—2 to Spurs a year ago, told me:

"I don't know whether we can win or not, but I promise you we're determined there's not going to be another catastrophe like that."

One of Crewe's keenest fans is the mayor, Councillor Sam Orwell, who was ill in bed but got up yesterday to see them off to London.

Last year, on their way to Tottenham, the Fourth Division boys left Crewe Station from Platform 13 and arrived on Platform 3. The result was 13—2.

This time they left PLATFORM 4—and pulled in on PLATFORM 1.

It's The Year For Success

By JOHN OAKLEY

CHEEKY Crewe, 2—1 conquerors of Chelsea, will run on to the White Hart-lane pitch to-day to tackle star-stacked Spurs determined to erase the memory of their 13—2 defeat in a Cup replay here last season . . . and if they win or draw three of their team will hold a special celebration.

Left-back Don Campbell, right-half Stan Keery and outside-left Merlyn Jones will be the celebrating trio if Crewe spring the biggest surprise of the season. For these three players are the sole survivors of the team thrashed unmercifully last February.

Spurs supporters, who consider to-day's match just another run-out for their talented side, might be in for a surprise.

Crewe proved when beating Chelsea at Stamford Bridge three weeks ago that they can produce football of a quality far higher than their normal Fourth Division fare.

Certainly Spurs are not taking the match lightly for nothing less than the Cup and League double, last achieved by Aston Villa in 1897, will please Tottenham fans.

And if you believe in cycles this must be Spurs' year. They won the Cup in 1901 and 1921. War stopped the 1941 competition so, according to the law of averages, 1961 should be the year for the London club to carry off the trophy for the third time.

FOOTBALL LEAGUE—DIV. I

Up to and incl. Jan. 28th.

	P.	W.	D.	L.	F.	A.	Ps.
Tottenham Hotspur	27	23	2	2	85	32	48
Wolverhampton W.	27	18	4	5	74	51	40
Sheffield Wed.	26	14	8	4	50	30	36
Burnley	26	16	1	9	73	48	33
Everton	26	14	4	8	60	48	32
Aston Villa	26	13	4	9	56	52	30
Arsenal	27	12	4	11	54	54	28
Leicester City	27	11	5	11	54	48	27
West Ham United	26	11	4	11	59	56	26
Manchester United	26	11	4	11	52	51	26
Blackburn Rovers	27	10	5	12	54	58	25
Cardiff City	27	9	7	11	37	46	25
Birmingham City	27	10	4	13	41	54	24
Nottingham Forest	27	9	5	13	42	55	23
Fulham	27	10	4	13	50	69	23
West Bromwich A.	28	9	4	15	44	55	22
Chelsea	26	9	3	14	61	68	21
Manchester City	25	8	5	12	51	62	21
Bolton Wanderers	26	8	5	13	39	50	21
Newcastle United	27	7	6	14	60	75	20
Blackpool	25	6	4	15	43	54	16
Preston North End	26	5	5	16	25	48	15

SPORTSMAIL AT THE BIG GAMES

THEY'RE STILL AT IT!

★ *Still hugging, kissing and cuddling their way in the LOVING Cup. Yet it's the Spurs' third as Terry Dyson (right) and scorer Dave Mackay celebrate as if it were a last-minute winner.*

★ *Look at disconsolate Crewe 'keeper Brian Williamson, hands stretched out in despair. It's like mocking his outclassed Div. 4 side to be so joyful when they're whacked.*

Goalkeeper Brian Williamson defied the mighty Spurs on Saturday. Now he's up for sale.

Tottenham triumph —but Williamson is the show-stopper

By BRIAN JAMES

Tottenham 5   Crewe 1

THIS was the Cup bet that Tottenham could not win, and that Crewe could not lose. After their 13—2 gallop last season, Tottenham could hardly do enough to satisfy their fans — and Crewe had scored three times before the kick-off.

Even after their masterly triumph in the mud, I heard it said "Spurs had an off-day." But Crewe's manager, Mr. Jimmy McGuigan, insisted: "A wonderful team —what a sight as they get going!"

The triple pre-match triumph of Crewe can be listed like this:

1. Whatever the result, the Cup has earned them some £6,000. "That is a tremendous help down in Division Four," says Mr. McGuigan.

2. The match was an education for McGuigan's novices—only four of the team have had previous big-time experience.

Value up

3. The Cup limelight has increased tenfold the value of the unknowns of a month ago. "We have really had the scouts buzzing round these past few days," says Mr. McGuigan.

"They have been after our goalie, right back, centre half, and inside left. We don't want to sell. But it's nice for a manager to know his players are wanted."

Goalkeeper Williamson stopped the show with four great saves in four minutes of the first half. As he went to take a goalkick the stands and terraces rose with a roar of applause.

It was several seconds before the astonished 'keeper collected himself enough to take the kick.

Tackling as fine as it was fast rattled Spurs till the last whistle.

Inspiration

Great and classic as Spurs are, I shudder to think what could have happened without Mackay. The big Scot revelled in the mud in an inspirational marathon.

But as soon as diving Dyson headed the first goal (4 minutes) only the score remained to be settled. Mackay, Jones, Smith, and Allen added the rest.

At 2—0, Tighe raised brief hopeless visions of an upset with a fine goal. But Crewe had to be content with the glory they earned by sweat and effort.

Tottenham.—Brown ; Baker, Henry ; Blanchflower, Norman, Mackay ; Jones, White, Smith, Allen, Dyson.

Crewe.—Williamson ; McGill, Campbell ; Keery, Barnes, Shepherd ; Stark, Tighe, Foster, Wheatley, Jones.

Les Allen—he regards Crewe as his "lucky" team.

Small winger . . . big jump. Sammy Lawrie (Charlton) climbs above Ron Henry (Spurs) at White Hart-lane.

Scorers Spurs: Mackay, Jones, Allen, Dyson, Smith
Crewe: Tighe
Halftime 3-1
Attendance 53,721
Receipts £11,120

DAILY MIRROR, Tuesday, January 31, 1961   PAGE 17

FIFTH ROUND

Birmingham v. Leicester or Bristol City
(Referee: K. Howley, Middlesbrough)

Brighton or Burnley v. Swansea Town
(J. Taylor, Wolverhampton)

Huddersfield or Barnsley v. Luton or Manchester C.
(R. Smith, Newport)

Leyton Orient v. Sheff. W. or Manchester U.
(R. Leafe, Nottingham)

Newcastle or Stockport v. Stoke or Aldershot
(H. Horner, Coventry)

Norwich City v. Sunderland
(J. Williams, Nottingham)

Peterborough or Aston Villa v. Tottenham Hotspur
(E. Crawford, Doncaster)

Sheffield United v. Bolton or Blackburn
(K. Aston, Ilford)

Ties to be played on Saturday, February 18.

They face trip to their Cup hoodoo ground

113

8

John White

1960/61	App/Gls	
League	42	13
FA Cup	7	0

1959-64	App/Gls	
All comps	219	47

Legend has a cruel habit of conferring itself on bright stars extinguished early and there is an air of romantic melancholy surrounding Tottenham's John White. What makes White different is that he had not merely hinted at his quality before his sudden death in 1964 at the age of 27; he had demonstrated it amply. And so any portrait of the Double side can focus on White the player and White the man, recognising that White the legend came later.

Inside-forward White was one of the four players to complete every game of the Double. Spurs historian Bob Goodwin put his finger on why. "With his perfect balance, incisive passing and ceaseless promptings, White made the whole team operate smoothly. He was not an eye-catching player or one for the spectacular, but as the ball hit the back of the net a quick analysis of the move that had led to the goal would invariably show White had been involved somewhere along the line."

While White's balance and technical ability led his manager at Falkirk to label him "the most complete footballer I have ever seen" and attracted the attentions of Bill Nicholson, he played a simple game. When he arrived at Spurs he replaced Tommy Harmer, whose tricks had made him a crowd favourite. He eschewed the fancy stuff, favouring the killer pass.

White had a profound understanding of space. "People talk about open spaces in soccer," he said. "They are not there to be seen. You have to create them by your own hard work and posi-

tional play." A perfect philosophy to place at the disposal of the masters of pass and move. His ability to drift away from his marker and pop up in space earned him the nickname The Ghost.

As a boy in Musselburgh, Scotland, White had been told he was "a nice wee player, but too small." But he had stamina and was an accomplished cross-country runner. His speed and mobility added to his technical ability and use of space to create a player who was not only devastating, but a joy to watch. On the pitch he embodied the aesthetic of quality.

Off the pitch, the pint-sized Scot with the Tommy Steele looks hated the attention his ability brought. His wife Sandra remembers John taking her to a dance in London's Piccadilly where, on recognising him, the band struck up the Tottenham anthem *MacNamara's Band*. "John came out in a sweat and was so embarrassed," Sandra says, "and yet he'd play football in front of all those crowds."

It's true, he was always in the limelight with his team-mates. He was one of the side's bigger personalities, genuinely loved by the team and the crowd alike and his death after being struck by lightning on a golf course in Enfield in 1964 was one of the greatest tragedies in the club's history.

Writing in the *Daily Mirror* on White's death, the great sports journalist Ken Jones – cousin of White's room-mate Cliff – said: "John White belonged to more than just one club and one country. He wasn't just of Spurs and Scotland, but of soccer."

Previous page: White in action v Burnley on 3 December 1960.
This page: Tender words on a family keepsake; his blazer badge.
Facing page: 'The Ghost's' boots and his personal diary that records a late New Year's resolution in May 1959: "Going to work hard at the game and try and make a name for myself." On 8 October the same year he wrote: "Signed Tott."

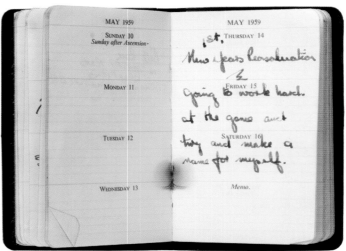

New Years Resolution & Going to work hard. at the game and try and make a name for myself.

> **A wonderful character, a joy to be around, a funny man who lifted the whole team and was great in the dressing room. Every time I think of John I smile and laugh** Cliff Jones

A selection of rare personal photos from the White family archive
Above: A youthful White in early action back home in Mussleburgh.
Above right: Trying his hand at the oval ball game in Scotland.
Right: Modelling one of his football international caps in the sun.
Far right: When White arrived at Spurs from Scotland, assistant manager Harry Evans gave him lodgings. John became part of the family, marrying Harry's daughter Sandra in 1961. Here the young couple show off their children Amanda and Robert.

Above: The proud owner of a gleaming Humber car – not quite the Baby Bentley of its day, but still a desirable set of wheels.
Above right: All smiles with Jimmy Greaves in 1962.
Right: Pith helmets to the fore, White celebrates in typical style with wife Sandra and team-mates Dave Mackay and John Hollowbread. White loved tricks and jokes and was always challenging his comrades to some elaborate skills test or other.
Following pages: White's death reported on the front page of the *Daily Mirror* and tributes from club, fans and family reflect the gravity of his loss.

Daily Mirror

3d. Wednesday, July 22, 1964 No. 18,844

International John White dies on golf course

SPURS STAR KILLED BY LIGHTNING

A Bloom chief in 'good news' riddle

By ROBERT HEAD

HOPES of an eleventh-hour reprieve for 5,000 shareholders in John Bloom's crumbling Rolls Razor washing-machine empire were raised—then dashed—last night.

A message on stockbrokers' ticker machines quoted Rolls Razor director Irving Jacobs as saying: "The good news we have been expecting all day will, if it comes, be later tonight."

But last night Mr. Jacobs told me: "I cannot understand how it happened. I made no such statement at all."

Mr. Bloom appeared at the door of his Park-lane flat shortly after 10 p.m. to say: "I will be making no statement tonight."

Meeting

Mr. Bloom's day began at 7.30 a.m. when he left his flat to meet accountants, bankers, and creditors at his Cricklewood headquarters.

The talks continued back at Mr. Bloom's flat.

On the Stock Exchange, Rolls Razor shares—worth more than 47s. each at one time last year—started the day at 1s. 6d., perked up hopefully to 2s. 7½d. then slipped back to 2s. 1½d.

Bills

Hopes centred on prospects that—

CREDITORS might be persuaded to give Rolls Razor another year or two to pay bills believed to total £1,000,000.

FINANCIERS might be found to put up an extra £1,000,000 working capital to keep the firm running until it can develop new washing machines, increase sales and slash costs.

But it seems certain that ... would agree to such a step only if they were given enough shares to give them virtual control of the company.

IT'S DANCING CILLA

LOOK who has joined the chorus . . . SINGING star Cilla Black, 21, DANCING in a glittering costume. Cilla, who has been taking dancing lessons, was rehearsing for "The Night of 100 Stars," the big charity show which is being staged at the London Palladium tomorrow to help orphan children of actors and actresses.

By MIRROR REPORTERS

SOCCER international John White, 26, star of the Spurs and Scotland forward lines, was killed by lightning yesterday in a storm which flailed a wide area of Southern England.

A flash struck him as he sheltered from the rain under an old oak tree at Crews Hill golf club, Enfield. He had been playing alone—and two groundsmen found him lying dead.

White, who was regarded as one of the finest inside forwards of recent years, was sometimes called "The Ghost" because of his will-o'-the-wisp play.

He played for Scotland twenty-two times and it is reckoned that it will cost Spurs an £80,000 transfer fee to get a replacement of his calibre.

Mr. C. F. Cox, a Tottenham director, said last night: "White's death is a tragic loss to Tottenham and football in general. He was a vital link in our successful run in recent years."

Weeping

Soon after White was found dead, his 24-year-old wife Sandra arrived at the golf course with their six-month-old son Robert. She intended to pick up her husband in the family car—but was met by police officers at the entrance to the club.

They broke the news to her, and fifteen minutes later she was driven away in tears.

Mrs. White, who has a two-year-old daughter, Amanda, married John in June, 1961.

Club steward Albert Burr, 55, said last night that Mrs. White had not wanted her husband to play golf, because their son was ill.

"But he decided to have a round while she went shopping," Mr. Burr added.

Sudden death came to John White—"a true man of Soccer," writes Ken Jones on Page 22—on the first fairway. A one-minute cloudburst sent him scurrying for cover under a tree at the side of the course.

As he sat beneath the tree, with his golf bags by his side, lightning struck. It is thought that he died instantly.

The club's professional, Leonard Mitchell, 42, said: "I was playing about 150 yards from where he was found. I could smell burning in the air, and there was a tingling in my fingers."

The savage summer storm held up rush-hour trains in London . . .

John White and his wife Sandra with their daughter Amanda and baby Robert—in one of his father's international caps.

Great storm holds up the rush-hour trains

Floodwater built up in a tunnel just outside King's Cross station and halted all trains, an Eastern Region spokesman said last night.

Jams

The centre two tracks of the station were flooded, and within fifteen minutes all outgoing tracks were swamped.

After a while, single-line working was started. "We are getting trains away, but up to seventy minutes late," said a railway spokesman.

Later, services were back to normal.

The last of the three Royal Garden Parties given by the Queen and the Duke of Edinburgh in the past week ended in a thunderstorm and torrential rain last night.

Huge traffic jams built up in several areas—the longest stretched almost eight miles from Hoddesdon to Waltham Cross.

People waded through 3ft. of water outside Chiswick Park Tube station.

Round the South coast, ships were battered by high winds and rough seas . . .

A record-breaking rescue was made off the Kent coast.

Less than thirty minutes after being thrown into the sea when their yacht capsized near the River Swale, three men were landed for treatment at Margate Hospital after being saved by helicopter.

Flood pictures—Back Page.

TELEPHONE: TOTTENHAM 1020   TELEGRAMS: SPURS·LOWER·TOTTENHAM

TOTTENHAM HOTSPUR FOOTBALL & ATHLETIC CO. LTD.
MEMBERS OF THE FOOTBALL ASSOCIATION AND THE FOOTBALL LEAGUE

LEAGUE CHAMPIONS	748 HIGH ROAD	WINNERS OF F.A. CUP
1950-1 · 1960-1	TOTTENHAM · N.17	1900-1, 1920-1, 1960-1
SECRETARY: R.S. JARVIS	CHAIRMAN: FRED. WALE	MANAGER: W.E. NICHOLSON

23rd July, 1964.

Mrs J. White,
    Church Street,
    Edmonton, N. 9.

Dear Mrs White,

    We were all very shocked and distressed at the fatal
and tragic accident which befell your husband John on Tuesday of this
week, and on behalf of my Chairman and Directors, the players, and all
the staff at the Club, I wish to offer you our very sincere sympathy
and condolence.

    The loss that the Club, and football in general, has
suffered is overshadowed by your own personal loss, and in the many
tributes we have received to John we have been asked to convey to you
the sympathy of a great number of supporters of the Club, and players
and officials of many other clubs with whom John had been associated.

    We will be keeping in close touch with you in the following
weeks, and once again please accept our very sincere sympathy, and kindest
thoughts for you and your young family.

                        Yours sincerely,

                        R. Jarvis
                        Secretary.

71, Semley Road,
    Norbury,
        S. W. 16.

Dear Mrs White,

    I have to write to tell
you how sorry I am about the
sudden death of your husband.

    My 17 year old brother and
myself idolized him, and we feel
as if he belonged to us.

    We shall miss him very much,
and so will Tottenham.

    To you and your children
we wish you all our sympathy.

        Yours Sincerely,
        Lewis Randell.

        (Age 12)

TO DARLING JOHN.
WITH ALL MY
LOVE
SANDRA..

LUCAS "King of the Road"
M & B
EXPORT PALE ALE
Swim and keep fit–
at your Local Baths
CLOTHIERS
WALKER

1961

February

League

4th   Spurs 2 Leicester 3

11th   Aston Villa 1 Spurs 2

22nd Spurs 1 Wolves 1

25th Man City 0 Spurs 1

FA Cup

18th   Aston Villa 0 Spurs 2

Left: Aston Villa's Geoff Sidebottom leaps in vain to stop a shot from Cliff Jones (not in picture) during a 2-0 FA Cup win for the Londoners.

As the league and cup intensified Tottenham were now battling for the Double on two competitive fronts. Try as Nicholson and his players might to take 'each game one at a time', potential unprecedented glories loomed large. The newspapers wrote excitedly of the prospect; fans dared to believe; the squad had emerged from the winter rigours relatively unscathed. Spurs were in good shape but the season was now reaching the stage when previous aspirants had found the Double a task too difficult to master. February was to provide a stern test of Tottenham's strength and character.

The month began badly with a third league defeat and one that did not bode well for future success. It was against Leicester, and would be seen as a worrying omen when the two sides later met in the cup final. Though Spurs were not at their best they should have won but instead, thanks to a disallowed goal and a magnificent display from Gordon Banks, Leicester ran out 3-2 winners and thus ended Tottenham's unbeaten home record.

The response was immediate. Blanchflower made the front pages the next day after he famously rejected Eammon Andrews' unbidden invitation to bare his metaphorical all on TV's *This Is Your Life*. Winning wide respect for his stance, Blanchflower instead focused on his job and the next game, a trip to Aston Villa. Though he was shackled for large parts of the match, the skipper was at his brilliantly motivational best, engineering an utterly professional 2-1 victory.

By a quirk of circumstance, the two sides met again a week later in the fifth round of the FA Cup. The clamour to see the tie was frenzied and the touts had a field day. Amid feverish claims of counterfeit tickets circulating before the genuine articles had gone on sale, Spurs fans began queuing at White Hart Lane for tickets at midnight, with a ten-hour wait before the office opened. Children were reportedly buying tickets on behalf of 'spivs'. Some Spurs fans even journeyed to Villa Park to purchase tickets for the home end. Spurs were the biggest draw in the country and anybody and everybody was desperate to see them play.

In the event Villa manager Joe Mercer made three changes to his side but to little effect, as Spurs ran out 2-0 winners thanks to a thumping drive from Cliff Jones and an own goal by John Neal. Mackay had been magnificent and even Bill Nick was moved to comment of the Double: "I think we have a great chance. The lads are playing with confidence."

That positive mood might have been dented by the next game with title rivals Wolves. Stringent examinations of Tottenham's abilities were coming one after the other and Wolves were determined to at least avoid a repeat of recent humblings. A defensive display earned the visitors a 1-1 draw. Tottenham's impetus was soon restored with a 1-0 win over Manchester City at Maine Road. A solitary goal from Terry Medwin suggested a narrow margin of victory, but Spurs had once again responded to a setback with an impressive statement of intent.

MARCH 28 SATURDAY 4TH FEB 1960

Walsh Darts in to Beat the League Leaders

From JOHN SCOTT

Tottenham Hotspur 2   **Leicester** 3

A WILD hysterical boot into the crowd by Baker, the Tottenham right-back, in the very first minute of the game, gave a direct hint as to his side's later play. Baker had space and time to construct rather than squander. It was a performance that was to be repeated by other Tottenham players during the afernoon, so it was not surprising that they met their first home defeat this season. Leicester, who tend to be fierce on their own ground and sleepy away, never gave Tottenham time o play like Tottenham. Their half-back line played superbly; White and Allen were forced into pockets of inactivity for most of the afternoon; and centre-half King was quite content to let Smith lumber about wihou allowing him many chances o shoot.

It was a strange game, often scrappy, often beautiful, often petulant. Always there was the roaring wind of Mackay charging up and down field, coaxing, yelling, tackling, tackling, tackling. He had his name taken for one tackle. But Mackay was at fault in that he allowed Walsh, the Leicester captain, masses of room to work.

As Mackay was darting up in attack, Walsh was waiting ready to pounce on the long clearance. It led to Leicester's third and decisive goal midway through the second half.

SCORERS

SPURS ALLEN
    BLANCHFLOWER (PEN)

LEICESTER LEEK
    WALSH (2)

HALF-TIME 1-2
ATTENDANCE 53,627

Norman Blunder

Jones dribbled through the Leicester defence and looked like putting Tottenham into the lead for the first time. But Banks saved his ground shot and the ball travelled rapidly downfield. Norman, in one tragic moment, miskicked and Walsh was on the ball like a flash to score. Mackay was nowhere to be seen.

Leicester have a very efficient forward-line, and it soon began to show the Tottenham defence that it was vastly different from the blunt knife of Crewe's. After 29 minutes, with a devilish miss by Smith a tthe other end recorded, Leek hooked in a great goal over the heads of the Tottenham defence, as they faced him, seemingly content to think he could do nothing at all so far out.

It brought retaliation, of course, from the League leaders, and Allen scored from close in after Jones had showed us that he is a mighty runner with the ball. But Leicester, led by Walsh, were not in the least upset, and they took the lead again after 34 minutes with a really cheeky goal. Leek headed Riley's cross against the bar and Walsh brought the ball down as casually as if he was looking at his wristwatch, and poked the ball through.

Tottenham equalised almost immediately after the restora when Blanchflower converted a penalty awarded when King sent Smith tumbling in the penalty area. The game at this stage was rough and undisciplined and Leicester gave away free-kicks galore.

Spurs.—Brown; Baker, Henry; Blanchflower, Norman, Mackay; Jones, White, Smith, Allen, Dyson.
Leicester.—Banks; Chalmers, Norman; McLintock, King, Appleton; Riley, Walsh, Leek, Keyworth, Wills.

No. 227

TOTTENHAM HOTSPUR
Football & Athletic Company Ltd.

Block M   **WEST STAND**

TOTTENHAM HOTSPUR
v
LEICESTER CITY

On SATURDAY, FEB. 4th, 1961
Kick-off 3.00 p.m.

Row X   23

Seat No. 8/-

The Tottenham Hotspur Company do not Guarantee that the proposed match will be played.

R. S. JARVIS
Secretary

PRICE 8/-

Ticket Holders are requested to be in their seats 15 minutes at least before the Kick-off.

Printed by Thomas Knight & Co. Ltd., The Clock House Press, Hoddesdon, Herts.

WEST STAND—Entrance HIGH ROAD

MARCH 29 SATURDAY 11TH FEB 1961

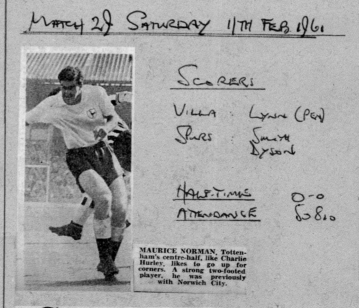

MAURICE NORMAN, Tottenham's centre-half, like Charlie Hurley, likes to go up for corners. A strong two-footed player, he was previously with Norwich City.

SCORERS

VILLA: LYNN (PEN)
SPURS: SMITH
       DYSON

HALF-TIME 0-0
ATTENDANCE 58,10

Villa scare Spurs

Aston Villa 1, Spurs 2

AFTER a week of secret tactical talks, Villa gave Spurs a scare and held the high-stepping League-leaders to a slender, single goal victory, writes Bill Holden.

This week manager Joe Mercer will again have daily discussions with his players, trying to plot the downfall of Spurs when the two teams meet in the FA Cup.

There is also a strong possibility that he will make changes in his attack.

Mercer would not say what the changes might be. But he told me:

"I shall announce my side early—on Wednesday, I think.

"I don't want the lads to be worried whether they are in or out of the team right up to the last minute."

He still believes Villa can beat Spurs—and so do his players.

It has become a point of honour with them to knock Spurs out and so end their hopes of the Cup-and-League double—last achieved by Villa themselves in 1897.

But Spurs certainly deserved their win on Saturday. What luck there was went Villa's way—their only goal was the result of a penalty decision that surprised even the Villa men.

Scorers.—Villa: Lynn (penalty). Spurs: Smith, Dyson.

Spurs flow on like oil

124

F.A Cup 5th Round   Saturday 18th Feb 1961

SPURS GOAL OF GLORY

F.A. CUP SPECIAL

By BOB PENNINGTON

ASTON VILLA 0, TOTTENHAM 2

IN one unforgettable move of supreme artistry, Spurs swept majestically towards that dream double with a goal that rates a purple passage, if not a chapter to itself, in the turbulent history of the F.A. Cup. . . . It is six minutes before half-time and these hard fighting men of Villa are hurling themselves against a white defensive wall in their frenzy to snatch an equaliser.

Just on the half-way line Spurs left-half Dave Mackay sweeps past three Villa forwards as if they were keen, green schoolboys. Then the ball starts to flow from man to man, with five Spurs collecting and caressing it away a split second before a lunging Villa boot.

From Mackay to Dyson . . . to White . . . on to Smith and Allen . . and there is Cliff Jones waiting on the edge of the penalty box to smash the ball wide of the clawing fingers of that gallant goalkeeper Geoff Sidebottom as a great hush falls over the 69,000 crowd.

The Brummies did not want to believe it. Even the Spurs' supporters could hardly credit that this goal of great beauty and bursting power had been created here on this, their Cup hoodoo ground.

At half-time a Southerner said to me: "I want it to stop now, to remember it just as it is." For there was much to remember and honour in this Tottenham team of teams.

CONTEMPTUOUS

The almost contemptuous mastery of this Scot Mackay! Last week's League "rehearsal" was undoubtedly skipper Danny Blanchflower's finest hour.

Now Mackay took over the mantle of greatness again, and we football writers were forced to ponder seriously on whether we should elect TWO Footballers of the Year in April . . . Dave and Danny, the greatest partnership in modern soccer.

Gone from the first minute were the nerves and self-doubts that forced Spurs to fight last week, instead of boxing for their points.

It was as if they had purged themselves of all weakness, as well as probing deeply and intelligently into the flaws of a Villa system of brawn and bite, heart and hammer.

Spurs were ahead in 18 minutes with Mackay inspiring the move. Cliff Jones' shot was deflected in the last yard by the lunging leg of left-back John Neal.

STUNNING

The second half was mostly a crowd-stunning demonstration of superiority by Spurs—marred in the last few minutes by boorish fouls on Mackay by Peter McParland and Bobby Thomson who were spoken to by the referee. Until then Villa had shown commendable ability to "take it."

I don't care who Spurs draw on Monday — with Mackay, Blanchflower, Norman, Henry, Jones, Dyson and White in this mood—the double is theirs for the taking.

COCKADOODLEDOO! 2-0 WIN

Scorer: Neal (o.g.)
*   Jones*

Half Time   0-2
Attendance 69,672
Receipts £539,140

ASTON VILLA FOOTBALL CLUB LTD.   No. 737

THE FOOTBALL ASSOCIATION CUP (5th Round)
AT VILLA PARK, BIRMINGHAM.
SATURDAY, FEBRUARY 18th, 1961. Kick-off 2-45 p.m.

Aston Villa v. Tottenham Hotspur

RESERVED SEAT 12/6

Row **V**   Seat No **40**

Entrance Door:

TRINITY ROAD B

THIS PORTION TO BE RETAINED

If composted, this ticket will be valid for the date on which the match is re-arranged. This ticket is issued subject to the By-laws and Regulations of the Football Association.

A GREAT TEAM? YES, AND HOW THEY FIGHT!

By JOE MERCER

Aston Villa manager, in an interview

TOTTENHAM HOTSPUR are a truly great side —not yet in the Real Madrid class, perhaps, but at least the equal of the 1948 Manchester United as the finest post-war club team in Great Britain.

I am confident that, provided they steer clear of a sixth-round tie at Sheffield Wednesday or Burnley, they will be home and dry by Aston Villa in 1896-97.

They have all the attributes of a great team—tremendous natural skill, intelligent planning, splendid team spirit and, though many people have doubted it, abundant fight and a real sense of endeavour.

MAGNIFICENT MACKAY

It has been this spirit of endeavour that has impressed me even more than their skilful football in the past two weeks, when Spurs have beaten us twice at Villa Park. For it had been suggested all along that Spurs would not last the pace in the Cup because of their lack of power.

That's all nonsense. In Dave Mackay (the finest wing-half in the world today) they have a magnificent tackler and a chap who can take care of himself in any situation.

Both backs can look after themselves and big Maurice Norman is a talented, commanding centre-half, who has matured immeasurably over the last year. Then Bobby Smith is a strong, dependable centre forward able to hold his own in any goal-mouth battle.

Now when you have these uncompromising characters around, I don't see how you can accuse Tottenham of being short of Cup-fighting potential.

In my opinion, the whole side revolves around Danny Blanchflower and Mackay. Stop this pair, and you stop Tottenham, you might say, but then tell me how in the name of football you stop such genius.

When Spurs are on the attack, they are so fluid that it is almost impossible to devise a plan to stop them. As one player moves upfield, so four and sometimes five players are floating around ready for the pass.

IMPROVISERS

You see, Spurs' most valuable attacking asset is their incredible ability to improvise or, shall I say, play it off the cuff. It shows their thoughtfulness and confidence.

And a team playing Spurs can so easily develop an inferiority complex. Take Saturday's match. They clinched a two-goal lead, then decided: "We'll close the game up."

This they did with cold efficiency, slowing the tempo down to just the pace they wanted. We hated being beaten at home, but there was nothing we could do about it.

I know Spurs have had quite a bit of luck this season, but while they are showing such poised perfection, it is a wonderful thing for the game—and a tremendous incentive for other English clubs.

THE AGONY OF NEAL

SPURS 1

JONES DUGDALE   NEAL   SMITH   CROWE   SIDEBOTTOM

THE AGONY of John Neal starts Aston Villa on the way to defeat against the master-footballers from Tottenham.

Goalkeeper Geoff Sidebottom is on his way into a dive to his left to clutch Cliff Jones's shot. Neal frantically tries to clear. He connects with the ball . . and sends it skimming in the net on Sidebottom's "blind" side.

Sixth round draw

SHEFFIELD WEDNESDAY v BURNLEY
Referee: K. G. Aston (Ilford).

BIRMINGHAM C. or LEICESTER C. v BARNSLEY
L. Kelly (Chorley).

SUNDERLAND v TOTTENHAM HOTSPUR
A. Murdoch (Sheffield).

NEWCASTLE UTD. v SHEFFIELD UTD.
K. A. Collinge (Altrincham).

To be played on March 4 (kick-off 3 p.m.), replays on or before following Thursday (kick-off 3 p.m. or not later than 7.30 if under floodlights).

SPURS 2

THOMSON   LYNN   SIDEBOTTOM   CROWE   JONES

● THE JOY of Cliff Jones ends Villa's bid to halt Spurs' sprint to the Cup and League double. The jet-paced winger sees his sharp-angled shot zoom past the clawing Sidebottom. His arms are flung high. And he's off in a dance of delight.

Match 30 Wednesday 22nd Feb 1961

*Match 31
Saturday 25th Feb 1961*

*Scorer Medwin
Half time 0-0
Attendance 40,278*

Thousands locked out at White Hart Lane

SPORTSMAIL AT THE BIG GAMES

Brilliant start—then comes the fade-out

10-MEN WOLVES TAME THE SPURS

Slater a passenger for 80 minutes

Tottenham 1   Wolverhampton 1   By ROY PESKETT

WOLVES are fighting to the last fingernail to prevent Spurs pulling off what seems an inevitable championship win. A 62,000 crowd—thousands more were locked out—saw Wolves, virtually reduced to ten men for 80 minutes, not only pull back a Spurs goal but check them, tame them, and finally humble them on their own pitch.

After Bill Slater had limped off in the tenth minute to have his ribs strapped following a collision with Bobby Smith, Wolves appeared to be in trouble.

The crowd waited expectantly for what seemed to be another runaway win.

But these Wolves are hardest to beat when up against long odds.

Clamp, Broadbent and Co. fell into their new positions so well that I noticed no difference.

Broadbent became a commanding half back. Clamp a dominant full back, and Showell switched to centre half to master Smith.

The giant Flowers joined Deeley and Durandt, and these three launched enough attacks to keep the Spurs defence fully occupied.

*Scorers: Spurs Smith
Wolves Farmer
Half time 1-1
Attendance 62,261*

DAVE MACKAY, Spurs' Scottish international left-half, is rated one of the best wing halves in the country. A native of Edinburgh, he cost the Londoners £30,000 when he was transferred from Hearts in March, 1959.

In pain

All Slater could do was to walk slowly up and down the touchline, obviously in great pain. He was injured when Smith tore round him in the ninth minute to hammer in a brilliant goal and set the seal on the fastest, finest, opening spell Spurs have had all season.

But this was all we saw of the super Spurs.

Wolves settled to their own pace. The more poised they became the more erratic were the Spurs.

Danny Blanchflower, usually so immaculate, gave away a goal in the 22nd minute when he attempted a tricky pass instead of clearing. A foot poked the ball away from him to the unmarked Farmer who equalised. Farmer had the ball in the net again four minutes after the interval but the referee ruled that he had punched it past Brown.

Even John White fell into the error of trying to be too clever when straightforward tactics were needed.

The wingers carried the ball up and into this cast-iron Wolves defence, and time and again groans of disappointment echoed from the crowd as attacks broke down.

Midway through the second half White chipped the ball against the bar, and Smith headed inches over. Then Allen missed an easy chance.

In a game of heavy tackles I admired the way Spurs held off tackling the injured Slater.

Slater left with the Wolverhampton party last night. He will have an X-ray examination in Birmingham this morning.

BILL SLATER
X-ray this morning

Tottenham: Brown; Baker, Henry; Blanchflower, Norman, Mackay; Jones, White, Smith, Allen, Dyson.
Wolves: Finlayson; Stuart, Showell; Clamp, Slater, Flowers; Deeley, Murray, Farmer, Broadbent, Durandt.

TOM FINNEY says: For sheer guts and glory on a glue-pot...

I SALUTE SPURS

Maestros march on—and a Medwin goal does it

MANCHESTER CITY 0, SPURS 1

THE tightly-packed terraces and every-seat-taken stands of Main Road stood in salute yesterday to 22 mud-clad men paddling their way off the pitch. Manchester City v. Spurs was now but a memory, but what a piece of splendid football it was.

I've sat in on more scientific games this season, I've basked in more breath-taking soccer displays. I've seen Spurs play better, too. But for sheer effort under appalling conditions, for sheer guts and glory on a glue-pot of a ground, this had the lot.

It had just one goal, from the Spurs stand-in outside-right, Terry Medwin, who had only to incline a nonchalant head at a precision centre from skipper Danny Blanchflower in the 90th minute.

It gave Spurs yet another win. I trust that they are suitably grateful.

In a driving down-pour of a first half, it was City who had the edge. Joe Hayes, Colin Barlow and young David Wagstaffe all had near-misses. Then came tragedy for Manchester.

Inside-left Joe Hayes, who had been giving the Spurs defence a real hammering, was injured and was forced to spend the entire second half as a hobbling, ineffective winger.

Add to this the fact that Denis Law, all over the field in the first half, faded badly after the interval and you have the measure of the second half.

Now those superb wing-halves Blanchflower and Dave Mackay were able to make their play, moving about the field at will and funnelling a steady stream of passes to the attack.

John White, Bobby Smith and Terry Dyson sent in some Spurs specials, but with City reserve goalkeeper Steve Fleet diving spectacularly for the ball and full-backs Leivers and Betts battling gamely on, it was all Spurs could do to deliver up that one goal.

Hugging

No wonder nearly the entire team hugged Medwin when he scored the solitary goal. But, frankly, I'd willingly have walked up and patted all the 22 men on the field.

For take away the goal which gave Spurs their win and there would still remain the glory of the men who made the most of mocking conditions, who played through a storm of rain, and on a swimming pool of a pitch—splendid, saturated Spurs, magnificent, mud-caked Manchester City.

● As told to DON EVANS.

LEAGUE POSITIONS							
DIVISION I							
	P	W	D	L	F	A	Pts
Spurs	31	25	3	3	91	37	53
Sheff. Wed.	30	18	8	4	61	24	44
Wolves	32	19	5	8	82	63	43
Burnley	29	17	2	10	73	53	36
Everton	31	15	5	11	63	50	35
Leicester	30	14	5	11	65	54	33
Aston Villa	30	13	6	11	61	59	32
Arsenal	32	13	6	13	65	67	32
Cardiff	32	12	8	12	49	58	32
Man. Utd.	31	13	5	13	62	59	31
Blackburn	31	12	7	12	58	60	31
Notts Forest	31	12	5	14	48	59	29
West Ham	30	12	4	14	63	65	28
Chelsea	31	11	5	15	69	75	27
Bolton	31	10	6	15	47	57	26
Birmingham	30	11	4	15	47	60	26
West Brom	33	11	4	18	52	66	26
Fulham	32	11	3	18	55	78	25

DANNY BLANCHFLOWER, Belfast's most famous footballing son, is in his seventh year at White Hart Lane after distinguished service with Aston Villa, Barnsley and Glentoran, the Irish League club.

Captain of Northern Ireland, he was elected "Footballer of the Year" in 1958.

His international career started as far back as 1949 and he now has well over 40 caps.

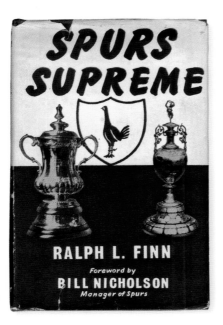

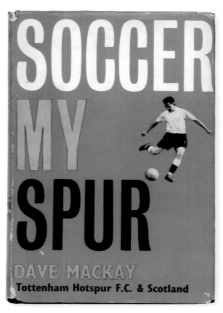

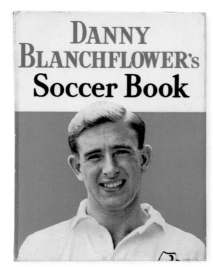

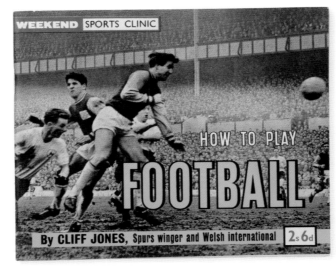

Double-related reading courtesy of Danny Blanchflower, Cliff Jones, Dave Mackay, Ralph Finn and Julian Holland. For Blanchflower it was a pointer towards his subsequent career as a journalist where he proved as creative as he was on the pitch.

9

Bobby Smith

BOBBY SMITH
(Spurs)

1960/61	App/Gls	
League	36	28
FA Cup	7	5

1955-64	App/Gls	
All comps	317	208

The cliché about having players you would want beside you in the trenches is one of football's cornier lines, but when it came to the physical crunch and bravery in the face of danger, few were more courageous (and physical) than Bobby Smith. A lion of a centre-forward, Smith risked pain and injury for the Spurs cause and had the scars to prove it. 'Putting himself in where it hurts' was a phrase never more resonant than when it referred to a player described by Brian Glanville as a "dreadnought" because the wear and tear of fearlessly leading the attack, compounded by pain-killing injections, has left him with arthritis. Every day Smith has a reminder of what he sacrificed to win the Double.

Not that Smith is one to feel sorry for himself. "I could take a lot of stick," is his modest self-assessment of the hazards he faced. He relished confrontation with uncompromising defenders, asked no quarter and gave none. When Spurs embarked on their European adventures, Smith struck terror in opposing goalkeepers who couldn't handle his fearsome penalty-area charges, nor his skill with the ball. Smith had an excellent touch and his physicality did not obscure his talents as a footballer. His dramatic equaliser in the Sheffield Wednesday game, the pivot, feint and thumping drive in the cup final, the hat trick against Blackpool in August that illustrated his full repertoire, all were evident examples of his skill and finesse.

Tottenham depended on Smith and he rarely failed them: as a target man he could hold the ball up and also bring others into play; when it was backs-to-the-wall time on mud-heap pitches away from home and hostile defenders were roared on by home fans demanding Spurs be cut down to size, Smith was a rallying figurehead of resistance; when the team needed a goal, he would oblige. But for Jimmy Greaves, Smith would rank as the club's all-time top goalscorer, and he scored an average of 23 a season in his nine years at White Hart Lane. Smith must score? He invariably did, notching a remarkable 33 goals during that incredible Double season.

In the midst of the glory years, Smith was an England international who deserved more than his 15 caps. Thirteen goals represented an outstanding ratio perhaps under-appreciated by the national team management of the time. There was no such sense of being undervalued at Tottenham. Signed as another recruit from Chelsea (and another shrewd purchase by Jimmy Anderson) Smith had an immediate impact at Spurs, breaking records and scoring aplenty well before the 1960/61 season.

Unlike several of his team-mates, his rich form continued after the Double until the knocks finally caught up with him. He left for the gentler surrounds of Brighton in the old Division Four before taking a well-earned rest beside the seaside in Hastings, then moved to Banbury and later back to suburban north London. In later life he was a painter and decorator and drove a minicab, which for some football-loving passengers must have made for the most interesting cab journey-conversation of their lives.

Previous page: Bobby Smith celebrates as Spurs score against an FA XI at White Hart Lane in the 1961 Charity Shield.
Left: Smith scores the opening goal v Chelsea on 3 April 1961 watched by Terry Venables.
Above: Bobby at home with wife Mavis and children Stephen and David in November 1960.

Right: In training, Spurs really did make players jump through hoops. In attendance is Bill Watson, the weight trainer employed after the Spurs team's visit to the Bolshoi ballet in 1959.
Following page: A Bobby Smith drive rockets towards the lens in pre-season training 1961. The photographer is braced for impact.

FOOTBALL
MONTHLY

Overseas price 2/-
Forces overseas 1/6   1/6

MAY 1961

BOBBY SMITH
Spurs and England

INSIDE: CUP FINAL SOUVENIR

BOBBY SMITH
TESTIMONIAL

EDGWARE TOWN FOOTBALL CLUB

SUNDAY 13th OCTOBER, 1968
KICK OFF 3.15 p.m.
ADMISSION BY PROGRAMME ONLY. 5/-

66 Bobby Smith provided
the physical side. He was our
minder. He used to sort one
or two defenders out for us.
But he was a very good, very
skilful player too 99 Cliff Jones

1961

March

Left: The FA Cup semi-final, Villa Park, and Bobby Smith jumps for joy after scoring the first Spurs goal. On his knees is Burnley goalkeeper Blacklaw, while showing his delight (far right) is Cliff Jones.

The excitement surrounding Tottenham's campaigns had reached feverish proportions by March and as the team strove for the first Double, the pioneering spirit of the age spread to the fans. Among the crowd of 61,000 who came to Roker Park to see if a promising Sunderland could stop the Lilywhites were a small band of 47 Spurs fans making their own piece of history. Led by Aubrey Morris, they had chartered a Viscount plane to become the first English fans to fly to an away game. Morris went on to build a business that took Spurs supporters all over Europe following their team, eventually becoming the Managing Director of holiday company Thomsons.

Morris described the atmosphere that day as "like a madhouse" with the passionate home crowd urging their side back into the game after Jones put Spurs ahead. Pandemonium greeted the equaliser as the fans spilled onto the pitch. Blanchflower calmed his team, organising a determined rearguard action that took the tie back to London.

There, more wild scenes occurred. The players had to battle through huge crowds and 15,000 fans stormed the gates when the 'full house' signs went up. The official attendance was 64,797, though the true number will never be known. Spurs, said the *Express*, showed "the icy arrogance of a team that knows its destiny is greatness," thumping five past Sunderland and prompting ecstatic young fans to swarm onto the pitch at the final whistle.

Then Spurs went to Cardiff and lost. Careless finishing was blamed. It was poor preparation for the FA Cup semi-final against the reigning League champions, Burnley, at Villa Park. Ten trains helped take 22,000 Spurs fans to see a Spurs side whose lead at the top of the table had been cut from 12 points to four. Nicholson took his players to the Welsh seaside town of Mumbles to prepare. It was here that the whisper of the Double became a roar as, according to Cliff Jones, the players became convinced they could really do it.

Tottenham's defence needed to be at its best in front of a 70,000 crowd as Burnley dominated the early play. Blanchflower's leadership was again crucial. Then, as is often the story in the cup, luck and controversy intervened. A gust of wind sent the ball past Burnley's Jimmy Adamson and Smith nipped in to score. An equaliser was disallowed, then the referee missed the ball striking Henry's hand on the goal line before Smith scored with a volley. Burnley tried to hit back through the middle, making it easy for Spurs to lock up. Jones sealed the win and again the fans poured on, this time chairing Smith off.

Spurs were in the final, but back in the league lost to struggling Newcastle at home before drawing at Fulham where Johnny Haynes eclipsed a visibly tiring Mackay. The shadow of a doubt was about to take hold when Spurs, as they so often did that season, banished it with a stunning Cliff Jones-inspired demolition of Chelsea.

F.A. CUP 6TH ROUND SATURDAY 4 MARCH 1961

POOLS CHECK

PINK CLASSIFIED

ROSA *The family* SHERRY GONZALEZ BYASS 15/-

Evening Standard

42,524   SATURDAY, MARCH 4, 1961   3d.

The best umbrellas have FOX Frames

Sunderland supporters hold up play when McPheat scores

SPURS MUST REPLAY
—PITCH INVADED

LEAGUE POSITIONS

DIVISION 1

	P	W	D	L	F	A	Pts
Spurs	31	25	3	3	87	43	53
Sheff. Wed.	30	18	8	4	61	24	44
Wolves	32	19	5	8	82	62	43
Burnley	29	17	2	10	78	59	36
Everton	31	15	5	11	63	58	35
Leicester	30	14	5	11	69	66	33
Aston Villa	30	13	6	11	61	62	32
Arsenal	32	13	6	13	65	67	32
Cardiff	32	12	8	12	49	55	32
Man. Utd.	31	12	5	13	62	59	31
Blackburn	31	12	7	12	68	63	31
Notts Forest	31	12	5	14	48	59	29
West Ham	30	12	4	14	65	65	28
Chelsea	31	11	5	15	69	75	27
Bolton	31	10	6	15	47	57	26
Birmingham	30	11	4	15	47	69	26
West Brom	33	11	4	18	53	69	26
Fulham	29	11	3	18	56	76	25

RESULTS

(Half-time scores in parentheses)

FA CUP (Sixth round)

Leicester City	(0) 2	Barnsley	(0) 0
Newcastle	(0) 1	Sheffield U.	(3) 3
Sheffield W.	(0) 0	Burnley	(0) 0
Sunderland	(0) 1	TOTTENH'M	(1) 1

TOTTENHAM ARE GIVEN A FRIGHT

SUNDERLAND 1, TOTTENHAM 1

From HAROLD PALMER: Sunderland, Saturday

Spurs and Sunderland fight again at White Hart Lane on Wednesday. And Spurs had to put up a terrific struggle to survive after scoring first in this exciting sixth round FA Cup-tie here at Roker Park.

Thousands of the 61,236 crowd rushed on to the field after McPheat, the man who had to pass a fitness test less than an hour before the kick-off, had scored the equaliser.

Police managed to clear the pitch and then patrolled the touchline at 10 to 15 yard intervals to prevent a further invasion.

There was a hostile reception from the crowd for Baker when he fouled Dillon in the first minute. Ashurst placed

SPURS FAN IS CARRIED OFF

Long before the start of the Sunderland-Spurs Cup-tie, the Roker Park ground was uncomfortably full—a 63,000 crowd.

First casualty was a Spurs supporter, who had to be carried off on a stretcher before the match started.

the free kick in the goalmouth, but Spurs got the ball away.

Spurs scored in the ninth minute. Sunderland defence was hesitant as Jones and Allen bored their way through the middle. Finally a corner was conceded and Hurley could only head Dyson's corner kick out to JONES. The winger, who had already started wandering across the field, was in front of goal about 12 yards and he carefully placed his header out of Wakeham's reach.

Jones was given the full cuddling treatment. But the goal in no way discouraged Sunderland. They applied themselves to their task with great energy and with Anderson, their half-half, distributing the ball thoughtfully they were keeping the Tottenham defenders on tenterhooks.

Fast, exciting

It was fast, exciting football with Sunderland fighting hard for the ball and using their wingers well.

The referee had words with Mackay and then with Anderson after hard tackles, but there was nothing vicious in the play.

Smith dribbled past the goalkeeper, but his shot hit the post. Dyson was inches wide with a really good effort and with five minutes to go to half-time Spurs should really have been three up. A tremendous 35-yard drive by Smith after Hurley had been brought down electrified the crowd at Wakeham saved. But a free-kick had been given to Sunderland.

Half-time: Sunderland 0, Tottenham 1

Four minutes after the interval Sunderland equalised. And this brought fantastic scenes. Thousands of fans invaded the pitch to mob the Sunderland players in midfield.

It was a corner by Hooper that led to the goal. Sunderland's tall centre-half was up there to head the ball in. Brown could only push it out and Anderson and McPHEAT, whom I must credit with the goal, rushed the ball between them into the back of the net.

The police took some time to clear the field and it was a frenzied home crowd that now roared their favourites on.

And what a storming game they played. They penned the Spurs in their half and the Londoners were badly rattled.

Three corners came in a minute for Sunderland. Tottenham's forwards just could not find any rhythm, largely because White was not putting his passes right.

McPheat was a constant menace and when his partner Dillon pushed the ball through Baker's legs it looked all set for a score. But Mackay, ever watchful, came from nowhere to kick the ball away from the winger's feet.

Temporary relief

A bad header by Henry gave Lawther a chance, but Blanchflower blocked the centre-forward's shot.

Spurs then forced a corner, taken by Allen, and Norman headed wide. But this was only temporary relief for Spurs. It was a brilliant interception by Henry that set Dyson and Allen moving down the left wing, but it all came to nothing.

Dyson, Jones and Smith all made bad passes when it looked so easy to make the right one. It seemed that none of the Tottenham forwards could find their form in the face of quick, firm tackling.

Jones caused some anxiety when he headed over the bar. Dyson nipped smartly through the middle before delivering a fierce shot that was well held by Wakeham.

Spurs were improving, but Dillon should have scored when he was put through the middle after clever approach work by Fogarty and Lawther.

Norman goes up

Spurs were so anxious to develop thrust in their attack that Norman went up to join in one of their spasmodic raids.

Sunderland: Wakeham; Nelson, Ashurst; Anderson, Hurley, McNab; Hooper, Fogarty, Lawther, McPheat, Dillon.

Tottenham: Brown; Baker, Henry; Blanchflower, Norman, Mackay; Jones, White, Smith, Allen, Dyson.

It's the first goal for Spurs. Sunderland goalkeeper Wakeham watches helplessly, with Ashurst and Nelson (right) on the goal line, as the ball goes in.

CUP PICTURE OF THE YEAR

Scorers
Sun. McPheat
Spurs Jones

Half-time. 0-1

Attendance. 61,236

Receipts £14,100

Moment of truth...

● Sunderland inside left Willie McPheat (stripes, centre) is poised for the kill as Spurs goalkeeper Bill Brown fails to hold the ball. A split second later McPheat hammered the ball in for Sunderland's equaliser.

	Home Goals	Away Goals	
	P. W. D. L. F. A.	W. D. L. F. A.	Pts
Tott'ham	31 11 3 1 51 21	14 0 2 40 16	53
Wolves	33 14 2 1 42 26	6 3 7 23 38	45
Sheff. W.	30 14 1 1 36 11	4 7 3 25 23	44
Burnley	29 8 1 6 41 30	9 1 4 37 23	36

Just Burnley to beat before Wembley
with the League already in the bag

The Double
F.A. Cup, League Championship
PRESTON NORTH END ... 1888—89
ASTON VILLA ... ... 1896—97

SPURS AT THE DOUBLE

Spurs one up—and the fans pour on. Their joy is complete as another giant step is taken towards the double.

Gallant Sunderland crushed by Soccer's aristocrats

WHO THEY PLAY NOW

By JOHN CAMKIN: Spurs 5   Sunderland 0

ONWARD now to Burnley and the grey towers of Wembley! Who now dare say that mighty Tottenham will not achieve the fabulous double of Cup and championship?

SCORERS ALLEN SMITH DYSON (2) MACKAY   HALF-TIME 3-0   ATTENDANCE 64,797   RECEIPTS £12935

MARCH 11, Cardiff (A); 18, Burnley (semi-final, Villa Park); 25, Fulham (A); 31, Chelsea (H).

APRIL 1, Preston (H); 3, Chelsea (A); 8, Birmingham (A); 15, Sheffield Wed. (H); 22, Burnley (A); 29, West Bromwich (H).

TO BE ARRANGED: Newcastle (H), Nottingham Forest (H).

Certainly not Sunderland! That gallant Second Division side were swept out of the Cup by brilliant and contemptuous football at White Hart-lane last night.

The thousands who stormed the gates in vain missed Spurs at their grandest, most aristocratic. Sunderland, beaten but once since October, were dismissed from audience of British football's kings.

The damage was done in 20 minutes of devastating football before half-time. It brought three goals and brought life surging back into Spurs' attack.

Of course the ball ran kindly for them in at least two of these vital goals. Only a great team can use luck as did Spurs.

Little John White, revelling on the firm, fast pitch, was the architect of victory. He sparked off the golden spell with a fine dribble and a shot which cracked the crossbar in the 25th minute.

But darting, menacing Cliff Jones was Sunderland's own executioner. He laid on all three of those vital first-half goals.

First he cleaved through the left flank of Sunderland's defence in the 27th minute and shot against a red and white striped shirt. Les Allen picked up the lucky rebound far away and scored goal No. 1.

Blindly

Next Jones darted past the right flank. This time goalkeeper Peter Wakeham could only parry his fierce drive out to the empty penalty area.

England's Bobby Smith, back to goal, shot blindly on the turn in the 32nd minute. The ball might have gone anywhere—but it ended in the net for one of Smith's finest goals.

Finally, as referee Clements looked at his watch, Jones laid on a third goal for little Terry Dyson as he himself slipped in the penalty area.

Even Burnley manager Mr. Harry Potts, making his semi-final plans, must have been impressed as Spurs shot almost at will in the second half.

Delightful, simple football brought goals for Dyson (65 minutes), and the lion-hearted Mackay (70). One for Jones in the 73rd minute was ruled out because Smith, apparently, was offside.

What can one say for gallant Sunderland? This side which fought so magnificently at Roker Park was reduced to shadows.

Majestic

Luck, too, deserted them. Martin Harvey, 18-year-old wing half, called in at the last minute, did not mark as tightly as would have Jimmy McNab, a flu victim. Wingers Harry Hooper and John Dillon, 18, were limping in the second half, but these things made no difference.

Nor did two simple chances wasted early by Ian Lawther and Ambrose Fogarty. Lawther, indeed, could have given Sunderland the lead in the 22nd minute when he prodded a chance over the bar.

The answer was that Sunderland had no White, no Jones, no Dyson, no Mackay, no Smith, no Blanchflower. They had only Charles Hurley to match Maurice Norman.

The half-back line, backbone of any side, was broken on its flanks by Spurs' majestic moves.

BIG CUP-TIE RIOT

DAILY SKETCH ★★★

THURSDAY, MARCH 9, 1961

By JOHN AUSTIN

A SOCCER-CRAZED crowd charged police guarding the main gates of Tottenham Hotspurs' ground last night.

The time 7.10—20 minutes before the kick-off of the Cup-tie replay between Spurs and Sunderland.

Minutes earlier, the loudspeakers blared: "The ground is closed. We have a capacity crowd. Ticket-holders only."

The crowd outside roared back: "Let us in."

'Mounties'

But the 20 police at the gates, backed by three "Mounties," looked out at the swaying mass of 15,000 football fanatics—and stayed put.

Ticket - holders? They climbed over the gates to get to the turnstiles 20 yards further in.

Players and officials spent half an hour fighting their way into the ground through the huge crowd.

Just before the gates closed, the crowd surged forward, scattering police and horses.

Helmets rolled. Small boys, women old and young were jammed shouting in the mass. Three passed out.

P.-c. Y265 told me: "Somebody pinched my helmet when I

REPORT AND MATCH PICTURES: PAGE 20

was knocked over. I can't remember how many times we have been pushed back to the turnstiles."

Another policeman said the scene was "murder."

A problem

After the game, which Spurs won 5-0, club chairman Mr. Fred Beardman said: "It is difficult to know what to do when you have 150,000 people trying to get into a place made for 65,000.

"However this is something we shall discuss at our next meeting."

Ticket-holders fight their way in—over the gates.

SPURS 15,000 STORM THE GATES

MATCH 32 SATURDAY 11TH MARCH 1961

BY A SPECIAL CORRESPONDENT

Cardiff City 3   Tottenham Hotspur 2

FAILURE to turn first-half superiority into more than two goals meant the fourth defeat of the season for Spurs. Revitalised Cardiff went into the lead at Ninian Park with two goals within six minutes after the interval and hung on grimly to the end.

That the Spurs led only 2-1 at half-time was an unfair reflection of the menace they had shown. But their forwards were careless finishers and it is fatal to give this vastly improved Cardiff side such an opportunity.

The result was that the cool, calculating play of the League leaders disappeared in face of the stern tackling and tremendous verve of the Welshmen. The tables were turned to an astonishing degree and Cardiff's biggest crowd of the season roared their team to victory.

Once again the Tottenham halfback line was admirable but Cardiff's middle line, too, was in peak form and Allen and White were blotted out.

SPURS TOTTER
Moore Outstanding

The Cardiff forwards, while not showing the same cohesion as their opposite numbers, nonetheless moved well enough to make the Suprs defence totter when under pressure. Moore was the schemer-in-chief and his clever distribution frequently caught Baker and Henry on the wrong foot.

A bad miss by Donnelly after two minutes proved to be costly for Cardiff for in their first attack immediately afterwards the Spurs went into the lead, Dyson scoring with a good shot.

Cardiff equalised through Hogg in the 11th minute but Allen took advantage of a partial clearance by Nicholls and shot hard and true to the corner of the net.

In the 50th minute Cardiff got the best goal of the match. They developed an attack on the left and the ball ultimately reached Walsh at outside right. He cut in before delivering a shot which Brown could not hope to save. A minute later Hole put Tapscott away and again Brown was beaten all ends up.

Cardiff City.—Nicholls; Harrington, Stitfall; Hole, Malloy, Baker; Walsh, Moore, Tapscott, Donnelly, Hogg.
Tottenham.—Brown; Baker, Henry; Blanchflower, Norman, Mackay; Jones, White, Smith, Allen, Dyson.

SCORERS

CARDIFF: HOGG
            WALSH
            TAPSCOTT

SPURS: DYSON
          ALLEN

HALF-TIME   1-2

ATTENDANCE: 45,463

Sensation in four fighting minutes !

SCORERS

SPURS   ALLEN
NEWCASTLE   HALF-TIME 1-0
ALLCHURCH   ATTENDANCE 46,470
SCANLON

MATCH 33 WEDNESDAY 22ND MARCH 1961

Smith injured as Hollins and Co. steal win

By ROY PESKETT: Spurs 1, Newcastle 2

TEN Newcastle heroes staggered off the field at White Hart-lane last night, unable to believe the luck that had given them two points when the battle to avoid relegation seemed hopeless. The other hero—Len White—hobbled on one leg.

White was injured on his own goal line with the very last kick of the match. Afterwards he went to hospital for an X-ray with a suspected fracture of the right ankle.

With the rest of his team White had packed the goal to hold on to the game Tottenham had so freely given them.

It was a fantastic and almost crazy night as Tottenham's double hopes took a painful clout on the nose.

CRAZY for the crowd who went almost crazy as they saw the match dramatically slipping down the drain.

TRAGIC for Tottenham, who never again will have so many chances to tot up a cricket score. **HAPPY**, so happy, for Newcastle.

They took one of the biggest first-half hammerings I have ever seen without flinching or collapsing; slowed the Spurs to their own pace then pounced twice when the League and Cup double chasers had run themselves out.

The luck which so many clubs claim has been Tottenham's 12th man this season finally left them.

In cold statistics, this is how it went against Spurs last night.
● Keith headed two headers from Smith off the line and kicked away a Jones shot.
● Both Dyson and Smith had amazing goal-line misses after getting in the way of team-mates' shots.
● Mackay headed against the crossbar with the entire Newcastle defence floundering.
● Smith and Jones had air shots when faced with open goals.
● Captain Danny Blanchflower's penalty was saved four minutes from half-time.

Fantastic

A Smith air shot may have even more unhappy repercussions than his missing a goal.

The England centre forward badly twisted his right knee and spent the last half-hour hobbling on the right wing.

Except for the Len White injury, Newcastle manager Charlie Mitten had a joyous evening.

He pitched two new boys into one of the most momentous and difficult matches of the season—goalkeeper Dave Hollins and inside-left Jim Harrower. And both came up trumps.

Hollins had a lot of luck during that fantastic first half when Tottenham might have had seven goals and gained confidence with every passing minute.

From Brighton "stiffs" to the roars of White Hart-lane. That's Newcastle's new goalkeeper Dave Hollins. Sample : This leap to hold a corner.

And this youngster finished a wonderful debut by stopping a seemingly certain Jones equaliser with his stomach a minute from the end.

Harrower had a much quieter game but made the pass for the equalising goal.

Two other recently signed players also shone. Centre-half McGrath was magnificent against this all-out Spurs attack, and Scanlon, formerly with Manchester United, hit the winner.

Strain shows

For Spurs it was just one long frustration after another. Yet it is obvious this quest for the double is sitting heavily on the shoulders of some of the players.

Only Maurace Norman and Ron Henry looked like championship players. Goals—

40 mins. : Dyson crossed from the left, Jones rolled the ball back and Allen scored with a terrific drive.

64 mins. : Harrower crossed from the right wing ; Allchurch rose high to head in from nearly 15 yards.

79 mins. : McGrath sent White away ; his neat pass found Scanlon far out on the line. A left-foot bang and the ball flashed between Brown's hands and the crossbar.

Hollins to the rescue again. He stops this Dyson shot for Spurs in the last minutes.

DOUBLE TROUBLE

By Bob Pennington

Tottenham have lost that golden glow

FULHAM 0, SPURS 0

A MIGHTY sigh of relief rolled across the Thames at the end of this most tense, tumultuous and thrilling but goalless game. The tension-tormented supporters and players of both Fulham and Spurs had to admit that a draw was only just. But there all unanimity ends.

For Fulham came the near ecstasy of so nearly toppling Tottenham by the excellence of their football and the sheer dedication of every man to pull them through this relegation crisis. Captain Johnny Haynes was the complete professional. Mullery, Macedo, Cohen, Langley and Leggat are names all London should honour this morning.

Eddie Lowe, bless his shining head, played his 400th post-war League match, with the fire and finesse of a youth tackling his 40th And Arsenal discard Bill Dodgin looked the snip of all time at under £5,000.

Fulham will not go down.

For Spurs this was near disaster. Their sorely-troubled manager, Bill Nicholson, was commendably blunt:

"We used to enjoy our football because we worked hard at it. But we are not working now," said Nicholson.

If Nicholson is to claim the Cup, let alone the double, he must use the whip. The slipping stars in his shoddy attack must be told: "Graft—or you won't play at Wembley."

Only the defence, and goalkeeper Bill Brown in particular, looked anything like the Super Spurs we know. Even Danny Blanchflower was bad — by Blanchflower standards.

The debt Spurs owe to Dave Mackay was made clear by his absence through injury. And the decision not to risk Bobby Smith's injured knee left the attack unbalanced. Seventeen-year-old Frank Saul shows promise, but is still an apprentice.

INCREDIBLE MISSES

The old Spurs would have won with five goals to spare; the old Fulham might have been crushed by 10.

Of the incredible misses by both teams, I single out two. Fulham centre-forward Maurice Cook, facing an empty net, leapt high to head a centre, only for the ball to break back and roll wide of the far post.

Then Spurs centre-half Maurice Norman came up in the closing seconds to groan as his superb, diving header went flashing inches wide of a post.

It was that sort of game from the first gasp to the last. Long before the final whistle, it was Tottenham who were only too happy to settle for a point.

DOWN to save goes Tony Macedo. At full-length he holds one of the few Spurs shots that were on target —a rasping drive from Cliff Jones, Spurs right-winger. A goal would have given Spurs a vital point in their bid for the title

DOWN in heap are Spurs stand-in centre-forward Frank Saul — he's the man underneath — and Fulham's Bill Dodgin. But Les Allen has eyes for other things.

MATCH 34 SATURDAY 25TH MARCH 1961
ATTENDANCE: 38.531

MATCH 35
31ST MARCH 1961
SCORERS
SPURS JONES (2) ALLEN SAUL
CHELSEA BRABROOK TINDALL
HALF-TIME 0.0
ATTENDANCE 65032

LEADERS FIND TITLE FORM AGAIN

CHELSEA HIT BY THAT OLD SPURS MAGIC

By ROY PESKETT :—Tottenham 4 Chelsea 2

IT took just 35 minutes of the old magic yesterday afternoon to give hitherto stuttering Spurs their most clear cut League win since they beat Arsenal by a similar score on January 21.

After a frustrating first half the touch came back.

But the start to the purple patch was as lucky as their previous efforts had been unlucky. In the 49th minute Chelsea centre-half Mel Scott pulled the ball back for Jones to tap it into the net.

Jones scored a second goal in the 54th minute. Allen made it 3—0 and young Saul, deputising for the injured Smith, smashed in the fourth.

Eased up

Spurs unwisely eased up after a penalty appeal had been turned down by referee George Pullin and Chelsea scored two "soft" goals in the last three minutes.

Now that they are back to something like their old form Spurs should make sure of the title in the next three games.

They may bring in Medwin for Dyson against Preston today (Saturday). Dyson took several knocks yesterday, and deserves a rest.

It is just as well for Tottenham that with Mackay out of action they have such a fine reserve in Tony Marchi. He was just about the best player on the field.

Brabrook and Tindall scored Chelsea's goals.

Cliff Jones, Spurs' Welsh international who is rated among the best wingers in the world, makes one of his thrilling bursts for goal.

	P	W	D	L	F	A	PTS
SPURS	35	26	4	5	98	44	56
SHEFF WED	35	22	9	4	69	35	53
WOLVES	36	21	7	8	90	66	49
BURNLEY	33	18	5	10	87	59	41
EVERTON	36	17	5	14	69	64	39
BLACKBURN	36	14	9	13	68	66	37
VILLA	34	14	8	12	65	63	36
ARSENAL	36	13	10	13	68	70	36
CARDIFF	35	13	8	14	52	64	34
LEICESTER	33	14	6	13	65	56	34
MAN UTD	35	13	7	15	65	68	33
WEST BROM	36	14	4	18	57	66	32
BIRMINGHAM	35	13	6	16	55	69	32
CHELSEA	35	12	7	16	82	85	31
WEST HAM	35	13	5	17	69	75	31
FOREST	35	12	7	16	50	65	31
FULHAM	36	12	6	18	61	83	30
BOLTON	34	10	8	16	49	60	28
BLACKPOOL	36	10	7	19	60	64	27
MAN CITY	34	10	7	17	65	80	27
PRESTON	35	10	7	18	38	57	27
NEWCASTLE	36	9	8	19	75	98	26

139

F.A CUP SEMI-FINAL

Saturday 18th March 1961

Mirror SPORT 4 PAGES

DAILY MIRROR, Saturday, March 18, 1961

Ten train-loads of fans follow London's pride

By BILL HOLDEN

EIGHTEEN train-loads of fans lead the big parade into Birmingham for today's F A Cup semi-final clash between Spurs and Burnley at Villa Park.

Ten will be from London, eight from Burnley.

Harry Potts, Burnley manager, would not announce his team until after his players had a training session on a works ground near their Leamington Spa headquarters yesterday morning.

Then he said the team which had been swept out of the European Cup 4—1 by Hamburg would meet Spurs.

Jimmy McIlroy, Irish international inside left, summed up Burnley's belief:

"Defeat in Germany has made us keener than ever. We can beat Spurs."

Burnley, whose triple trophy bid was smashed by Hamburg, still hope to become the first team to win the F A Cup and Football League Cup in the same season. But I take the highly-skilled, dearly-bought blend of talent which has

become the pride and joy of London to beat Burnley—and their Villa Park Cup bogey.

Three times Spurs have lost a semi-final there since the war.

Today they should stride on triumphantly toward the Cup and League double—last achieved in 1897.

Great Chance

Manager Bill Nicholson told me: "We must have a great chance."

Sheffield United, lone Second Division survivors also bid for a double.

They aim for Cup and promotion—last achieved by West Bromwich in 1931.

All their players were given a final fitness test yesterday morning, and all were passed fit—so it is a full-strength team.

Derek Pace, centre forward, told me: "It has always been my dream to play at Wembley in the Final. I really believe we shall get there."

But I agree with Mirror Sport's man-on-the-spot.

VILLA: HELP US BEAT SPIVS

Aston Villa last night appealed to Spurs and Burnley fans: "DON'T come if you have not got a ticket. We have sold out.

"Help us beat the spivs by staying away if you have been unlucky."

Peter Ingall, and tip Leicester to get through.

They have only one object: to win the Cup for the first time. They have the most unimpressive record of the four left in the competition: Once beaten finalists; only twice before in a semi-final.

Now manager Matt Gillies says: "I never prophesy. But the lads are fully confident we can do it."

And so for my own bid for a treble.

Having accurately forecast the EIGHT clubs to reach the sixth round, and then the FOUR to reach the semi-finals, I plunge on the two Wembley teams being SPURS and LEICESTER.

THUMBS UP!

● We'll win, say Spurs' trio Cliff Jones (left), Les Allen (centre) and Ron Henry as they leave London yesterday. Destination: Villa Park.

Special

FOOTBALL OUT-OF-TOWN

Saturday, 18 March
Burnley v. Tottenham
Euston 8.35, 9.10, 9.40, 9.55
and 10.5 a.m. .... } 18/6
South Tottenham 8.10 and
8.45 a.m. .... }

(Buffet Car trains—Book early)

Manchester Utd. v. Arsenal
Euston, 8.20 a.m. 34/-

Newport Co. v. Brentford
Paddington, 10.55 a.m. 20/6

Saturday, 25 March
Southampton v. Charlton
Waterloo, 3.30, 4.35 p.m. 12/-

Please retain this Bill for Reference   O/54R. (S.Day)

FOOTBALL

SEMI-FINAL F.A. CUP
at VILLA PARK
KICK-OFF 3.0 p.m.

SATURDAY 18th MARCH 1961

BURNLEY
v.
TOTTENHAM HOTSPUR

SPECIAL EXCURSION EUSTON TO BIRMINGHAM AND WITTON - REFRESHMENTS AVAILABLE

OUTWARD		Lavender Tickets	Pink Tickets	Yellow Tickets	Grey Tickets	Buff with Red Line Tickets	
		a.m.	a.m.	a.m.	a.m.	a.m.	
EUSTON	Dep.	8.35	9.10	9.40	9.55	10.5	SECOND CLASS
BIRMINGHAM New St.	Arr.	11.27					RETURN FARE
WITTON	Arr.		12.13	12.36	12.45	12.57	

RETURN		ALL WITTON TICKETS				Lavender Tickets only.	18/6
		p.m.	p.m.	p.m.	p.m.	p.m.	
WITTON	Dep.	5.10	5.22	5.35	5.47	7.45	
BIRMINGHAM New St.	Dep.						
EUSTON	Arr.	7.40	8. 9	8.17	8.35	10.28	

ON OUTWARD JOURNEY COLOURED TICKETS AVAILABLE ONLY BY TRAINS AS SHEWN

CHILDREN under three years of age, free: three years and under fourteen, half-fares.

HOW TO REACH THE GROUND

FROM BIRMINGHAM - Special bus service at frequent intervals from Dale End or Bull Street. 15 minutes journey.

FROM WITTON - Villa Park is adjacent to Witton Station

SPECIAL NOTICE - In the event of the Match being postponed, the Special Arrangements will be cancelled and Excursion Tickets will not be issued, provided notice of postponement is received at the Station of departure in time to cancel such Special Arrangements.

TICKETS CAN BE OBTAINED IN ADVANCE AT EUSTON AND AT THE TOTTENHAM TRAVEL BUREAU, 562, HIGH RD. N.17, OR BY PRIOR NOTICE BEING GIVEN AT OTHER STATIONS AND OFFICIAL RAILWAY AGENTS.

Further information will be supplied on application to Stations, Official Railway Agencies, or to the District Passenger Manager, Euston House, London, N.W.1.

MARCH, 1961.   BRITISH RAILWAYS   B.R. 358/4.

No. 629

:: ASTON VILLA FOOTBALL CLUB LTD. ::

AT VILLA PARK, BIRMINGHAM

SATURDAY, 18th MARCH, 1961.   Kick-off 3.0 p.m.

F.A. CHALLENGE CUP

SEMI=FINAL
25/=

Row **S**   Seat No. 2

Entrance Door:
TRINITY ROAD B

Secretary,
Aston Villa F.C. Ltd.

THIS PORTION TO BE RETAINED

This ticket is issued subject to the Rules and Regulations of The Football Association.

BILLY NICHOLSON
Spurs manager

The Spurs' victims

Round III: Charlton Athletic (h), won 3—2 (Allen 2, Dyson).

Round IV: Crewe Alexandra (h), won 5—1 (Dyson, Smith, Mackay, Jones, Allen).

Round V: Aston Villa (a), won 2—0 (Neal o.g., Jones).

Round VI: Sunderland (a), 0—0. Sunderland (h), won 5—0 (Allen, Smith, Dyson 2, Mackay).

HARRY POTTS
Burnley boss

Burnley's progress

Round III: Bournemouth (h), won 1—0 (Connelly).

Round IV: Brighton (a), 3—3 (Miller, Carolan o.g., Robson). Brighton (h), won 2—0 (Miller, Robson).

Round V: Swansea Town (h), won 4—0 (Connelly, Robson 2, Pointer).

Round VI: Sheffield Wednesday (a) 0—0. Sheffield Wednesday (h), won 2—0 (Robson, McIlroy).

Leicester and Sheffield U. replay

3-0 SPURS STRIDE ON TO WEMBLEY

Smith shoots Spurs into the Final

by PETER HEWITT

GOALS by Spurs' leader Bobby Smith in the 30th and 49th minutes blasted battling Burnley off the road to Wembley in the F.A. Cup semi-final at Villa Park.

Those golden goals by Smith were the real hammer blows which sank Burnley's hopes of a Cup Final appearance, but a minute from the end Jones crashed in Spurs' third goal.

A record was set up even before the semi-final began, for the receipts of £20,565 15s. were a record for any match at Villa Park.

TOTTENHAM HOTSPUR
Brown
Baker   Henry
Blanchflower   Norman   Mackay
Jones   White   Smith   Allen   Dyson
●

Harris Robson Pointer McIlroy Connelly
Miller   Adamson   Joyce
Elder   Angus
Blacklaw
BURNLEY
Referee: Mr. K. A. Collinge (Altrincham).

The official attendance was 69,968.

Burnley, kicking off, launched the first raid on the right wing, but Norman robbed Pointer and made a 20-yard back-pass to Brown.

But Spurs were not long in getting into their studied stride. A neat right-wing move between Blanchflower, White and Dyson ended in White crossing over Blacklaw's head—but Angus headed away.

The first real threat came from Connelly when he broke away on the right and beat the Spurs defence with his cross, but the ball swerved away as Harris ran to intercept.

The first shot came from Connelly. Left-back Elder intercepted a clearance, banged the ball back into a crowded penalty area, and as 'Spurs defenders fumbled, Connelly nipped in and tried a first-time shot which Brown held confidently.

Burnley, eager to make up for their European Cup failure in Hamburg this week, had a little more of the attacking play in the tentative opening minutes, and as McIlroy split Spurs defence with a through ball to Robson, but Norman was on hand to intercept.

McIlroy was the chief menace to Spurs and in a spell of all-out attacking by Burnley, the Irish international had a foot in most of the moves. Brown was thankful to clutch one swirling right-wing centre from the scheming inside-right.

Little had been seen of 'Spurs' famed attack, and Mackay dashed up to try and ease the slight Burnley pressure and came off second best in a shoulder charge with Blacklaw.

In trouble

A long, swirling cross by Elder had Spurs in trouble again but the ball beat everyone and curled to Mackay who blasted it upfield.

After Blacklaw had clutched a white corner, Burnley surged back and a crossfield pass from Harris to Angus, who had come right up, had Spurs wavering again.

The full-back's cross to the far post looked dangerous, but Brown just managed to grab Robson's header on the line.

It was so close that many Burnley fans were shouting "goal."

Spurs fans had not had much to shout about but that all changed in the 30th minute when England centre-forward SMITH shot Spurs into the lead.

Adamson was drawn out of position to tackle Allen and completely missed the ball, leaving Smith a simple task to run on and blast it past a helpless Blacklaw. That was the confidence boost that Spurs needed and it was Burnley's turn to come under pressure.

A shot from Allen whistled just wide and Dyson bobbed up in the next raid to head just over the bar.

No penalty

Spurs appealed for a penalty when Dyson volleyed a right-wing corner from Allen and claimed that Angus stopped the ball with his hands but the referee, right on the spot, waved play on.

The game had completely changed and now it was Burnley's defence who were glad to kick into touch.

Half-time: Tottenham .. 1 Burnley 0

Spurs surged back on attack after the interval with their forwards inter-changing positions skilfully and Blacklaw just managed to catch an awkwardly bouncing left wing cross.

Three minutes after the interval Burnley had the ball in the Spurs' net. Elder swept the ball over into the middle and Robson just beat Norman to it and headed it in, but Burnley's moment of triumph was dashed when the referee awarded a free-kick against Robson.

Seconds later Burnley appealed for another goal when in a fantastic scramble Miller and Connelly had shots blocked on the line, but once again the referee ruled in Spurs' favour.

Before both sets of supporters had finished arguing about the decisions Spurs were two goals up and once again SMITH was the scorer.

The ball bobbed around the edge of the Burnley penalty area and suddenly Smith tried a speculative shot and the ball flashed well out of Blacklaw's reach into the net.

Burnley were not going out without a fight and Brown had to move smartly to tip a fierce angled shot from Harris over the bar.

Onslaught

With the blustery wind in their favour, the Lancashire side continued to storm down, and Brown handled everything cleanly despite several awkward moments.

Spurs penalty area was just a mass of players at times. Even Adamson dribbled his way upfield, but Burnley could not quite break down the white-shirted barrier.

A delightful move across field between McIlroy, Connelly and Harris saw the left-winger hit the ball into Spurs' goalmouth, but everyone missed the ball.

For all Burnley's pressure and the skilful promptings of McIlroy, Brown was not being severely tested as Blanchflower had Norman usually snuffed out the raids before they could become dangerous.

Little seen of the 'Spurs attack which was quite content to play the ball around and use up valuable time.

It was still Burnley on the attack at the end and Joyce headed narrowly over the bar from a right-wing corner, but it was all not enough to stop 'Spurs continuing their march to Wembley—and the double.

One minute before the end Spurs clinched it when White flicked the ball inside from the left and JONES swung his left foot and Blacklaw had no chance. Then the whistle blew and Spurs' supporters rushed on to the field to carry Smith to the entrance to the dressing room.

On the way to Wembley . . . Bobby Smith shoots Spurs' first goal.

An exciting moment at Villa Park — Blanchflower, Norman and Baker leap for the ball but are beaten by Burnley's Connelly.

A GOAL? YOU BE THE JUDGE

F.A. CUP SEMI-FINAL DETAILS

Leicester (0) 0		**Sheffield Utd. (0)** 0	
£16,000		52,095	
(Replay March 23, at Nottingham Forest ground, 3.0.)			
Tottenham H. (1) 3		**Burnley (0)** 0	
Smith (2), Jones		69,968	
£20,565			

TOTTENHAM will contest the Cup Final at Wembley for the first time in their history. In 1901, at Crystal Palace, they beat Sheffield United 3—1 in a replay. Twenty years later, they beat Wolves 1—0—but at Stamford Bridge.

BURNLEY have now been knocked out of two Cup competitions in four days—they were beaten 4—1 (aggregate 5—4) by Hamburg in the second leg of their European Cup quarter-final tie on Wednesday.

TEAM OF CENTURY

'Double is do-able', says Danny, the master

10

Les Allen

LES ALLEN
(Spurs)

1960/61	App/Gls	
League	42	23
FA Cup	7	4
1959-65	App/Gls	
All comps	137	61

Goals ultimately won the Double and inside left Les Allen supplied this most basic yet precious of football commodities in abundance – 27 in all, ranking him as second only to Bobby Smith in the list of top goalscorers during that epic season. Yet such bare statistics do not do justice to Allen's all-round contribution. Like each member of the side, he complemented his team-mates, enabling him to not only flourish as an individual but to help bring out the best in his colleagues.

Allen was the ideal foil to the barnstorming Smith. While the burly Yorkshireman wreaked merry havoc in opposition penalty areas, Allen played off his shoulder, exploiting a knockdown, playing a killer pass, springing from deep to rattle home match-winning goals. He did not quite play 'in the hole' in the modern parlance and neither was Allen an artist in the mould of White, Jones and Blanchflower. But he was brilliantly effective.

Originally tried out as an amateur at Spurs, he had returned from Chelsea in December 1959 to replace the popular Johnny Brooks. Brooks had a decent track record for Spurs and had played for England; Allen had struggled to make an impact with 'Drake's Ducklings' and it took some time for the White Hart Lane crowd to accept him back into the Tottenham fold. Bill Nicholson had other ideas, however, and had been perceptive enough to realise that given time to adapt to the system and his new surroundings, Allen would prosper. So it proved. A five-goal haul in the famous 13-2 FA Cup demolition of Crewe in 1960 won over

the doubters and by the start of the Double season Allen was firmly established in the side. He scored eight goals during the opening 11-victory sequence, helping to lay the foundations for the success at the end of the season.

The pinnacle of Allen's contribution was to smash the winning goal in the title-deciding epic against Sheffield Wednesday. "Always be looking to join as the third man in a movement," he had advised youngsters and he put that principle into blistering practice when he seized on Norman's header down from Blanchflower's free kick to power a glorious shoulder-high volley home. Anyone in the crowd who may still have had reservations about Allen's talent now had no reason to question his ability.

He was never to reach such glorious heights again. The arrival of Jimmy Greaves restricted his first-team opportunities in the following season and, once Alan Gilzean arrived three years later, Allen's Spurs days were numbered. He switched to QPR in 1965 for a successful three-year spell. He then managed with the west Londoners and at Swindon, then in Greece before leaving football to become a modelmaker back in his home county of Essex. He was also to oversee a footballing dynasty, with sons Clive and Bradley and nephews Martin and Paul continuing the family's footballing tradition.

Clive went on to coach at the club, maintaining the Allen connection decades on, and in his playing days was a pretty useful Tottenham goalscorer in his own right. Like father, like son.

" Les Allen was a very underrated player. I think he underrated himself – he was a bit of a glass-half-empty merchant. But he scored 27 goals that season and was very important to the side **"** Cliff Jones

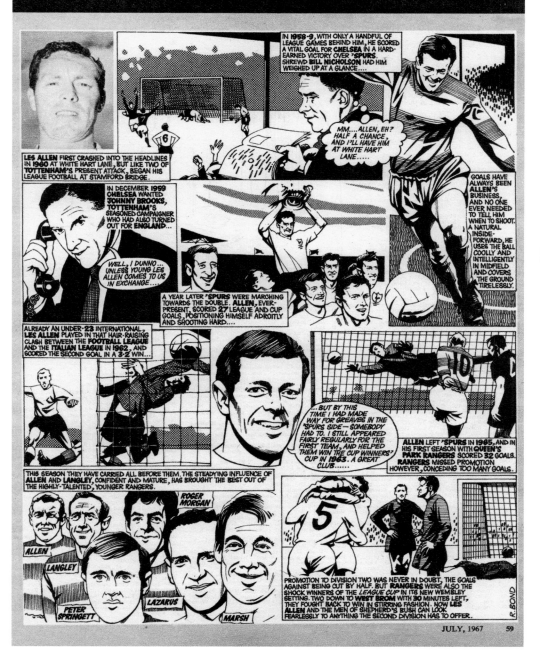

STAR STRIP— **LES ALLEN**

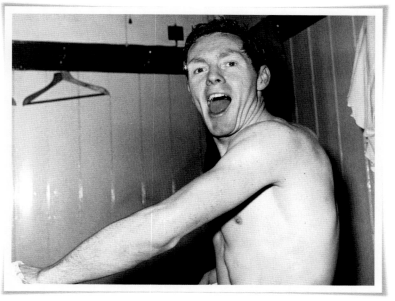

Previous spread: Les Allen runs in the snow during a period of rehabilitation.

Facing page: Allen goes for goal during the Double-season opener against Everton at White Hart Lane.

Left: Allen's career in pictures, as illustrated by Bob Bond for *Charles Buchan's Football Monthly*.

Above: Allen shows his delight in the Spurs dressing room after the title was secured in April 1961.

1961

April

Left: Hail the conquering Lilywhite heroes. The old champions sportingly pay tribute to the new on 22 April 1961.

With the cup final place safely secured for May, Spurs could turn their attention to ensuring the other part of the Double equation was completed. The run in had tripped up other sides before them and Wolves's near-miss the previous season, when Burnley seized the title on the final day, was a reminder that a job wasn't done until the last ball had been kicked.

Ahead lay a daunting seven games in the space of just over four weeks – 29 days of destiny to make sure the League Championship trophy resided at White Hart Lane for only the second time in the club's near 80-year history. It was with a neat symmetry that the sequence began against the first club to win the Double and the team whose white shirts Spurs had copied in admiration, the 1889 'Invincibles' of Preston. The visitors had fallen on leaner times and, doomed to relegation, were lambs to the Spurs slaughter as they suffered a demoralising 5-0 defeat.

Next up was a London derby away to Chelsea. Jimmy Greaves was on top form and gave the home side a 2-1 lead in front of a Stamford Bridge crowd baying for Tottenham blood. Spurs looked to be heading for defeat but Medwin equalised. A Blanchflower masterstroke won the day. The captain motioned Norman forward for a free-kick and the defender did the rest with a header. It was proof that guile, spirit and application was as vital to winning the Double as the silky football.

Another 3-2 victory, this time against Birmingham, set up the decisive clash of the season. Sheffield Wednesday had doggedly clung to Tottenham's coat-tails, chipping away at the points advantage through the winter and still in contention by the time Easter had passed. Yet on April 17th, Spurs could finally put the challenge to rest and win the league on their own turf. A ferociously competitive night crackled with expectation; nerves frayed especially when, against the run of play, Megson powered Wednesday into the lead.

But yet again, Spurs showed their class and spirit. Smith's outstanding equaliser sent the crowd into raptures; Allen's winner just a minute later shook the old stadium to its rivets. The second half was a composure-shredding torture, save for Blanchflower's measured display. The final whistle eventually blew, fans streamed onto the pitch to chant their captain's name and the title was won.

"As I write these words," the *Mirror's* chief football correspondent Bill Holden despatched, "pandemonium reigns at White Hart Lane… the song is ringing in our ears: 'Glory, glory – the Spurs go marching on.'" In an era long before today's saturation coverage, the nation's television viewers would have to wait until 11.15 that night for the BBC's report of the tumultuous scenes, but Londoners might have just as well have heard the cheers simply by opening their windows.

A win against Forest and two defeats to Burnley and West Brom provided an anti-climactic end to the league campaign, but the first instalment had been completed. Now for the Double.

MATCH 36 SATURDAY 1ST. APRIL 1961   MATCH 38 SATURDAY 8TH APRIL 1961

IT'S 100 UP FOR SPURS

● Another magic moment for Super Spurs—their 100th goal of the season leaves Preston 'keeper Alan Kelly sprawling. Forwards Frank Saul, John White, and Les Allen, and centre-half Tony Singleton watch Cliff Jones's shot enter the net at White Hart Lane.

THOSE TOTTENHAM BOYS HIT THEIR PEAK AGAIN

Tottenham 5 Preston 0: by ALAN HOBY

IT was as great a goal as we have seen at White Hart-lane all through this wonderful season—and the happy Tottenham thousands streamed away at the end bubbling over with the magic enchantment of it. . . .

The golden goal came in the 21st minute. Inside-left Les Allen began the move when he stood casually—almost arrogantly—by the ball while he waved back skipper Danny Blanchflower from an offside position.

Then, with the Preston defence as petrified as stone statues, Allen swept the ball across to the magnificent Marchi at left half. Dave Mackay's "stand-in" pushed it forward to right-winger Cliff Jones who thereupon plunged into the realm of pure fantasy.

Shrugging off one massive tackle, Spurs' Welsh star twice pulled back the ball from the wildly lunging boots of his opponents. Incredibly side-stepping two men, Jones impudently cracked the ball into the net with his right foot. And that was how the super-Spurs scored their 100th League goal of the season.

A lucky lead

Earlier, after two and a half minutes Spurs had snatched a lucky lead when Preston's young reserve goalkeeper Alan Kelly made his one tragic mistake of the match. Diving to field a 20-yard drive from John White, he allowed the ball to wriggle like a fish out of his hands and slither with tormenting slowness over the line for Preston.

Even that vast Tottenham crowd, rabid for the League-Cup "double," hushed in sympathy with the stricken young 'keeper as he held his head in his hands.

But for the rest of this joyous springtime football fiesta by Tottenham there was no luck—and no hope—for Preston.

Spurs, with Marchi, White, Blanchflower, and Jones at their imperious best, toyed with North End.

Frank Saul, 18-year-old centre forward deputising for England's

Bobby Smith, headed their third goal following a dazzling two-pass Marchi-White move down the left wing.

Just before half-time the sinuous Jones darted in to nod home an impudent Blanchflower free kick.

What can I say about poor Preston? That they made pretty patterns in the mud? That their finishing wouldn't have dented a paper bag? That they were up against a football machine which, on this form, cannot fail to clinch the double? All these arguments are valid.

But the elementary truth cannot be avoided: despite the energy and spirit shown by centre-half Tony Singleton, inside-right John Fullam, and left-half Frank O'Farrell, Preston were annihilated.

We had hardly recovered from the stunning roar which greeted the half-time Sheffield Wednesday score when Jones scored again with an acrobatic overhead kick—5—0.

After this final goal the game became even more of a one-sided canter for Tottenham. Spurs suddenly seem to be released from the terrible tension which was threatening to submerge their treasure house of talent.

Now, with the beauty and rhythm of their game fully restored, I am certain that the genius of these artistic Spurs will bring them the reward of the League championship and the Cup.

Dave Mackay and Bobby Smith are fit for tomorrow's return with Chelsea: but what a debt Spurs owe to "reserves" Marchi, Medwin, and Saul. They calmed and steadied the whole team.

SCORERS
WHITE
JONES (2)
SAUL

HALF-TIME 4-0

ATTENDANCE 46325

MATCH 37 MONDAY 3RD APRIL 1961

AMAZING FIGHT FAILS

Norman leaps into attack, sinks Chelsea

By JOHN CAMKIN

| Chelsea | 2 | Tottenham | 3 |

BIG Maurice Norman, Tottenham centre half, probably brought the championship to White Hart-lane in the 75th minute yesterday. He also quenched an amazing Chelsea fight that almost achieved the impossible.

Norman, so strong in defence, went upfield to head the goal that cheated ten gallant Chelsea fighters, if not of victory, of an honourable draw.

Consider the fright these Chelsea heroes gave to Danny Blanchflower and his men. Sillett and Ron Tindall, both injured. They started without Peter Brabrook, their deputy centre forward, went to hospital with a dislocated right shoulder after a firm, fair tackle by Norman.

Five minutes later Jimmy Greaves waltzed past two defenders and rushed a cross from Harrison into the net. More than 57,000 people hailed a brilliant equaliser to Smith's sixth-minute goal for Spurs.

Linesman T. Clapperton thought otherwise. His offside flag brought such vehement protests from Greaves that England's inside right had his name taken for the first time in his career.

Perplexing

Some of Mr. Clapperton's decisions were, in my view, perplexing. Both he and referee Jack Kelly, probable Cup Final referee, were booed at half-time.

These calamities were enough to sink 20 men. Instead, Chelsea's ten were leading by 2—1 nine minutes after half-time.

First, the tireless Blunstone fired a fine 18-yard drive past Brown in the 48th minute. Then Greaves popped up in the 55th minute, ran on to Blunstone's pass and ended a picture move with a picture shot into the roof of the net.

Spurs were clearly shaken, but recovered their poise and confidence like the champions they almost certainly are.

Medwin equalised after Smith headed Blanchflower's long-pass back to the penalty spot.

Chelsea: Bonetti; Sillett (J.) Harris Venables, Scott, Anderson; Blunstone, Greaves, Brabrook, Tambling, Harrison.

Tottenham: Brown; Baker, Henry; Blanchflower, Norman, Mackay; Jones, White, Smith, Allen, Medwin.

SCORERS
CHELSEA   BLUNSTONE
            GREAVES
SPURS   SMITH
            MEDWIN
            NORMAN

HALF-TIME 0-1

ATTENDANCE 57103

SPURS

They prove their greatness under Brum's onslaught

| Birmingham 2, Spurs 3. | By JOE HULME |

BIRMINGHAM put on one of the greatest recovery acts I have ever seen and their wonderful second-half fight was worthy of a point.

Three goals down after 33 minutes, all due to their own fault, they had stood mesmerised by a super Spurs team which did just as it liked.

Then Birmingham realised they had got to fight for the ball and after half an hour got stuck into these slick Spurs.

As a result, Tottenham lost their poise and were given a tremendous hammering.

In this superb battle Dave Mackay played a tremendous game, but Danny Blanchflower found the pace and pressure too much and long before the end his ageing legs were flagging.

The Birmingham fight-back hinged on a 39th-minute penalty when Peter Baker fouled Jimmy Bloomfield, one of the stars of the Birmingham side.

OFF THE TARGET

Harris shot wide from the spot, but referee Tirebuck ordered a retake because Brown was moving, and Harris made no mistake at the second attempt.

Three minutes after the change-over Harris got a second when Norman missed a cross from Bloomfield.

From that moment it was nearly all Brum, but Spurs, covering brilliantly, got out of trouble without any panic, and to prove they are forever dangerous, Les Allen made the crossbar quiver with an 86th-minute drive.

That opening half-hour by Spurs was truly great, and here I give Leicester a personal warning: John White has run into form at the right time.

I thought he had a magnificent first half, beating men with his passing and footwork.

He had a part in nearly every attack and in the first minute headed against the cross-bar and presented Bobby Smith with the simplest of goals.

Then in the 33rd minute White took advantage of yet another Birmingham defensive error to run on and score.

In between Peter Baker's error obliged by passing the ball to Bobby Smith, who presented Les Allen with an open goal.

Leicester must also watch Cliff Jones, the most dangerous winger in football today.

His electrifying bursts, when he often beat four men at a time, were one of the highlights of the game.

BIRMINGHAM—Withers 7; Farmer 8, Allen 7; Hennessy 7, Smith 7, Neal 8; Hellawell 8, Orritt 7, Harris 7, Bloomfield 8, Taylor 6.
TOTTENHAM—Brown 7; Baker 7, Henry 8; Blanchflower 8, Norman 8, MACKAY 9; Jones 8, White 8, Smith 7, Allen 7, Dyson 6.
Referee: L. J. Tirebuck (Halifax) 7.

SCORERS
B'HAM   HARRIS (2) (1 PEN)
SPURS   SMITH
          ALLEN
          WHITE

HALF-TIME 1-3.

ATTENDANCE 40960

148

The More than two and a quarter million have watched Spurs this season . . . **39** They have won more games than any other team in the history of the First Division. **Steps** Their total of 16 away wins is a record for the League Championship. **To** . . . Spurs started by winning 11 games in a row . . . have won the title in 39 games. **Glory**

SPURS—THE SUPER CHAMPIONS!

	P.	W.	D.	L.	F.	A.	Pts.
Tottenham H.	39	30	4	5	111	49	64
Sheffield Wed.	39	22	12	5	74	41	56

TOTTENHAM CLINCH TITLE

CHAMPIONSHIP SPECIAL

Spectacular Spurs march on Europe

SMITH PIERCES WALL OF STEEL

By JOHN CAMKIN: Tottenham 2, Sheffield Wed. 1

THE Football League championship is triumphantly, worthily home at last—at White Hart-lane. The proud name of Tottenham Hotspur shines in the record books of British Soccer. And now on to the Cup Final and the double!

The hard work of manager Mr. Bill Nicholson and his great team has its first reward, and England has a worthy representative in next season's European Cup.

Seconds after the last victory kick against Sheffield Wednesday, the only League challengers to the idols of half London, happy crowds streamed over the brown pitch.

Command appearance

"We want Danny," they chanted in their hundreds. "Glory, glory," they sang when Tottenham's captain did not appear. Finally Blanchflower and his team bowed to popular demand, and the grimy, white-shirted, heroes filed into the director's box.

So the thousands left happily to wait hopefully for another triumph at Wembley on May 6.

The bitter acrimony of Soccer politics and the wage dispute is forgotten for a moment as England's outstanding side ascends its throne. Here is a victory for everything good in the game; a triumph for the irresistible combination of great artistry and unselfish dedication.

The influence of Tottenham will spread to every level of the football pyramid. It will be an influence completely for the good.

The final act, perhaps inevitably, was scarcely typical of the brilliant season which has produced 64 points and 111 goals from 39 First Division games.

Slightly nervous Spurs produced only rare flashes of football as they fought their way to victory against a Wednesday as hard as Sheffield steel.

Free kicks were frequent. Referee T. Dawes (Norwich) took the names of Tottenham's Mackay and Wednesday's Johnson. Two goals came directly from infringements.

Spurs proved they can be hard in a hard match, and their brilliant finishing power did not desert them in a moment of crisis.

Bobby Smith, gently flicking the ball past England colleague Peter Swan, finally crashed the ball past England's Ron Springett for a magnificent first goal in the 42nd minute.

JON'S SPORTING TYPES

BUDGET

". . . and, finally, the item you've been waiting for—Spurs won!"

The smile of a man who planned a victory with his head and welcomed it with his heart . . . the smile of Danny Blanchflower.

A bath-towel is Les Allen's banner of triumph as jubilant Spurs file into the directors' box to a flare-lit ovation from these shouting, singing fans.

Rumbustious

Les Allen, the other half of Tottenham's goal-scoring partnership, crashed in the winning volley on the stroke of half-time.

Before these goals Tottenham had struggled, trailing, after Don Megson, Wednesday's left back, fired in a fine first goal in the 29th minute.

After the goals Spurs played with some of the poise and confidence of champions. Smith and Cliff Jones were brilliant in attack.

Rumbustious Smith joyfully challenged his England colleagues at every chance. One hefty charge in the 80th minute drove Springett on to a goalpost and off the field for five minutes' treatment.

Now Spurs need three more points from three games to seal the championship record of 66 points from neighbouring Arsenal.

Tottenham: Brown; Baker, Henry; Blanchflower, Norman, Mackay; Jones, White, Smith, Allen, Dyson.
Sheffield Wed: Springett; Johnson, Megson; McAnearney, Swan, Kay; Finney, Craig, Ellis, Fantham, Wilkinson.

Same men 22 times

SPURS have two main ambitions left this season: (1) To beat Arsenal's First Division record (1930-31) of 66 points. (2) To become the first club since Aston Villa (1897) to win the Cup and League.

So far Spurs have played 39 League matches this season. In 22 the team has been the same:

Brown; Baker, Henry; Blanchflower, Norman, Mackay; White, Smith (R.), Allen, Dyson.

Blanchflower, Henry, White, and Allen have played in all 39. Other appearances: Baker, Brown, Norman (38), Dyson (37), Mackay (34), Smith (R.) (33), Jones (28), Medwin (12), Saul (6), Marchi (2), Barton, Hollowbread, Smith (J.), one each.

Scorers

League scorers: Smith (R.) 26, Allen 23, Jones 15, White 13, Dyson 12, Blanchflower 6, Mackay 4, Medwin 4, Norman 4, Saul 3, opponent 1.

Spurs have won all except nine matches this season. The nine:

LOST: Newcastle and Leicester (home), Cardiff, Sheffield Wednesday, and Manchester United (away).

DRAWN: Wolves, Manchester City, Burnley (home), Fulham (away).

GAMES TO COME: Nottingham Forest and W.B.A. (home), Burnley (away).

THE GOALS THAT DID IT

THE FIRST: Bobby Smith, extreme right, beats Springett

THE CLINCHER: Scored by Allen and Smith jumps for joy

SCORERS
SPURS SMITH
ALLEN

WEDNESDAY
MEGSON

HALF-TIME
2-1

ATTENDANCE
61,200

TOTTENHAM'S TITLE

	P	W	D	L	F	A	Pts
TOTTENHAM							
SHEFF. WED.							
WOLVES							

Wait till you hear my COCK-A-DOODLE-TWO for the 2nd leg!

LEAGUE CHAMPIONSHIP CUP
THIS SPACE RESERVED FOR FA CUP
1ST DIVISION

149

Above: Bobby Smith smashes the equalising goal that sent White Hart Lane into a deafening frenzy and launched Spurs towards clinching the title against Sheffield Wednesday. *Above right*: At the final whistle, thousands of supporters piled on to the White Hart Lane pitch. It was a night of intense emotion and raucous celebration that no one who was present will ever be able to forget. *Right*: The winner itself was scored by Les Allen, pictured celebrating in the bath with his ecstatic team-mates. *Facing page*: Danny Blanchflower makes time to shake a hand.

MATCH 40 SATURDAY 22ND APRIL 1961

SPURS TAKE A DIVE IN CLASS WARFARE

Burnley 4, Spurs 2.   By JOHN LEONARD

IT was billed as "The Battle of the Champs"—Spurs, the new silk-smooth Pride of the South, versus Burnley, the fitful Cocks of the North. In theory it should have been the match of the season. In fact—it was.

A magnificent pulsating game with ice-cool, clinical Soccer from Spurs and tempestuous lightning flashes from Burnley. From the minute those two brilliant Irishmen, Jimmy McIlroy and Danny Blanchflower, shook hands as the two captains to the moment they walked off the field as the men of the match, it was a superb struggle.

And the result—an undisputed triumph for the North, who pulled back from two goals down to slam the new champions 4—2. But for some amazing goalkeeping by Spurs' Bill Brown the margin might have been even greater.

Tottenham—at full strength everywhere except on the right-wing where they swopped one Welsh international for another—were spurred on on the one hand by the prospect of breaking Arsenal's long-standing points record, but hunted on the other hand by fears of injuries with the biggest prize of all, the Cup and League double, lying temptingly before them.

They cast their fears aside and sometimes played football worthy of all the lavish praise which has been heaped upon them.

But even at that they were not good enough for a mercurial flat-out Burnley

Spurs' first goal came unexpectedly and entirely against the run of play when full-back Peter Baker strolled unchallenged half the length of the field to score with a speculative shot from fully 20 yards.

FINAL WHISTLE. *Off trots Blanchflower. "Win or lose, I always enjoy the game..."*

Lifted roof

Then after 40 minutes Terry Dyson switched over to the right wing and lobbed the ball into the centre for Bobby Smith to rise above the Burnley defence and put the Londoners two up.

And then after 58 minutes the Burnley crowd lifted the roof as McIlroy opened Spurs defence for Harris to score.

Nine minutes later the ground positively exploded as Pointer crossed from the left for McIlroy himself to fire the ball home.

From that moment Spurs lost much of their poise, and when in the 84th minute McIlroy initiated another piercing move for Harris to score there seemed to be little doubt which way the game must go.

BURNLEY.—Blacklaw 7; Angus 7, Elder 7; Joyce 7, Cummings 7, Miller 7; Connelly 7, *McILROY 10, Pointer 9, Robson 7, Harris 9.
SPURS.—Brown 9; Baker 8, Henry 7; *BLANCHFLOWER 10, Norman 7, Mackay 8; Medwin 7, White 8, Smith 7, Allen 8, Dyson 7.

SCORERS

Burnley: HARRIS (2)
         McILROY
         ROBSON

SPURS: BAKER
         SMITH

HALF TIME 0.2

ATTENDANCE 28397

MATCH 41 WEDNESDAY 26TH APRIL 1961

By ROY PESKETT
Tottenham 1   Nottingham Forest ... 0

CHAMPIONS Tottenham need one point from their last League game on Saturday — against West Bromwich at home—to set a First Division points record. Last night, before the smallest crowd at any first-team match at White Hart Lane this season (35,700) they scraped a one-goal win.

That goal by Terry Medwin, 26 minutes from time, gives Spurs 66 points, to equal the record Arsenal set when they won the Division I title in 1930-31.

Persistent rain turned the pitch into a skating rink on which Spurs found it difficult to maintain their usual slick pace.

Except for an earlier effort from Medwin which struck the cross-bar, two magnificent saves by the 18-year-old Grummitt, and some skidding near-misses in front of goal their forwards did not look impressive.

Often the red-shirted Forest looked more like champions. They gave an extremely competent display and I think that manager Mr. Andy Beattie is building a team that will go places next season.

It is sprinkled with youngsters who already know the game and the only "old man" is 27-year-old centre half and skipper Bob McKinlay.

Smart wingers

Forest's smart young wingers, 19-year-old Rowland and 18-year-old Channel Islander Le Flem, often worried the Tottenham full-backs.

Former Tottenham wing-half Jim Iley started as if he was going to show his former club just what they had lost, but in the second half he did not look as effective as either Blanchflower or Mackay.

Spurs were without Welsh international Cliff Jones who, I understand, will be fit to play on Saturday. Though White and

TERRY MEDWIN
... shot the vital goal

Blanchflower schemed many openings the resolute Forest defence gave Smith and Allen little room to manoeuvre.

But it was Smith who started the move which brought the all-important goal. He chipped the ball through to Medwin, who flicked it round Patrick and ran in to ram it past Grummitt.

Tottenham : Brown; Baker, Henry; Blanchflower. Norman. Mackay; Medwin, White, Smith, Allen, Dyson.
Nottm. Forest: Grummitt; Patrick, Palmer; Whitefoot, McKinlay, Iley; Rowland, Booth, Vowden, Quigley, Le Flem.

SCORER. MEDWIN   HALF TIME 0.0   ATTENDANCE 35473

EAGER ALBION GIVE SPURS A FRIGHT

TOTTENHAM 1, WEST BROMWICH ALBION 2
From HAROLD PALMER: Tottenham, Saturday

An eager West Bromwich side gave Spurs the run-around here at White Hart Lane today. The new champions, with one eye on Wembley, had a fright when Derek Kevan scored for Albion. Although Spurs equalised in the second-half through Smith, Robson hit a second for Albion after 62 minutes.

Spurs were looking their best in new white shirts but after they had started aggressively, the former England forward, Derek KEVAN snatched a chance to put West Bromwich ahead.

There was an element of luck about Albion's goal. Hope, a 17-year-old discovery had his shot blocked by Blanchflower but the ball went to Clark. Over came a quick centre and Kevan stabbed a fast shot past Brown. It was a real opportunist effort.

Spurs were nearly two down in 12 minutes. Robson shot from the corner of the penalty area and the ball struck the inside of the far post and rebounded across the face of the goal a foot in front of the line.

Spurs could not complain about their luck. Clark, slightly limping, slipped a pass inside to Kevan. It was another measured shot that beat the goalkeeper. This time the ball hit underneath the bar and again rebounded into play.

The post—again

Spurs' luck really was in. With four minutes to go before half-time, another bright Albion attack ended with Hope cracking a great 25-yard shot against the left upright—the third time Albion's shots had hit post or bar in this half.

Half-time: Tottenham 0, West Bromwich Albion 1.

Spurs were still shy of a good old-fashioned tackle in the second half, but within four minutes they had equalised.

White centred, the ball went to Allen, who carefully stabbed it for the far side of the goal. Wallace did not get hold of the ball and SMITH, falling as he did so, pushed the ball past the goalkeeper.

A few minutes later Blanchflower found Smith with a wonderful pass. The centre-forward was all on his own some eight yards out and all he could do was to thump the ball straight into Wallace's arms.

Free-kick

After 11 minutes of the half, Wallace caught a cross from Mackay and was buffeted over the goal line by the charging Smith. The crowd roared for a goal but the referee indicated that Smith had used an elbow and gave Albion a free kick.

Albion regained the lead in the 62nd minute. ROBSON was being tackled by Mackay when he shot for goal. A slight interception probably put some spin on the ball which bounced awkwardly to beat the surprised Brown.

Spurs tried hard for an equaliser. But they seemed more concerned when Mackay went down on one knee and limped when he got up than they were in the score.

No wonder team, says Nicholson

Spurs ..1   West Bromwich ..2
By IAN WOOLDRIDGE

BILLY NICHOLSON, the manager who has led Tottenham to 66-point League championship victory, told a 52,000 crowd through a microphone yesterday: "As you've seen today, our team are not wonder men. I only hope they will get in the groove again and COPY West Bromwich at Wembley next Saturday."

Beside him stood the glittering League trophy. Beneath him thousands of clamouring fans struggled with police.

But Nicholson never smiled. And with reason. Just seven days short of the Cup Final—and the historic double that goes with it—his team had reeled, tottered and finally collapsed to their poorest performance since the curtain went up last August.

Nicholson, in fact, had never spoken a truer word. West Bromwich—sounder in defence, more probing in attack, and more urgent in their entire approach to the game—gave Spurs a lesson in the art of intellectual Soccer from first minute to last.

Fourth-minute lead

Derek Kevan had swept West Bromwich into a fourth-minute lead. Robson scored their second from 20 yards in the 62nd. But Spurs solitary answer was a 49th-minute goal which Smith bundled into the net with the grace of a dustman aiming a crude kick at a cat.

So Arsenal's 30-year-old record of 66 points remained only equalled, not beaten. But that right now must be the least of Spurs' legion anxieties.

They looked battle-fatigued almost to the point where they had lost faith in their own ability. The proud, arrogant, elegant patterns were gone. In their place came a sterile stream of high crosses from the corner flags which goalkeeper Wallace always cut off.

But let me add that it was never a sad day on which to end a League season.

West Bromwich informed us that more and more teams intend to play the Tottenham way and, regardless of what happened at White Hart-lane yesterday that is fine news for English football.

Billy Nicholson

SCORERS
Spurs : Smith
WBA : Kevan
Robson

HALF-TIME   0-1
ATTENDANCE   52,05†

FINAL TABLE

	Home Goals				Away Goals					
	W.	D.	L.	F. A.	W.	D.	L.	F. A.	Pts.
Tottnhm ..	15	3	3	65 28	16	1	4	50 27	66
Sheff. W.	15	4	2	45 17	8	8	5	33 30	58
Wolves ...	17	2	2	61 32	8	5	8	42 43	57
Burnley ..	11	4	6	58 40	11	3	7	44 37	51
Everton ..	13	4	4	47 23	9	2	10	40 46	50
Leicester ..	12	4	5	54 31	6	5	10	33 39	45
Man. U. ..	14	5	2	58 20	4	4	13	30 86	45
Blackburn	12	3	6	48 34	3	10	8	29 42	43
A. Villa ..	13	3	5	48 28	4	6	11	30 49	43
W. Brom.	10	3	8	41 33	8	2	11	24 19	41
Arsenal ..	12	3	6	44 35	3	8	10	33 50	41
Chelsea ..	10	5	6	61 48	5	2	14	37 52	37
Man. C. ..	10	5	6	41 30	3	6	12	38 60	37
Nottm. F.	8	7	6	24 33	6	2	13	28 45	37
Cardiff ..	11	5	5	34 26	2	6	13	26 59	37
W. Ham ..	12	4	5	53 31	1	6	14	24 57	36
Fulham ..	8	5	8	39 39	6	0	15	33 56	36
Bolton ..	9	5	7	38 29	3	6	12	20 44	35
Brmngham	10	4	7	35 31	4	2	15	27 53	34
Blackpool.	9	3	9	44 33	3	6	12	24 39	33
Newcastle	7	7	7	51 49	4	3	14	35 60	32
Preston ..	7	6	8	28 25	3	4	14	15 46	30

TOTTENHAM HOTSPUR FOOTBALL AND ATHLETIC COMPANY LIMITED

SATURDAY, APRIL 29th, 1961   PRICE TWOPENCE

A Message from the Chairman

MY co-Directors join me to-day, at the end of this unforgettable season, in congratulating our players on their success in winning the Championship of the League. They have indeed written another memorable page in the history of the Club, and by the high skill and excellence of their play they have delighted countless followers of the game both at Tottenham and on the grounds of other clubs. Looking back over the season we have many memories of the dramatic quality of their football, which has received so many tributes from supporters. Congratulations also to our Manager, Mr. W. Nicholson, who has been such an inspiring personality in this happy season, his second in the capacity of Manager, and incidentally his 25th season with the Club. This is a proud day for him, and for all associated with the Club, and may Tottenham Hotspur continue to win new fame in the future. That is the wish of us all.

At the conclusion of to-day's game the League trophy and medals will be presented by a member of the League Management Committee.

FRED J. BEARMAN

The Football League
Div. I Championship Cup

Souvenir Programme

This page: This set of pictures was taken by a fan at the final home game of the season against West Brom. Despite winning the title almost two weeks before, Spurs players had to wait until this game to get their hands on the trophy.

Facing page: A press shot taken from the back of the directors' box as Danny Blanchflower finally lifts the precious silverware.

11

Terry Dyson

TERRY DYSON
(Spurs)

1960/61	App/Gls	
League	40	12
Cup	7	5

1954-65	App/Gls	
All comps	209	55

A diminutive combination of feisty energy and whipcrack pace, Terry Dyson fitted the Double team's attack like a handmade glove. Standing at just 5ft 3in, his small stature belied a competitive nature and an all-action style that provided dashing left-sided verve to the team's relentlessly attack-minded approach.

This proud son of Yorkshire could have slipped into the stirrups of his jockey father, but football was his forte. Dyson signed for Spurs in a café opposite Arsenal's traditional home at Woolwich barracks, where he had completed his national service. Like a number of the Double team, his was no easy passage into the side; he had to compete for his place and made only occasional appearances in a six-year period. But his patience was rewarded. He timed his development to perfection and seized his opportunity when it arose, making the left-wing berth his own in 1960.

His impact was immediate. He scored twice in the second-game win over Blackpool and his level of performance barely wavered right through to May. Speaking to *Charles Buchan's Football Monthly*, Cliff Jones said of Dyson: "He played so well on the left wing when I was injured that he could hardly be dropped. Terry seemed to get better and better." The in-form Dyson thus became a key player in the Double side, to the extent that he missed just two matches of the 49-game campaign, scoring, providing or contributing to a good number of the 136 goals. He was ideally suited to the fluidity of Tottenham's venomous attack, interchanging with his team-mates and providing options with his imaginative movement. And he had a left foot to dream of, wielding it like a wand to cast neat, incisive passes and beautifully measured crosses. He was a grafter, too, not averse to battling for possession deep in his own half.

After missing an easier chance, Dyson scored what proved to be the winning goal in the cup final, earning praise from Bill Nicholson who was not disposed to handing out plaudits to his players. It was an appropriate denouement to Dyson's and Tottenham's finest season. There was still time in his Spurs career to register another famous match-winning display as he inspired Spurs towards their European Cup-Winners' Cup triumph two years later. Bobby Smith said to him at the final whistle: "You better retire now, you'll never play better." It was to prove prophetic. The game became known as 'Dyson's Final' but it was also his swansong, preceding a period in which he wound down his Spurs career before joining Fulham in 1965.

Dyson went on to play and manage in non-league football, and then taught PE in schools. He now works with the Hertfordshire Education Authority, helping children with emotional and behavioural difficulties, and for the FA as an Academy assessor. In this role he can still sometimes be seen at Tottenham's academy matches, pacing the wing and running an expert eye over the inheritors of his craft – and no doubt passing on a few reminiscences about his glory years to any youngster with the sense to listen to one of wing-play's finest exponents.

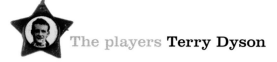

Previous page: Dyson limbers up before the 1961 semi-final.

Top: Dyson (front row, far right) prior to the 1954 Army Cup final against the Royal Corps of Signals with his Royal Artillery team-mates, including Ron Henry (front row centre).

Above: On tour and enjoying the sun in North America in 1957 with Ron Henry, Bobby Smith and Ron Reynolds.

Right: Carry on follow that camel in Cairo, November 1962.

Facing page: Celebrating a goal in 1964 in characteristic fashion.

 **"** Terry Dyson's strength was his enthusiasm. And he was a very good footballer as well, a good passer and he scored important goals **"** Cliff Jones

12

The squad

Bill Nicholson famously called on just 17 players to secure the Double. The star names are thus rightly lauded for their stamina as well as their skill, but behind every great team there are the less acclaimed members who featured briefly yet were integral to the achievement.

Terry Medwin almost merits status as a first-choice player. He made 14 league appearances, just under half that of Wales team-mate Cliff Jones, for whom he was a superb deputy. Medwin played in six of the opening 11 wins and over the season scored five vital goals, including the winner against Manchester City in February. He had been a prominent and popular Spurs player before the Double and continued to feature as a key man for the next two seasons until a leg break in 1963 ended his playing career. He coached at Fulham and was assistant manager at Swansea before retiring to life in Wales in 1983.

Another long-server was Tony Marchi. Born in Edmonton, he joined Spurs in 1949 and just missed out on appearing for the 1951 title-winning side, but had become skipper by 1956 and was set for a long and fruitful Tottenham career. Instead he went to play in his father's homeland of Italy, but the parting was brief. Marchi returned in 1959 to provide redoubtable back-up to the Mackay-Blanchflower half-back axis. The pair had big boots to fill, but Marchi slotted in perfectly. He played more extensively in subsequent seasons, including in the 1963 Cup-Winners' Cup campaign, before becoming player-manager at Northampton in

1965. He left football in 1967 and opened a decorating shop in Maldon, Essex, where he now lives.

Home-grown striker Frank Saul was also to enjoy more appearances in Spurs colours after the Double, but his six league games in 1960/61 featured three important goals, including the opener in the 3-2 win over Arsenal. Saul had made his debut three days before at the age of just 17, and would go on to become an FA Cup winner, scoring in the 1967 final against Chelsea before leaving for Southampton in 1968 in the deal that brought Martin Chivers to London. Saul went on to work as a builder in Essex.

Three other players made just single appearances. Had the system of non-tactical substitutions been introduced before 1965, it's likely this trio would have featured more. But the record books show they were part of a legendary team. Locally-born John Hollowbread stood in for the injured Bill Brown for the Boxing Day win against West Ham, saving superbly from Bobby Moore. Hollowbread was a loyal understudy in 14 years at Spurs, before leaving for Southampton and then retirement in Spain where he died in 2007. Full-back Ken Barton and inside-forward John Smith had the unfortunate distinction of making their only appearances in the 2-0 defeat at Manchester United in January. Barton left for Millwall and then Luton. He died aged just 44 in 1982. Smith appeared 24 times for Spurs, but would taste Wembley glory as part of the Swindon team that beat Arsenal in the 1969 League Cup. He died in 1988, aged only 49.

League 1960/61	App/Gls	
Terry Medwin	14	5
Frank Saul	6	3
Tony Marchi	6	0
Ken Barton	1	0
John Hollowbread	1	0
John Smith	1	0

FA Cup 1960-61	App/Gls	
Terry Medwin	1	0

Mirror Sport

SPURS ARE SOCKED BY STIFFS!

Pre-Cup defeat by 4-1

By KEN JONES

A RED-FACED Tottenham Cup team got a 4-1 walloping as a semi-final send-off from their reserves yesterday.

Back from their Welsh coast hide-away, Spurs wound up their training at White Hart-lane with a full-scale crack at their star-studded "Stiffs" —forty-eight hours before they clash with Burnley at Villa Park tomorrow.

And with only skipper Danny Blanchflower missing from their F A Cup line-up, they were hustled and bustled to defeat.

Centre half Maurice Norman gave away an own-goal. Frank Saul, Barry Aitcheson and John Smith made it 4—0 before the senior stars hit back with a goal by Terry Dyson

Usual Line-up

Spurs are taking Terry Medwin, Mel Hopkins and Toni Marchi to Birmingham as reserves, but will announce their usual line-up before leaving today.

Public Trial Match   August 13th, 1960   Kick-off 3 p.m.

WHITES
White Shirts, Blue Shorts

RIGHT WING   LEFT WING

GOAL
BROWN

BACKS
BAKER   HENRY

HALF-BACKS
BLANCHFLOWER (Capt.)   NORMAN   MACKAY

FORWARDS
JONES   WHITE   SMITH, R.   ALLEN   DYSON

Referee: F/Lt. A. L. MASON, Kent
Linesmen: Mr. H. L. COOK, Surrey (Red Flag)
Mr. D. LEWIS, Herts (Yellow Flag)

FORWARDS
AITCHISON   COLLINS   F. SAUL   HARMER   MEDWIN

HALF-BACKS
MARCHI (Capt.)   RYDEN   SMITH, J.

BACKS
HOPKINS   HILLS

GOAL
HOLLOWBREAD

BLUES
Blue Shirts, White Shorts

LEFT WING   RIGHT WING

ANY ALTERATION WILL BE NOTED ON THE BOARD

Previous page: Pre-season training. Frank Saul is no 9.

Above: The only team to beat Spurs twice in 1960/61? Answer: The Spurs reserves. "No disrespect to some fine footballers, but we called them Tuesday morning players," remembers Jones. "What mattered was producing on the Saturday."

Right: Terry Medwin, a key performer in the Double side.

Facing page: John Smith (left) and John Hollowbread (right) celebrate the 1962 cup win with Terry Dyson.

TERRY MEDWIN
Tottenham Hotspur
and Wales

163

1961

A date with destiny

THE FOOTBALL ASSOCIATION CHALLENGE CUP COMPETITION

FINAL TIE

LEICESTER CITY
v
TOTTENHAM HOTSPUR

SATURDAY, MAY 6th, 1961   KICK-OFF 3 p.m.

EMPIRE STADIUM

WEMBLEY

OFFICIAL PROGRAMME · ONE SHILLING

6 May 1961

Spurs 2 Leicester 0

Scorers: Smith, Dyson
HT: 0-0
Attendance: 100,000

"To tell you the truth, I didn't think we could do it."
"To tell you the truth, neither did I."
If Bill Nicholson had known David Niven and Gregory Peck would close the film he took his players to see on the eve of the cup final with those lines he may have opted for an alternative way to relax them ahead of their date with destiny. *The Guns of Navarone* was billed as 'The Greatest High Adventure Ever Filmed' and Tottenham Hotspur's own adventurers were about to hit the heights. The *Radio Times* flagged the game up on its cover and, for once, the favourites were the team everyone wanted to win.

The Double had caught the popular imagination and it was big box office, with tickets like gold dust. Not for the first time, and certainly not the last, complaints that the ordinary fans were passed over raged in the build-up. Bobby Smith, meanwhile, had other problems, slipping away twice to his doctor's in Palmers Green for painkilling injections on the morning of the game, desperate to overcome a knee injury that might make him miss out.

Since winning the league, the players' minds had been on the game no one wanted to miss. Now it was here. It is the little details that continue to glimmer. That trip to the Odeon Leicester Square; Smith's nocturnal flit; Blanchflower telling the Duchess of Kent pre-match that Spurs did not have names on their tracksuits like Leicester because "we know each other, Ma'am."

Perhaps they have such resonance because the game itself failed, as these big-billed bouts often do, to be the classic anticipated. Spurs were nervous, Blanchflower out of step, the team more conservative than they had been all season. Only Cliff Jones showed the spark of the super Spurs, perhaps because he was underwhelmed by the occasion.

In fact, Leicester looked the better side, probing and threatening with some slick football. When Peter Baker got knocked momentarily senseless making a last-ditch interception it seemed a metaphor for a groggy Spurs showing. But no football tale would be complete without a cameo from Lady Luck and the Wembley jinx which had been visited upon many teams had an influential part to play. This time it struck Leicester after right-back Len Chalmers injured his ankle in a tackle in the 19th minute. With no substitutes allowed, Leicester were as good as a man down and the game turned.

Spurs ground them down, finally breaching a heroic defence in the 69th minute when Wembley goal king Smith turned and dummied on the penalty spot before shooting home. Dyson headed a second on 77 minutes and Spurs cruised home. They had achieved the impossible. The Double was done.

Blanchflower didn't much care for the shenanigans of celebration and paraded the cup before the ecstatic crowd more out of duty than anything else. Afterwards, typically, he kept it all in perspective. "I'm glad it has come in the twilight of my career," he said. "It's the right time for it. I feel sorry for the younger lads. The rest of their soccer lives must be an anti-climax."

Radio Times (Incorporating World-Radio) May 4, 1961. Vol. 151; No. 1956.

BBC RadioTimes
tv and SOUND

5D

The F.A.
Cup Final
BBC TELEVISION
AND LIGHT PROGRAMME

Tottenham Hotspur
CAPTAIN DANNY BLANCHFLOWER

Leicester City
CAPTAIN, JIMMY WALSH

The cup final

WEMBLEY
1961

ROSETTE WORN AT WEMBLEY SATURDAY 6th. MAY 1961

FOOTBALL ASSOCIATION
CUP FINAL

EMPIRE STADIUM
WEMBLEY

LEICESTER CITY
v
TOTTENHAM HOTSPUR
SATURDAY MAY 6 1961

DAILY EXPRESS
COMMUNITY SINGING

Top left and right: Tottenham Hotspur players go through exercises with weight trainer Bill Watson at Cheshunt, Hertfordshire, 2 May 1961, in preparation for the FA Cup final against Leicester City.
Far left: Dave Mackay stretches in his cup final tracksuit.
Left: Supporters' Club organ *The Lilywhite* looks forward to Wembley in a special issue.

Leicester City & Tottenham Hotspur

GOOD FOR YOU!

Let's take the cup
And fill it up
With what is good for you
And give three cheers
For all this year's
Cup Final twenty-two!

KICK OFF WITH

GUINNESS

Before and after the game

The Evening News & THE STAR

Milady TOFFEES

World's largest evening sale

No. 24,678   LONDON, SATURDAY, MAY 6, 1961   PRICE 3d.

WEMBLEY SPECIAL

WEMBLEY 1961

THE CUP FINAL LINE-UP

SPURS
(White shirts, blue shorts)

BROWN

BAKER   HENRY

BLANCHFLOWER (capt.)   NORMAN   MACKAY

JONES   WHITE   SMITH   ALLEN   DYSON

Referee: J. Kelly   Linesmen: H. New. W. Downer
(Chorley)

Kick-off 3 p.m.

CHEESEBROUGH   KEYWORTH   McILMOYLE   WALSH (capt.)   RILEY

APPLETON   KING   McLINTOCK

NORMAN   CHALMERS

BANKS

LEICESTER
(Royal blue shirts, with white collars and cuffs; white with royal blue striped stockings)

The Lucky Number ?

By VICTOR RAILTON

THERE are two lucky omens to encourage the eleven pride of North London as they start the nerve-tingling trot through the dark tunnel under the terrace to face the blare and glare of the Cup Final against Leicester City this afternoon.

They have won the cup at each of the cold, gripping them the black dressing room used by victorious Wolves last season; and they can point gladly to the year on the calendar ending in a one.

They won two previous final appearances were in 1901 and 1921. Both those occasions brought victory; the last time in the incomparable Jimmy Dimmock matched the only goal that beat Wolverhampton.

Tottenham is on have been England's top team from the first week of the season. It was a fabulous performance to lead the League all the way.

Recent results have shown that the train has had it. If Spurs are to achieve the first team to achieve the double of League and Cup this century—Aston Villa were the last in 1897—they will need all of fortune's favours.

Success will mean the trophy coming to London for the first time since Arsenal won it 11 years ago. It will be the first time the two major F.A. trophies have been held by clubs so near to each other. Walthamstow Avenue, neighbours of Spurs, already hold the Amateur Cup.

Their headquarters are less than four miles from Tottenham. In comparison with Spurs, Leicester's achievements this season have been modest.

They were involved in the largest semi-final in history, taking 354 minutes to score the first of two goals that ended the challenge of Sheffield United.

But they have been to Wembley before—they lost to Wolves in 1949—and they were the first team to beat Spurs at Tottenham this season when the campaign was five months old.

TOTTENHAM HOTSPUR F.C.

versus

LEICESTER CITY F.C.

Back row (from left): Frank McLintock, Ian King, George Heyes, Ken Keyworth, Gordon Banks, Len Chalmers and Derek Hines. Middle row : Mr. A. Dowdells (trainer), Colin Appleton, Howard Riley, Albert Cheesebrough, Hugh McIlmoyle, Jimmy Walsh, Gordon Wills and Mr. Mat Gillies (manager). Front row: Ian White and Dick Norman.

Kelly's in charge

"THIS is the most wonderful thing that has ever happened to me. When I started refereeing in junior football 26 years ago I dreamed of this."

That was how Jack Kelly, 45-year-old Chorley insurance broker (pictured above) reacted when he heard that he would referee the Cup Final on May 6.

And a few hours after the news reached him from the F.A. he was asked if he could referee a village match four days before his Wembley date. His answer? "Of course I will."

Mr. J. G. Williams (Nottingham) will referee the Amateur Cup Final at Wembley on April 22.

SCOUTS' LEADER

ASSISTANT manager Harry Evans has played his part in the 'Spurs success story. He has taken over much of the correspondence that kept Bill Nicholson tied to his desk, and he is also responsible for the whole scouting system.

Two years ago the bottom dropped out of Harry's soccer world, when he was sacked as Aldershot's manager. At that time Jesse Carver had resigned as assistant manager at Tottenham and Harry hopefully applied for the post.

Bill Nicholson once again proved his shrewdness when he chose Harry to become his assistant from a long list of applicants. They have formed a highly successful partnership.

A cheerful man, he spreads happiness among everyone, and is one of the most popular members of the staff.

Mrs. Barbara Wallace, a member of 'Spurs' office staff for four and a half years, and the only woman member, will provide the blue and white ribbons which will adorn the F.A. Cup if 'Spurs win at Wembley. The ribbons used at the two previous finals have been lost. Mrs. Wallace is a granddaughter of the late 'Spurs chairman, Mr. Morton Cadman, whose family have always had charge of the ribbons.

NORTH TERRACE SEAT (Uncovered)

ENTER AT D TURNSTILES
(See plan & conditions on back)

ENTRANCE (LEFT)   4

Row 22   Seat 302

EMPIRE STADIUM, WEMBLEY
The Football Association
Cup Competition

FINAL TIE

SATURDAY, MAY 6th, 1961
KICK-OFF 3 p.m.

Price 10/6

Bracewell Smith
Chairman,
Wembley Stadium Limited

THIS PORTION TO BE RETAINED
This ticket is issued on the condition that it is not re-sold for more than its face value.

Previous page: Bill Nicholson leads his team out at Wembley for their appointment with destiny. *Top left:* Danny Blanchflower introduces the players to the Duchess of Kent. *Top right:* Cliff Jones thought he'd broken the deadlock, but the goal was disallowed for offside. *Bottom left:* Bobby Smith swivels on the penalty spot to open the scoring in the second half. *Bottom right:* Terry Dyson's header flies past Leicester goalkeeper Gordon Banks for the second goal.

SPURS—THE DOUBLE

SPURS GET THAT DOUBLE: THE FIRST THIS CENTURY

Injury—then two great goals seal Leicester's fate

TWO goals in nine minutes gave Tottenham victory in the Cup Final this afternoon against Leicester City. Spurs thus become the first team to win the Cup and League double this century.

Despite Chambers' injury in the first half Leicester kept the score sheet clean up until half time. The reshuffled rearguard held well, but the attack was naturally blunted. Spurs did net once, but the goal was disallowed for offside.

TOTTENHAM HOTSPUR

R   Brown   L
Baker
Blanchflower   Norman   Mackay   Henry
     White   Smith   Allen
Jones   Dyson

      ●

Cheesebrough   McIlmoyle   Riley
   Keyworth   Walsh
Appleton   King   McLintock
   Norman   Chalmers
        Banks

L   R

LEICESTER CITY

Referee: Mr. Jack Kelly, of Chorley.

Linesmen: H. G. New (Hants) and W. J. Downey (Co. Durham).

The morning sunshine gave way to a dull, breezy afternoon at Wembley for the FA Cup Final between the double seeking Tottenham Hotspur and Leicester City.

Rain threatened, but the turf looked in a superb condition for good football.

The 100,000 crowd, who had paid gate receipts of £49,813 gathered early. Among the huge crowd were five of the Australian cricketers, including Richie Benaud, the captain.

Headed by their managers, the teams came out to a great roar of welcome. Leicester had blue track suits and Spurs white windcheaters, covering their shirts.

They lined up before the Royal box and were presented to the Duchess of Kent who later was presenting the trophy.

RED CARPET

A red carpet had been spread out on to the pitch for the Duchess to walk on, possibly an indication that the turf was soft.

In the hour before the kick-off the touts claimed that they were losing money.

"The market has collapsed and we are now selling tickets for less than we gave for them," said one.

There were plenty of buyers.

"There were hundreds of tickets for sale along Olympic Way. Operating in twos and three's, the touts thrust out handfuls of 3s. 6d. tickets to the crowds, asking £4 for them which dropped to £3 with bargaining."

There was plenty of play. Blanchflower, of Spurs, spun the coin and won, but there did not appear to be

much advantage in the toss, which was of the swirling nature associated with Wembley.

Leicester were first to attack, a free kick by Chalmers from near the halfway line taking play well into the Spurs half, but the ball was quickly cleared.

Spurs at once swept down field and a long cross field pass by White found Allen, who had switched to the outside-right position.

The little winger, however, could not control the ball and the move came to nothing.

A long free kick by Mackay on the left—almost as good as a corner—brought danger to Leicester. The ball was passed to Dyson, still on the right, and he sent a short ground pass to White who, from about 10 yards, blazed a splendid chance high over the bar.

NO NERVES

When Leicester responded McIlmoyle, their surprise choice at centre-forward, showing no trace of nerves, sent Cheesebrough away with a good pass.

The winger, however delayed his centre too long and it was charged down.

Leicester continued on the attack to force a time and a better centre on the left by Keyworth looked dangerous, but Blanchflower headed away.

Then McIlmoyle got in a strong ground shot which was diverted for a fruitless corner.

White and Blanchflower inter-passed neatly in the next Spurs raid, but the Leicester defence was in no

Goals time table

SMITH (Tottenham) 66 mins.

DYSON (Tottenham) 75 mins.

Wembley crowds and watching TV millions saw exciting duels with Leicester City goalkeeper Gordon Banks (left) and Tottenham Hotspur centre-forward Bobby Smith taking the leading roles.

PINK UN's BISCUIT AWARDED TO!

Tottenham Hotspur

LEICESTER CITY (for gallantry)

way overawed and they were soon back on the attack.

Walsh, tackled by MacKay, gained a free kick near the edge of the penalty area, but the massed Spurs defence cleared without trouble.

Close marking and quick tackling by the Leicester defence was a feature of the early stages, and when Smith tried to burst his way through, a good shoulder charge by King took him off the ball.

Then Jones tried to dribble through. He beat two men, but a third succeeded in dispossessing him.

At the other end a long cross-field ball by Riley found McIlmoyle, who hit the ball over the head of Norman, but also over the goal.

The ball did not seem to run fast enough on the holding turf to suit Spurs' style, and their moves developed too slowly to cause serious concern to Leicester.

A fine pass down the middle by Walsh sent McIlmoyle running strongly for the Spurs goal, and he managed to round Norman, but Henry, on the Spurs' left back, had covered his centre half well, and he robbed the Leicester centre

forward before he could get in a shot.

Then a centre from the right by Cheesebrough found Baker, and Baker was knocked down in making the clearance.

Baker was quickly up on receiving attention from the trainer, as Jones had been just before when he was seen to receive a knock in the stomach.

Soon after Chalmers, the Leicester right back, lay writhing on the ground after losing the ball to Allen in a tackle.

He seemed to have hurt his right leg, and lay for some time with an anxious cluster of Leicester colleagues bending over him.

This mishap came after 19 minutes, and raised thoughts of the Wembley injury bogey which has affected so many recent finals.

NASTY INJURY

Players of both clubs assisted Chalmers, whose right boot was taken off. When it proved that it's possible to do his feet, Chalmers hobbled badly, and it seemed clear that he had suffered a nasty injury to his right ankle.

McLintock took the right

Contd. on back page

WEMBLEY HOODOO THE TRAINER'S MAGIC SPONGE CAN'T CURE

ROLL OF MISFORTUNE
1952 WALLEY BARNES
1953 ERIC BELL
1955 JIMMY MEADOWS
1956 BERT TRAUTMANN
1957
RAY WOOD 1959
ROY DWIGHT 1960
DAVE WHELAN 1961
LEN CHALMERS

HAIL SUPREMOS!

Give Leicester proud badge for courage

By DESMOND HACKETT: Spurs 2 Leicester 0

TREMENDOUS, terrific Tottenham Hotspur are the greatest. There will never be another team like them. Never-again will 11 unpretentious young chaps make up a side to defy every sporting spectre in bogeydom and land the League and Cup double.

Spurs will become The Unforgettables. Their names will be recited when great deeds of football are told.

Well, that is what they will be saying in a very few years. So why not say it now?

Give praise to a team whose superb football at least gave them the opportunity of succeeding where all others had failed since Aston Villa in 1897.

But right now millions agonise over the crippled player—that annual woe of Wembley—and the inevitable demand that there must be substitutes.

When Leicester right back Len Chalmers was reduced to a pain-ridden, hobbling crock of a man in the 19th minute, a game which had been flowing with good football sagged.

THE HANDICAPS

Because out-dated legislators insist "We never have had substitutes and we do not see why we should change," these handicaps were inflicted upon the showpiece of Soccer.—

The inhumanity of Leicester being reduced to 10 men in the most exhausting football test of the year.

The shattering handicap of Leicester having to endure the eighth Final out of the last 10 to be spoiled by injuries.

And Spurs, on this orbit to football fame, having their golden immortality slightly tarnished by an unavoidable "if."

If John White had not achieved the near-impossible by shooting over from five yards in the fifth minute.

If that tingling goal which Cliff Jones streaked in five minutes before the interval had not been promptly judged offside.

If these had been goals, then maybe Spurs would have forgotten their tension and decorated the muscle-nagging

Wembley turf with wondrous football.

Instead, even against 10 men, Spurs were staggering back under Leicester attacks blazed off by that dazzling, bewildering little man Howard Riley.

THE DUEL

The Riley duel with Ron Henry became the most absorbing thing in the game. In the end Henry was the winner. But he had to become the greatest player on the field to earn that distinction.

No wonder that in the after-match capers this kingpin player Henry crowned himself with the silver lid of the Cup.

Leicester, who move by move swept away the label they were mere stooges in this Wembley dimension, reduced Spurs to teeth-chattering fright.

Eight minutes, starting at 4.22, decided the result.

Terry Dyson, who had just headed over from five yards, centred hard and low to his particular team buddy, Bobby Smith.

This burly, heavy-thighed Smith became a thing of delicate precision as he pivoted clear of centre-half Ian King and sent the ball blurring beyond the resistance of 'keeper Gordon Banks.

MY 'DOUBLE'

Dyson, the smallest man on the field, impudently headed in the second goal from Smith's high cross. And the two men I said would score had settled the double.

At this historical point, Chalmers was finally advised to end the terrible risk he had been taking and limped sadly off the field.

Every Cup Final compels a special memory. I will always remember with admiration the Leicester players lining up at the exit from the pitch to applaud the Spurs. Fame was the Spurs, but Leicester at least can claim courage and dignity.

The cup final

Above: The cup final ball, which was inscribed with details of the match to mark the historic achievement. *Right:* The cup bedecked in Spurs ribbons, a tradition instigated by the wife of a Spurs director after the club's FA Cup win of 1901. *Far right:* An exhausted Danny Blanchflower descends the Wembley steps.

Left: Terry Dyson is in impish mood, ducking under the arched arms of Danny Blanchflower and Bobby Smith as the trophy is paraded. *Top left:* TV's David Coleman gets a few words from Blanchflower. *Top right:* Smith bumps into PFA chief Jimmy Hill after the match. *Bottom left:* Only 14,000 Spurs fans were officially allocated tickets, but those present will never forget the day.
Bottom right: Typically sporting, Bill Nicholson visits the Leicester dressing room.

The Double
in colour

For those who did not witness it in person, the Double season is documented in monochrome images that lock it firmly in a bygone age. Colour movie footage of the cup final – and a bizarre Pathé News feature in which Spurs players visit The White Hart pub to be shown the landlord's ornamental guns – do exist, but black and white images are so prevalent it's sometimes hard to imagine that a colour world existed at all.

For most press photographers there was simply no demand for colour work. None of the newspapers required it and colour magazines and supplements rarely covered sport. The exceptions were *World Sport* magazine (see p58) and *Charles Buchan's Football Monthly,* but these often used hand-tinted photos, creating a surreal virtual colour effect (for example p106). To celebrate the Double a 'true' colour photoshoot was commissioned. In a now famous set-up the players were precariously posed on a step ladder. Pictures from the session made the cover of *Charles Buchan* (p200) and the official Spurs players' publication (p186). If there's one image that crystallises the spirit and comradery of the Double team, it's perhaps this picture of the players together in the Paxton Road goalmouth in the summer of 1961.

Now a colour shoot in controlled lighting conditions was one thing, but attempting to shoot action photography in bad light and with rudimentary equipment was a near technical impossibility. However, some rare colour match photography was unearthed in the *Mirror* archives for this book and is featured on the following pages. Looking at the final pictures in this feature, the vibrancy of the photographs is such that it is hard not to feel temporarily transported back to the streets of north London on the day the Double came to Tottenham – in glorious technicolour.

The Double
in colour

It was a murky November day in 1960 when Spurs took on Fulham at White Hart Lane and this is a rare view of matchday as it would have looked to the naked eye.
This page: Cliff Jones is congratulated by Terry Dyson after scoring one of his two goals in the 5-1 win.
Facing page, top left: Jones leaps to head for goal again.
Top right: Fulham's Jimmy Hill appeals to the referee as Spurs protect their goal.
Bottom left: Danny Blanchflower and Peter Baker offer consolations to Johnny Haynes after the match.
Bottom right: A mud-soaked Bobby Smith heads for the players' tunnel.

179

The Double
in colour

This page, right: Danny
Blanchflower leads the team
out for the FA Cup semi-final
at Villa Park in April 1961.
Far right: The cameraman gets
a keeper's-eye view as Cliff
Jones heads for goal.
Below, left and right: Bill
Brown in his cap, protecting
the Spurs goal from attack.
Facing page: Spurs players
trot back to their half, after a
goal in the 3-0 win against the
imposing Holte End backdrop.

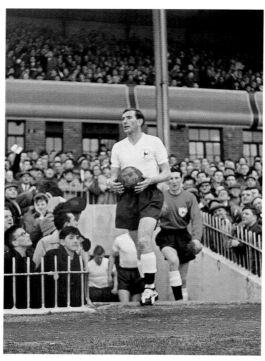

You've got to believe by Julie Welch

It's odd how when the floodlights come on, nothing about Tottenham seems to have changed much. Odd how the sounds and smells and sights of modernity are all around you and yet the presence of the awe-inspiring Double side is so strong that you feel yourself transported back to White Hart Lane as it was half a century ago. Odd, too, how the sense of the sublime persists and how even if you weren't born when the Double side was playing you somehow know what the expectation in the air was like – know the feeling of wonder at what you were seeing, exactly the same as the crowd who were there might have seen it.

And then you pause to marvel at the immensity of what that team did, the effort and wizardry and struggle and commitment and the pure, astonishing self-belief and chutzpah that it must have taken. Football has evolved since then and while doing the Double will never be commonplace it no longer feels as out of reach as Mars. The Double that Spurs achieved in 1960/61 will always be the best and most special. They were the side that made the impossible a reality.

As the brilliance of that team became almost a weekly exhibition, you felt happy and lucky that you supported them. But even if you didn't follow Spurs it was easy to look at them impartially and respond to the artistry, inventiveness and power. If you never get to witness that kind of football – not just read about it or see it on television but actually be physically present when it happens, right there in the stadium, contributing to the passion

and rapture and adrenaline because you're part of the spectacle – it's tempting to say you haven't really lived. It's a feeling like no other – almost disbelief that a team can be that good coupled with gratitude that you're seeing the stuff of legend take place.

How did they do it? It's a mystery. As a player, Bill Nicholson had been a no-frills, cautious, pragmatic defender. When it came to coaching he was an out-and-out romantic. After a decade of football dominated by Wolves, hitting long balls from the back to their skyscraper strikers and flying wingers, this was a team that changed everything. It had brains and speed and muscle and creativity. It took chances. They believed they could do it; they didn't need us to tell them how good they were. They knew it.

There was the lean and rangy Bill Brown, dominating his goal area; Maurice Norman like a great hill in the centre of defence; Peter Baker and Ron Henry, sound and composed. There was the way that Danny Blanchflower and John White somehow seemed to know where each other was, as if they were joined by invisible cords; there was the inimitable Dave Mackay, storming through the fog and mud to get a point, a player who combined exceptional skill with raw bravery and inspirational bloodymindedness.

Goals came easily. Every now and then, like a silver rocket, Cliff Jones would launch himself; a move from him would often be the start of the fireworks: from Cliff himself, from John, Danny and Dave; from Bobby Smith, the target man who'd run through brick walls to get his head to the ball; from Les Allen, a

"TOTTENHAM HOTSPUR. F.C. 1960-61

DOUBLE-EVENT TEAM F.A.CUP WINNERS & CHAMPIONS.DIV.1

R. Henry   M.Norman   W,Brown   R,Smith   P,Baker

C,Jones   J,White   D,Blanchflower   L,Allen   T,Dyson   D,Mackay
Captain

The personal view

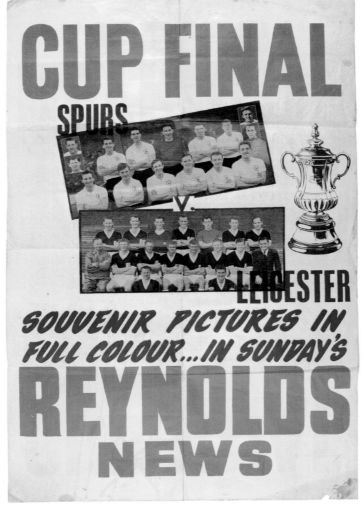

Julie Welch grew up on the Double side, and went on to be the first woman to report football for the national press. She continues to write articles, books and novels – and to follow Spurs.

There's only one way to deal with such pessimistic thinking. You get yourself along to White Hart Lane any matchday or night and as you take up your position and look down onto the pitch, you think yourself back into 1960, on the cusp between summer and autumn. Think of Bobby Smith's hat trick against Blackpool. Of Les Allen ripping through the Manchester United defence. Of John White making all those goals against Aston Villa.

And as you imagine the packed stands and terraces of White Hart Lane 50 years ago, the scale of the achievement comes back to you, the sheer heady delight of that season, so enchanting that you can feel it even now. It will only take a moment and the air will fill with the noise of 60,000 people; the next minute those familiar dazzling shapes and patterns are being made on the pitch and your mind sketches out for you the sublime promise of a season like no other.

That's what we follow Spurs for. All those hours and days and weeks and years of hope; they're the price we pay for one glorious season when everything came together like a massive, beautiful piece of music. And the memory – or if you weren't around in 1961, then imagination is a powerful thing – of Danny Blanchflower with that odd crouching run of his; of John White, appearing like an angel to receive his pass; of Dave Mackay, brilliant-eyed with mad resolve; of Bobby Smith sorting out a defender or two; of Terry Dyson leaping twice his height to reach a ball; of Cliff Jones emerging victorious from one of those hardly believable supercharged head-first flights down into the tangle of boots and legs; and of the Spurs Double team as magical and fleet-footed and potent in our dreams as they once were on the pitch all those years ago.

quiet and modest man who scored crucial winners; from Terry Dyson, moving around the pitch like fat spitting in a frying pan. And as these last images come to mind, it's possible that the melancholy seeps into your soul at the realisation that it was a moment in time we'll never have back again. In that gloomy mood it's easy to see Danny, Dave and John, Les and Terry, Bobby and Cliff, Peter, Maurice, Ron and Bill fading from memory the way that the sporting giants of the 1920s and 1930s have faded into obscurity until they're as far away from our experience as Romans and Anglo-Saxons.

The Double wives, a photo from Sandra White's collection. *Left to right, back row*: Joyce Medwin, Mavis Smith, Pat Hopkins, Elaine Brown, Marie Marchi, Jacqueline Norman, Sandra White, Pat Allen, Edna Henry. *Front row*: Joan Jones, 'Darkie' Nicholson, Betty Blanchflower, Alma Evans, Vera Hollowbread.

The Double on film

Above: Zoe Nathanson played the young 'Julie' in the film, seen in a scene in the team bath at White Hart Lane.
Facing page: (clockwise from top left) agonisingly close to a cup final ticket; chatting with 'Danny Blanchflower'; the gang initiation on the pitch.

Julie Welch was a schoolgirl when Spurs won the Double and the inspiration of that great side and its captain is clear to see in the short semi-autobiographical film she wrote in 1984 for Channel 4. It's not easy to make a decent film about football, but *Those Glory, Glory Days* succeeds because it is as much about the human condition as it is about the game.

Much of it was filmed in and around the ground, with the back of the Paxton Road stand and the ticket office featuring large. So too do the passageways under the West Stand and the changing rooms, where Julia Herrick, the 'Julie' character in the film, explores by torchlight after she bunks into the ground the night before cup final tickets go on sale. In one memorable scene, she climbs into the vast, empty team bath and imagines she's giving a team talk.

The film opens with football reporter Herrick being patronised by the male hacks in the White Hart Lane press box. Julie Welch persuaded some of her Fleet Street friends, such as David Lacey, to appear in those opening scenes alongside Richard Wilson, who later found fame as Victor Meldrew in the sitcom *One Foot In The Grave*. Leaving the ground, a frustrated Julia is almost run down by a Mercedes. The car stops and a soft Irish voice asks if she wants a lift. Julia climbs in, cursing the lack of taxis and the grit in her contact lenses, before looking up to see her childhood hero Danny Blanchflower (who played himself) is the driver. "I used to watch you play," she says, almost imme-

diately regretting the feebleness of the comment. The incident prompts a flashback, to Julia as a schoolgirl and the gang of Tottenham fans she hung around with in the Double season.

It's the flashback that forms the substance of the film, showing young Julia's initiation into the gang via a comically-observed initiation involving a piece of West Stand seat and Bobby Smith's chewing gum and their mounting excitement as Spurs edge closer to the Double. All this happens against a backdrop of Julia's unhappiness at home, and it's the interplay between the sadness and confusion of Julia's family circumstances and the comically observed antics of the gang that gives the film its heart.

At one stage the young Julia uses Bill Nicholson's maxim, "When not in possession get into position," and the scene gave author Julie Welch one of her proudest moments when the film was first screened. "I was sitting with David Puttnam," she remembers, "and Bill was sitting in the row just in front. When she says that line, he said 'That's right.' It was a great moment."

It's the understanding of what people are all about that makes this film worthy of repeated viewing and it ends with a great piece of philosophy, as true for life as it is for football, that comes from Danny Blanchflower. Julia asks him: "Do you think I'm daft, wanting to be a football reporter?" Danny answers: "Well, I think you are a bit daft, yes, but you've got to be a bit daft sometimes, if you want to change things. You've got to fight for your place – if you want to get into the team."

1961

Glory, glory

Danny Blanchflower did not feel The Glory during that strangely deflating lap of Wembley with the FA Cup. He did not expect to feel it the day after as the team prepared for another parade down Tottenham High Road. "There was a queue at The Royal Dance Hall, but that was for the bingo," he observed.

But by 3.30pm on that bright Sunday, he felt it. "The roads were packed from one Town Hall to the other," he said. "I have never seen so many people crowding pavements, clinging to trees and hanging out of windows down the three-mile route.

"Here was the real glory. The trust and respect of the fans in their team, for a season for skill and style and crowds, and the triumph of the first Double this century."

In so many of the pictures of the day's joyous scenes it is kids who are to the fore – thrilled and excitable as kids are, but also showing signs of the abandon with which their generation would shape the sixties and the future. In contrast, the official celebration at the Savoy Hotel on the Saturday gave the establishment a chance to show their appreciation, Minister for Transport Ernest Marples striking a Cholmondely-Warnerish note as he told the super Spurs: "You have been showing us the arts and graces of the game with a great deal of poise, balance and rhythm. You have tried always to play football, and I do congratulate you."

Even here were signs of how The Glory was part of something bigger, a leaving behind of one age and the embracing of a new. The establishment figures of the Minister and the beknighted FA chairman rubbed shoulders with showbiz stars – Harry Secombe, Roy Castle and Shirley Bassey among them. Four of the 1921 cup-winning team were there and Bill Nicholson typically fretted about whether his 1951 team-mates would feel pushed aside. History positively swirled.

It was left to John Arlott, that great poet of British sport, to give a speech concluding the proceedings on behalf of the guests, elaborating on the observations he had made in the programme for the last home game of the season.

"Not all champions have been recognised at the true bar of footballing judgment – the opinion of those who play against them. The Tottenham Hotspur side of 1960/61 however, made friends on all levels – on delighted terraces, among the critics (applause from the press is frowned upon as undignified, but this team moved some very hard reporters to unchecked admiration) and the best of players and managers. Footballing Britain realises that no other team is so fitting to be 'England' in the coming European Cup... Not even the great Hungarian side surpassed these men in the unhurried, lulling, short-ball creation of a position and then exploited it with the long ball, sent like a javelin into the gap in the shield."

Fifty years on Cliff Jones put it in more perfunctory but no less profound style. "It was a season of unbelievable excitement. We played to over two million people in the league and 500,000 in the cup. We put bums on seats and, boy, did we entertain."

Daily Mirror

3d.   Monday, May 8, 1961   No. 17,849

HOME WITH THOSE TWO CUPS!

THE all-conquering Spurs came home in triumph yesterday

The great double had been achieved. And on the balcony of Tottenham Town Hall yesterday (above) skipper of super-Spurs, Danny Blanchflower, holds aloft the FA Cup won by his team in the final on Saturday.

Beside him is the Mayor of Tottenham, Councillor Harry Langer, with the Football League Championship Cup, also won by the Spurs.

Tottenham greets its heroes

Left: Young fans prepare for the start of the parade in Knight Lane, Edmonton.
Top left: Crowds wait at the gates of White Hart Lane. *Top right:* The team bus edges down the High Road. *Bottom left:* Passing the Red House offices. *Bottom*

right: The vast crowd that thronged the High Road stunned the players and manager. "Tottenham's never seen anything like it before," said Bill Nicholson. "I am most moved by your loyalty and support," he announced at the Town Hall.

Previous pages: John White is just visible as the cup is shown off to a vast crowd stretching back up the High Road, and fans go to extraordinary heights to catch a glimpse of their heroes.

Above: At the Town Hall, the bus is mobbed by fans who burst through the police cordon. *Right:* Tottenham mayor, councillor H Langer, shares the trophy limelight with Danny Blanchflower.

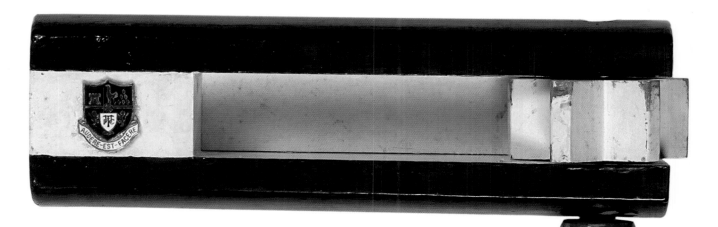

This recently discovered photo was taken by Spurs fan Liam Frost's father in the garden of the Bell and Hare pub after the parade. Says Liam: "My father, as a child, discovered the players used to go to the Bell and Hare after each home game. He and his mates used to hang around the back after matches where the players would be waiting for it to open for the evening session. They got to know them." Here Dyson, Mackay, Jones and White smile for their pal's camera. Mackay's bowler is a nod to the hat worn by chairman Fred Bearman.

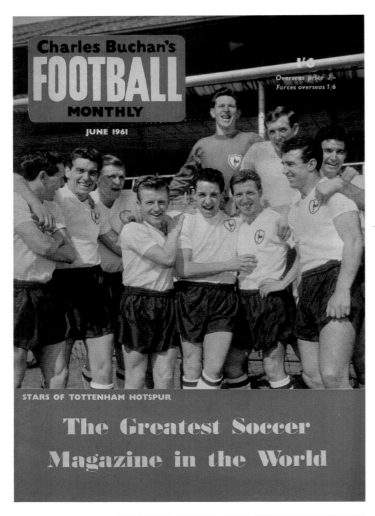

STARS OF TOTTENHAM HOTSPUR

The Greatest Soccer Magazine in the World

Drink a toast to the

SPURS

from a solid English Pewter Tankard - engraved with the actual reproduced autographs of the record-breaking Spurs Double Team of season 1960-61

HALF-PINT 45s.   PINT 55s.
Postage and Packing 2s.

Personal Callers Welcomed

A. & J. COHEN, Watchmakers and Jewellers, 677 High Road, Tottenham, N.17

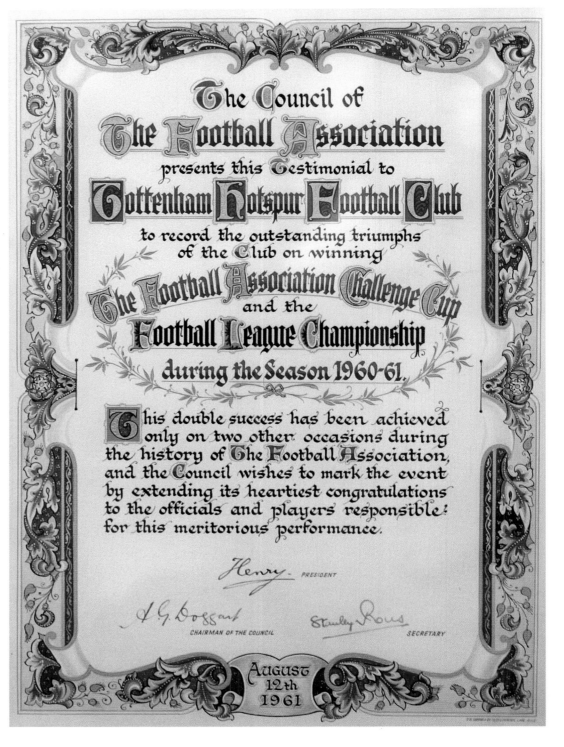

The Council of The Football Association presents this Testimonial to Tottenham Hotspur Football Club to record the outstanding triumphs of the Club on winning The Football Association Challenge Cup and the Football League Championship during the Season 1960-61.

This double success has been achieved only on two other occasions during the history of The Football Association, and the Council wishes to mark the event by extending its heartiest congratulations to the officials and players responsible for this meritorious performance.

Henry. PRESIDENT

A. G. Doggart
CHAIRMAN OF THE COUNCIL

Stanley Rous
SECRETARY

AUGUST 12th 1961

HIGHLIGHTS FROM
CUP FINAL 1960-61

SPURS WIN THE DOUBLE!

LEICESTER
CITY

TOTTENHAM
HOTSPUR

Facing page, top left: Somewhat opportunistically *Charles Buchan's Football Monthly* uses a shot of The Double team to declare itself 'The Greatest Soccer Magazine in the World.'
Bottom left: A special commemorative tankard produced by a local jewellers.
Right: A beautifully illustrated presentation made by the FA to the club in recognition of the achievement.
This page: Listen to the cup final again on 33rpm vinyl!
Following pages: Bobby Smith, Terry Dyson and Dave Mackay show off the League Championship trophy in the Spurs dressing room and the same trio celebrate with the FA Cup at Wembley.

The Double

The players promised they would celebrate winning the Double when it was finally secured and did so in some style at the Savoy on the evening after the cup win. Showbiz celebrities including Roy Castle added some glitz and glamour. The Tottenhamites' new record *Tip Top Tottenham Hotspur* was played and a copy presented to all the players by singing superstar of the day, Shirley Bassey. Tributes and speeches lavished plaudits on the team, but with an appreciation of the less celebrated figures so typical of the man, Bill Nicholson made sure the whole squad received due recognition, saying of the reserves, "They did not win any honours but have always been pulling their weight and have played above themselves when they have come into the first team."

Right: Harry Secombe cracks a smile with Terry Dyson.

Below left: Cheers all round from Dyson, Smith, White and Henry.

Below right: Players break into song accompanied on piano by assistant club secretary Alan Leather (in the glasses). Leather was also official food taster on the 1959 Soviet tour.

204

CELEBRATION DINNER

BOROUGH OF TOTTENHAM

In honour of the outstanding achievements of the Tottenham Hotspur Football Club during the 1960-61 Season

FRIDAY
12th MAY
1961

TOWN HALL TOTTENHAM N.15

White, Blanchflower and Jones sign souvenir footballs at the Cafe Royal in July 1961, one of the many functions held at venues including Tottenham Town Hall and the Mecca Ballroom. The inscribed tankard is one of those presented to the players at the Café Royal event. The trophy (far right) was awarded by the BBC's *Sportsview* for Team of the Year 1961. On the following page, the glittering prizes: the trophies (left) and on the facing page the winners' medals for the League (left) and FA Cup (right)

After the Double

Pennant from Spurs's first game in European competition against Gornik in the 1962 European Cup.

Following some thrilling Tottenham victories in April 2010, football writer David Lacey wrote that the performances "stir memories of things past," referencing the wing-wizardry of Cliff Jones, the guile of John White and the reflexes of Bill Brown to make his point. Fifty years on, the Double side is still the benchmark.

In 1961/62 a second successive Double was only prevented by former Spur Alf Ramsey's Ipswich, who beat Spurs home and away to take the title. Ipswich's effectiveness stemmed from using a withdrawn left-winger to supply a pair of battering ram centre-forwards. It wasn't pretty, but it worked. Only Bill Nicholson saw how to neutralise the tactic, by using the full-backs to come inside and pick up the centre-forwards while the half-backs smothered the withdrawn left-winger. The players disagreed and lost both league games. In the following season's Charity Shield Nicholson put his foot down. Spurs beat Ipswich 5-1.

The FA Cup was won again in 1962 and in Europe Spurs innovated once more. With Tony Marchi played as an extra defender away from home in place of Les Allen, Spurs effectively pioneered a fluid 4-3-3. They thrilled the Continent and reached a semi-final against Bela Guttmann's Benfica. In one of the finest European games ever seen in England, Spurs just fell short, victims of three marginal decisions but also of mistakes which cannot be made against sides as good as that Benfica were.

In the following season, Spurs did conquer Europe, becoming the first British team to win a European trophy. They not only beat Atletico Madrid, then one of the finest teams in Europe, they destroyed them 5-1 in the final of the Cup-Winners' Cup. And for the third season running they contested the league title until its final days.

Three victories on tour in South Africa in May and June 1963 were to be the Double side's swansong. But what they achieved amounts to far more than a list of trophies – as vital as they are when judging greatness. Achieving something for the first time can never be matched. But the achievement endures because of the manner in which it was attained. And this means far more than just referencing Danny Blanchflower's famous quote about glory – although that is as fine a maxim for the game as there is.

Tottenham Hotspur's Double side moved football into a modern era. An era of international competition instead of insularity and one in which the joy of the spectacle became as valued as the satisfaction of the result. Look at the Total Football of Cruyff's Ajax and draw a line back to the fluidity of the Double side; look at the flexibility of formation employed by the most successful of today's sides and do the same.

It is not too fanciful to say that it was the Spurs Double achievement that opened football to new possibilities and a new audience. And whenever the quality of a great side is discussed, it is still the Spurs Double side that is used as a comparison. Even after 50 years. And that is because football is not just about winning. It is about glory. Hallelujah!

209

CUP FINAL 1962 — **Evening Standard** — COLOUR SOUVENIR

SPURS ALL SET FOR 'DREAM' CUP FINAL

BACK (left to right): Baker, Allen, Norman, Brown, Henry, Smith, Mackay.
FRONT (left to right): Medwin, Greaves, Blanchflower, White, Jones.

Colour pictures by Evening Standard cameraman, ARTHUR JONES

Previous page: One of the greatest ever strikers,
Jimmy Greaves, joins one of the greatest ever teams.
Above: Ready for the 1962 FA Cup Final against Burnley,
which saw Spurs win the trophy for a second successive
year, but a double Double just eluded them.
Top right: Spurs brought home the Cup-Winners' Cup in 1963.
Bottom right: The coming of a new generation – a young Pat
Jennings takes to the air with Bill Brown in 1964.

South Africa 1963

In the summer of 1963 the club went on tour to South Africa. The trip to the southern hemisphere was the last summer in which this brilliant band of footballers would all be assembled as a team, bookending an adventure that had started on the tour of the Soviet Union in 1959 when the side came together.

Left: John White, Cliff Jones and John Hollowbread take a ride on the cable car which took tourists up Table Mountain.

Above: White gets a playful kick down the mountain from Danny Blanchflower. In November 1963 Blanchflower finally succumbed to long-standing injuries and retired. In December the same year Dave Mackay broke his leg and didn't play again until 1965. Most heart-rending of all, John White was killed in the summer of 1964. The Double side were no more.

BLACKPOOL FOOTBALL CLUB v. TOTTENHAM HOTSPUR — FOOTBALL LEAGUE — MONDAY, 22nd AUGUST, 1960 — Kick-off 7.15 p.m. — PRICE: THREEPENCE — OFFICIAL PROGRAMME

BLACKBURN ROVERS F.C. — SEASON 1960-61 — OFFICIAL PROGRAMME — 3d

BOLTON WANDERERS FOOTBALL CLUB — BURNDEN PARK, BOLTON — Season 1960-61 — Wednesday, September 7th — BOLTON WANDERERS v. TOTTENHAM H. — OFFICIAL PROGRAMME — 3d.

Arsenal FOOTBALL CLUB — Football League Division I — June 1960-61 — ARSENAL v. TOTTENHAM HOTSPUR — OFFICIAL PROGRAMME — 6d

OFFICIAL PROGRAMME 4d. — LEICESTER CITY FOOTBALL CLUB — SEASON 1960-1961 — Saturday, 17th September 1960 — LEICESTER CITY v. TOTTENHAM HOTSPUR

OFFICIAL PROGRAMME 3d — WOLVERHAMPTON WANDERERS — FOOTBALL LEAGUE DIVISION I — SEASON 1960-61

Nottingham Forest FOOTBALL CLUB, City Ground, Nottingham — Football League, Division One — Saturday, October 15th, 1960 — Nottingham Forest v. Tottenham Hotspur — 4d.

NEWCASTLE UNITED FOOTBALL CLUB — ST. JAMES' PARK, NEWCASTLE — WE WELCOME TODAY — TOTTENHAM HOTSPUR — Saturday, 29th October, 1960 — Kick-off 3 p.m. — OFFICIAL PROGRAMME — 3d

FOOTBALL LEAGUE DIVISION ONE — 4d — SATURDAY 12th November 1960 — Kick-off 3 p.m. — OFFICIAL PROGRAMME — SHEFFIELD WEDNESDAY v. TOTTENHAM HOTSPUR — Hillsborough

OFFICIAL Albion NEWS PROGRAMME — 3d — ALBION v. TOTTENHAM HOTSPUR

PRICE 3d — PRESTON North End FOOTBALL CLUB LTD. — OFFICIAL PROGRAMME — No. 11 — SATURDAY, DECEMBER 10th, 1960 — YOUR CHANCE TO WIN £75,000 — SEE SATURDAY'S LAST FOOTBALL "POST" AND HAVE-A-GO AT THE WEEKLY "ODD-ONE-OUT" COMPETITION

EVERTON FOOTBALL CLUB — GOODISON PARK, LIVERPOOL — FOOTBALL LEAGUE — DIVISION I — EVERTON v. TOTTENHAM HOTSPUR — Saturday, 17th December 1960. Kick-off 3 p.m. — OFFICIAL PROGRAMME 4d

WEST HAM UNITED v. TOTTENHAM HOTSPUR — FOOTBALL LEAGUE — Division One — MONDAY 26th December 1960 at 3 p.m. — No. 29 — OFFICIAL PROGRAMME 6d

UNITED REVIEW — MANCHESTER UNITED FOOTBALL CLUB — 4d — MANCHESTER UNITED v. TOTTENHAM HOTSPUR — SEASON 1960-61 — OFFICIAL PROGRAMME

The VILLA news and record — 3d — THE FOOTBALL LEAGUE — FIRST DIVISION — SATURDAY, FEBRUARY 11th, 1961 — Tottenham Hotspur — Match No. 25 — KICK-OFF 3.0 p.m.

The VILLA news and record — 3d — THE FOOTBALL ASSOCIATION CHALLENGE CUP (FIFTH ROUND) — SATURDAY, FEBRUARY 18th, 1961 — Tottenham Hotspur — KICK-OFF 3.0 p.m.

MANCHESTER CITY FOOTBALL CLUB — SEASON 1960-61 — TOTTENHAM HOTSPUR — Official Programme Fourpence

SEASON 1960-61 OFFICIAL PROGRAMME — 4d — SUNDERLAND A.S.N. FOOTBALL CLUB LTD., ROKER PARK — F.A. CUP SIXTH ROUND — Saturday, 4th March — Sunderland v. Tottenham — Kick-off 3.0 p.m.

OFFICIAL 3d PROGRAMME — CARDIFF CITY A.F.C. LTD. — Football League Division I — Saturday, 11th March 1961 — Kick-off 3 p.m. — CARDIFF CITY v. TOTTENHAM HOTSPUR

OFFICIAL PROGRAMME — THE FOOTBALL ASSOCIATION CHALLENGE CUP — SEMI-FINAL TIE — TOTTENHAM HOTSPUR v. BURNLEY — VILLA PARK, BIRMINGHAM — SATURDAY, MARCH 18th, 1961 — PRICE 6d

FULHAM FOOTBALL CLUB — SEASON 1960-61 — OFFICIAL PROGRAMME — 4 — FULHAM v. TOTTENHAM HOTSPUR — SATURDAY, MARCH 25th, 1961 — FOOTBALL LEAGUE DIVISION I

LEAGUE CHAMPIONS 1954-55 — Chelsea Football Club — FOOTBALL LEAGUE—DIVISION I SEASON 1960-61 — CHELSEA v. TOTTENHAM HOTSPUR — Monday, 3rd April, 1961. Kick-off 3 p.m. — Official Programme 6d

BLUES News — THE OFFICIAL PROGRAMME OF BIRMINGHAM CITY FOOTBALL CLUB — SEASON 1960-61 — PRICE THREEPENCE

Burnley FOOTBALL CLUB — FOOTBALL LEAGUE CHAMPIONS 1959-60 — No. 29 TOTTENHAM HOTSPUR, Saturday, April 22nd, 1961 — OFFICIAL PROGRAMME SEASON 1960-61 — PUBLISHED BY Burnley Football & Athletic Co., Ltd. — 3d

1960/61 record

Division One

Date	Opponent	Result	Att	1	2	3	4	5	6	7	8	9	10	11	
Aug 20 (h)	**Everton**	W 2-0	50,393	Brown	Baker	Henry	Blanchflower	Norman	Mackay	Jones	White	**Smith**	**Allen**	Dyson	
22 (a)	**Blackpool**	W 3-1	27,656	Brown	Baker	Henry	Blanchflower	Norman	Mackay	**Medwin**	White	Smith	Allen	**Dyson 2**	
27 (a)	**Blackburn Rovers**	W 4-1	26,819	Brown	Baker	Henry	Blanchflower	Norman	Mackay	Medwin	White	**Smith 2**	**Allen**	Dyson	
31 (h)	**Blackpool**	W 3-1	45,684	Brown	Baker	Henry	Blanchflower	Norman	Mackay	Medwin	White	**Smith 3**	Allen	Dyson	
Sep 3 (h)	**Manchester United**	W 4-1	55,442	Brown	Baker	Henry	Blanchflower	Norman	Mackay	Medwin	White	**Smith 2**	**Allen 2**	Dyson	
7 (a)	**Bolton Wanderers**	W 2-1	41,565	Brown	Baker	Henry	Blanchflower	Norman	Mackay	Medwin	**White**	Saul	**Allen**	Dyson	
10 (a)	**Arsenal**	W 3-2	59,868	Brown	Baker	Henry	Blanchflower	Norman	Mackay	Medwin	White	**Saul**	**Allen**	Dyson	
14 (h)	**Bolton Wanderers**	W 3-1	43,559	Brown	Baker	**Henry**	**Blanchflower p**	Norman	Mackay	Jones	White	**Smith 2**	Allen	Dyson	
17 (a)	**Leicester City**	W 2-1	30,129	Brown	Baker	Henry	Blanchflower	Norman	Mackay	Jones	White	**Smith 2**	Allen	Dyson	
24 (h)	**Aston Villa**	W 6-2	61,356	Brown	Baker	Henry	Blanchflower	Norman	**Mackay**	Jones	**White 2**	Smith	**Allen**	**Dyson**	
Oct 1 (a)	**Wolverhampton W**	W 4-0	52,829	Brown	Baker	Henry	**Blanchflower**	Norman	Marchi	**Jones**	White	Smith	**Allen**	**Dyson**	
10 (h)	**Manchester City**	D 1-1	58,916	Brown	Baker	Henry	Blanchflower	Norman	Mackay	Jones	White	**Smith**	Allen	Dyson	
15 (a)	**Nottingham Forest**	W 4-0	37,248	Brown	Baker	Henry	Blanchflower	Norman	**Mackay**	**Jones 2**	**White**	Smith	Allen	Dyson	
29 (a)	**Newcastle United**	W 4-3	51,369	Brown	Baker	Henry	Blanchflower	**Norman**	Mackay	**Jones**	**White**	**Smith**	Allen	Dyson	
Nov 2 (h)	**Cardiff City**	W 3-2	47,605	Brown	Baker	Henry	**Blanchflower p**	Norman	Mackay	**Medwin**	White	Smith	Allen	**Dyson**	
5 (h)	**Fulham**	W 5-1	56,270	Brown	Baker	Henry	Blanchflower	Norman	Mackay	**Jones 2**	**White**	Smith	**Allen 2**	Dyson	
12 (a)	**Sheffield Wednesday**	L 1-2	53,988	Brown	Baker	Henry	Blanchflower	**Norman**	Mackay	Jones	White	Smith	Allen	Dyson	
19 (h)	**Birmingham City**	W 6-0	46,010	Brown	Baker	Henry	Blanchflower	Norman	Mackay	**Jones 2**	**White**	**Smith p**	Allen	**Dyson 2**	
26 (a)	**West Bromwich Albion**	W 3-1	39,017	Brown	Baker	Henry	Blanchflower	Norman	Mackay	Jones	White	**Smith 2**	**Allen**	Dyson	
Dec 3 (h)	**Burnley**	D 4-4	58,737	Brown	Baker	Henry	Blanchflower	**Norman**	**Mackay**	**Jones 2**	White	Smith	Allen	Dyson	
10 (a)	**Preston North End**	W 1-0	21,657	Brown	Baker	Henry	Blanchflower	Norman	Mackay	Jones	**White**	Saul	Allen	Dyson	
17 (a)	**Everton**	W 3-1	61,052	Brown	Baker	Henry	Blanchflower	Norman	**Mackay**	Jones	**White**	Smith	**Allen**	Dyson	
24 (h)	**West Ham United**	W 2-0	54,930	Brown	Baker	Henry	Blanchflower	Norman	Mackay	Jones	**White**	Smith	Allen	**Dyson**	
26 (a)	**West Ham United**	W 3-0	34,351	Hollowbread	Baker	Henry	Blanchflower	Norman	Mackay	Medwin	**White**	Smith	**Allen**	Dyson	OG
31 (h)	**Blackburn Rovers**	W 5-2	48,742	Brown	Baker	Henry	**Blanchflower**	Norman	Marchi	Medwin	White	**Smith 2**	**Allen 2**	Dyson	
Jan 16 (a)	**Manchester United**	L 0-2	65,535	Brown	Barton	Henry	Blanchflower	Norman	Mackay	Smith J.	White	Smith	Allen	Dyson	
21 (h)	**Arsenal**	W 4-2	65,251	Brown	Baker	Henry	**Blanchflower p**	Norman	Mackay	Jones	White	**Smith**	**Allen 2**	Dyson	
Feb 4 (h)	**Leicester City**	L 2-3	53,627	Brown	Baker	Henry	**Blanchflower p**	Norman	Mackay	Jones	White	Smith	**Allen**	Dyson	
11 (a)	**Aston Villa**	W 2-1	50,786	Brown	Baker	Henry	Blanchflower	Norman	Mackay	Jones	White	**Smith**	Allen	**Dyson**	
22 (h)	**Wolverhampton W**	D 1-1	62,261	Brown	Baker	Henry	Blanchflower	Norman	Mackay	Jones	White	**Smith**	Allen	Dyson	
25 (a)	**Manchester City**	W 1-0	40,278	Brown	Baker	Henry	Blanchflower	Marchi	Mackay	**Medwin**	White	Smith	Allen	Dyson	
Mar 11 (a)	**Cardiff City**	L 2-3	45,463	Brown	Baker	Henry	Blanchflower	Norman	Mackay	Jones	White	Smith	**Allen**	**Dyson**	
22 (h)	**Newcastle United**	L 1-2	46,470	Brown	Baker	Henry	Blanchflower	Norman	Mackay	Jones	White	Smith	**Allen**	Dyson	
25 (a)	**Fulham**	D 0-0	38,536	Brown	Baker	Henry	Blanchflower	Norman	Marchi	Jones	White	Saul	Allen	Dyson	
31 (h)	**Chelsea**	W 4-2	65,032	Brown	Baker	Henry	Blanchflower	Norman	Marchi	**Jones 2**	White	**Saul**	**Allen**	Dyson	
Apr 1 (h)	**Preston North End**	W 5-0	46,325	Brown	Baker	Henry	Blanchflower	Norman	Marchi	**Jones 3**	**White**	Saul	Allen	Medwin	
3 (a)	**Chelsea**	W 3-2	57,103	Brown	Baker	Henry	Blanchflower	**Norman**	Mackay	Jones	White	**Smith**	Allen	**Medwin**	
8 (a)	**Birmingham City**	W 3-2	40,961	Brown	Baker	Henry	Blanchflower	Norman	Mackay	Jones	**White**	**Smith**	**Allen**	Dyson	
17 (h)	**Sheffield Wednesday**	W 2-1	61,205	Brown	Baker	Henry	Blanchflower	Norman	Mackay	Jones	White	**Smith**	**Allen**	Dyson	
22 (a)	**Burnley**	L 2-4	28,991	Brown	**Baker**	Henry	Blanchflower	Norman	Mackay	Medwin	White	**Smith**	Allen	Dyson	
26 (h)	**Nottingham Forest**	W 1-0	35,743	Brown	Baker	Henry	Blanchflower	Norman	Mackay	**Medwin**	White	Smith	Allen	Dyson	
29 (h)	**West Bromwich Albion**	L 1-2	52,054	Brown	Baker	Henry	Blanchflower	Norman	Mackay	Jones	White	**Smith**	Allen	Dyson	

FA Cup

Date	Opponent	Result	Att	1	2	3	4	5	6	7	8	9	10	11	
Jan 7 (h) 3rd	**Charlton Athletic**	W 3-2	54,969	Brown	Baker	Henry	Blanchflower	Norman	Mackay	Medwin	White	Smith	**Allen 2**	**Dyson**	
28 (h) 4th	**Crewe Alexandra**	W 5-1	53,721	Brown	Baker	Henry	Blanchflower	Norman	**Mackay**	**Jones**	White	**Smith**	**Allen**	**Dyson**	
Feb 18 (a) 5th	**Aston Villa**	W 2-0	65,474	Brown	Baker	Henry	Blanchflower	Norman	Mackay	**Jones**	White	Smith	Allen	Dyson	OG
Mar 4 (a) 6th	**Sunderland**	D 1-1	61,236	Brown	Baker	Henry	Blanchflower	Norman	Mackay	**Jones**	White	Smith	Allen	Dyson	
8 (h) 6th replay	**Sunderland**	W 5-0	64,797	Brown	Baker	Henry	Blanchflower	Norman	**Mackay**	Jones	White	**Smith**	**Allen**	**Dyson 2**	
18 (Villa Park) SF	**Burnley**	W 3-0	69,968	Brown	Baker	Henry	Blanchflower	Norman	Mackay	**Jones**	White	**Smith 2**	Allen	Dyson	
May 6 (Wembley) F	**Leicester City**	W 2-0	100,000	Brown	Baker	Henry	Blanchflower	Norman	Mackay	Jones	White	**Smith**	Allen	**Dyson**	

Reproduced from *Spurs – A Complete Record* by Bob Goodwin

Acknowledgements

This book would not have happened without the invaluable assistance of:
Cliff Jones, Julie Welch, Andy Porter, Neville Evans, Rob White, Bob Goodwin,
Jim Drewett and Toby Trotman at VSP, Justyn Barnes at Kraken Opus,
Donna Cullen, Victoria Howarth, John Fennelly and all at THFC.

Thanks also to: Paul Trevillion, Malcolm Jenkins, Peter Coles, Bob Bond,
Liam Frost, Richard Havers, Paul Moreton, Daren Burney, Jane Haville,
Graham Rowe, Simon Keeping, Paul Thompson, Robert Waite and all at
Bruce Castle Museum, Damian Dent and Matthew Butson at Getty Images,
David Scripps, Vito Inglese and Manjit Sandhu at Mirrorpix, Andy Cowie at
Colorsport, Callum McLennan at Topfoto, Mark Leech at Offside, Edd Griffin
at Rex features, Colin Campbell at Ohub, Ball Li and Dave Yan at Hung-hing.

The authors would like to thank the Cloake, Powley and Cheeseman families
for their support and understanding.

Select bibliography

Tottenham Hotspur The Complete Record by Bob Goodwin, Breedon
The Double by Ken Ferris, Two Heads
The Ghost of White Hart Lane by Julie Welch and Rob White, Yellow Jersey
And the Spurs go Marching On by Phil Soar, Hamlyn
Alan Mullery: The Autobiography Headline
When Saturday Comes: The Half Decent Football Book, Penguin
Rothmans Football Yearbook (various years) Queen Anne Press/Headline
The Real Mackay Mainstream
Inverting the Pyramid by Jonathan Wilson, Orion
Spurs The Double by Julian Holland, Heinemann
Spurs Supreme by Ralph L. Finn, Robert Hale
Danny Blanchflower, A Biography of a Visionary by Dave Bowler, Victor Gollancz
Glory Glory by Bill Nicholson, Macmillan 1984

Image sources

Photo libraries
Getty Images: 6, 24(2), 27, 29, 37, 103, 104tr & br, 105tr, 106bl, 130,
131r, 132, 143, 144, 145r, 150br, 155, 158l & r, 167(3), 170bl & br, 173, 202,
205t, 206, 210br
Mirrorpix: Cover, 10, 39, 79, 82, 115, 131l, 151, 161, 175tr & br, 176-183(14),
192, 194, 195, 197, 204tr & bl
PA Photos: 23, 32, 40, 47, 52, 57, 62, 104tl, 108, 122, 134, 150tl & br,
175bl, 204br, 209
Colorsport: 17, 157, 169, 174, 185, 203
Rex Features/ANL: 70l & r, 77tr, 129, 210tr
Topfoto: 77br, 150tr
Offside: 107, 159

Collections
Neville Evans: Back cover, 8, 11, 14, 18-19, 28, 30r, 31(2), 36, 38l, 46, 48-51,
56, 58, 59l, 60, 67, 68, 70t, 78, 80l, 84-101, 102, 105b, 114, 128, 133r, 142, 146,
156, 159r, 160(3), 164, 166r, 186, 190, 198c, 201, 205bl, 207, 208, 210l, 216
Rob White: 25r, 71, 80tl, 83br, 106tl, 116-121, 187, 211
Football Monthly Ltd: 38r, 105l, 106r, 133l, 145l, 162r, 199(2), 200tl
Bruce Castle Museum – Haringey Culture, Libraries and Learning Service:
9, 13, 25, 163, 184, 193br, 196, 198r, 205tr, 215
THFC: 15, 21, 174, 200r, 205br
Julie Welch: 188-189
Paul Trevillion: 81, 131b
Liam Frost: 198l
All other material from private collections

Any unacknowledged copyright holders please contact the publishers

FROM THE OPEN MARSHES OF TOTTENHAM ··· TO THE RICH TURF AND OPULENCE OF WHITE HART LANE! FROM THE MINOR GAMES OF AMATEUR SOCCER TO THE TOP OF ENGLAND'S ELITE DIVISION 1. A STORY STUDDED WITH GREAT NAMES AND GREAT ENDEAVOUR ····
A STORY THAT COULD HAVE ANOTHER CHAPTER ADDED, BEGINNING ··· "THIS YEAR THE LEAGUE AND CUP DOUBLE WAS ACHIEVED AT LAST!"

The End 5-50